WHAT DO CORPORATIONS WANT?

Communicative Capitalism, Corporate
Purpose, and a New Theory of the Firm

Timothy Kuhn

BRISTOL
UNIVERSITY
PRESS

First published in Great Britain in 2024 by

Bristol University Press
University of Bristol
1–9 Old Park Hill
Bristol
BS2 8BB
UK
t: +44 (0)117 374 6645
e: bup-info@bristol.ac.uk

Details of international sales and distribution partners are available at bristoluniversitypress.co.uk

British Library Cataloguing in Publication Data
A catalogue record for this book is available from the British Library

ISBN 978-1-5292-1427-7 hardcover
ISBN 978-1-5292-1429-1 ePub
ISBN 978-1-5292-1430-7 ePdf

Cover design: Lyn Davies Design
Front cover image: Unsplash/CHUTTERSNAP
Bristol University Press uses environmentally responsible print partners.
Printed and bound in Great Britain by CPI Group (UK) Ltd, Croydon, CR0 4YY

FSC
www.fsc.org
MIX
Paper | Supporting
responsible forestry
FSC® C013604

Contents

List of Figures and Tables

Figures

Table

Acknowledgements

I've had quite a bit of help in assembling and assessing this argument over the past decade or so. The intellectual collaborators are many; I'd like to recognize and thank them before delving into the book itself. First is Karen Lee Ashcraft, my Colorado colleague, friend, and inciter of bold intellectual imaginativeness. Also the best person with whom to practice immaturity and snarkiness in stuffy academic settings. Not far behind are two people who read, and commented on, the entire manuscript: Veronica Dawson and Matt Koschmann. I know that must have been painful and time-consuming, but it improved the argument significantly.

And then there are those who contributed to this book, often without even knowing they were contributing. In conversations or other writing projects together, I owe a significant debt of intellectual gratitude to François Cooren, Dennis Mumby, Gail Fairhurst, Dennis Schoeneborn, Bryan Taylor, Linda Putnam, Paul Leonardi, Joëlle Cruz, Joel Iverson, Jody Jahn, Bob McPhee, Consuelo Vásquez, Stan Deetz, Steve Corman, Scott Poole, Shiv Ganesh, and the late Jim Taylor. You shaped my thought here – sometimes as a sounding board, sometimes as an exemplar, and sometimes as a coach – and I appreciate it. And while I'd love to be able to shift the blame for errors and shortcomings (and there are undoubtedly many in the pages to follow) to these people, all inadequacies and deficiencies are mine alone.

The greatest appreciation, however, I reserve for the greatest parts of my life: Sophia, Ella, and Sam. None of this would have been possible without your love, encouragement, tolerance, and curiosity.

I also enjoyed the privilege of presenting this book's contents in many venues, where I tried out the material (and learned what didn't work). There were quite a few papers presented at the Academy of Management, National Communication Association, and International Communication Association conferences, along with a Professional Development Workshop J-C Spender and I co-organized at the 2014 Academy of Management meetings. In addition to sessions at the University of Colorado Boulder, kind colleagues also invited me to present some of this work at Fudan University (China), the University of Vienna, the Vienna University of Economics and Business,

HEC Montreal, the University of Montréal, the University of Innsbruck, and the University of Texas at Austin.

And special gratitude to Paul Stevens, the Bristol University Press editor I first met way back in 2019 and who expressed endless enthusiasm for this project, even during the significant challenges I (and the world) encountered between then and now. Ellen Pearce, who replaced Paul, was equally fantastic and supportive, and Isobel Green's work as senior editorial assistant has been exceptional.

Finally, a note about the book's cover image. At first glance, it's obvious that this is a geometric pattern assembled into a large building (or a large building covered by an almost innumerable set of hexagons), the sort that marks the presence of a powerful corporation. Perhaps it's a company's headquarters, the construction and ongoing maintenance of which required/requires many more corporate entities. The curved wall of seemingly endless hexagons signals that there's an entity here, one that practices rational planning and systematic design. It's also potentially imposing, the façade appearing impenetrable and intimidating – but it's also clearly a façade. Those are all associations people have with the dominant firms on our social scene, and the common conception of *What Corporations Want* mentioned previously (that their dogged-yet-sometimes-noxious pursuit of those profits is as unyielding as this image). But if you look just above the title box, you'll see some greenery, only slightly visible. Indeed, I missed it the first time I saw this. There's hope for corporations and their *wanting* to 'become other.'

Preface

Corporations have always fascinated me. From dinner table conversations where my father inveighed against the foolish superiors with whom he dealt at work, to a college job working on an overly ambitious business ethics training program in one of the world's largest private companies, to learning the ropes (and quickly becoming disillusioned with) a sales position at a consumer products company after completing my undergraduate degree, to hearing decades of university students' impressions of corporations as necessary but toxic actors, to public debates about corporate personhood, corporations have always been curious *and* frustrating creations. Not only are they the screens upon which a wide array of hopes and dreams are projected (my own included), but they also often appear, at least in the popular consciousness, as unitary entities with well-defined interests. Across those many experiences with corporations, I gradually came to understand that, like all organizations, they are significantly messier and less predictable than we participants and observers would like to admit. And in that complexity we can find something captivating.

The title *What Do Corporations Want?* is intended to be provocative in its deceptive simplicity. As I've had conversations about this book with colleagues, friends, and family, they tell me the answer to the title's question is simple: corporations want profits. End of story. (That's usually followed by a joke about how short a book this'll be.) Obviously, that's not wrong, but I'd suggest – keeping with the preceding paragraph – that answering the question is significantly more complex (and interesting) than it might at first appear.

This book engages with that complexity, but its message is relatively simple: the phase of capitalism in which we find ourselves – what I'll call 'communicative capitalism' in Chapter 1 – makes corporations *want* (makes them pursue purpose) in ways that interfere with new 'becomings.' In other words, corporations' efforts to organize to meet the demands of a new form of capitalism produce *dis*/organizational consequences that threaten their capacities to shift and grow in directions that serve the purposes they purport to desire. I then argue that the book's central theoretical contribution, a Communicative Theory of the Firm, provides a resource to make sense of both the complexity and the ironic consequences of action. It does not, however, offer anything like a recipe for 'better' performance or a route to avoid complexity. In fact, it argues that because corporations are ontologically multiple, their purposes and trajectories are sites of contestation. Understanding contestation implies a rich conception of authority (richer than organization studies scholars typically employ, that is), and I provide a conceptual apparatus for examining it.

Developing a new theory of the firm for a new capitalist order is not, in itself, a good thing. But because corporations are some of the most prominent and influential actors on our socioeconomic scene, we'd better understand what (and how) they want. And as I mention in the Introduction, unless we can answer those questions, we can't grasp the issue of whether those wants are worthwhile. So, while the book addresses the conventional themes encountered by theories of the firm well-known in strategic management and managerial economics, it moves beyond those to address more thorny issues associated with organizing as well.

Getting there, however, will require a mode of interrogation that may appear peculiar, perhaps even abstruse. I'll present the central notion, communication, in a light that violates many taken-for-granteds in its encounter with Communicative Constitution of Organization and new materialist thinking. But I hope to show that the payoff is worth the effort.

Introduction

The problem of the firm is purpose.

Starting a book with a statement like 'the problem of the firm is purpose' could be the height of banality. And banality would certainly be the case were this yet another entry in the pop-management genre arguing that an inspiring statement of mission or vision is key to motivating employees and producing corporate success. Or were it pointing to the need for strategic managers to articulate purpose in just the right tone to navigate numerous stakeholder demands. Or were it merely a justification for the sudden pervasiveness of corporate 'Chief Purpose Officers.'[1] Or if it represented the belief that companies need a moral touchstone to prevent irresponsible action or atone for past sins. In any of those cases, the statement would simply repeat well-worn, and increasingly uninteresting, tropes about contemporary corporations. Banal to be sure.

Yet I'd suggest there's something more stimulating and provocative in that opening line than might appear at first blush. This book argues that *purpose* tells us more about corporations than any other concept. Purpose is implicated in every element of being, and becoming, a firm: how it structures its operations, establishes boundaries, develops products, selects markets, appeals to (and defends itself from) publics, and how it comes to be considered an 'it' in the first place. Purpose is thus a *problem* – a question, a challenge, a premise, a puzzle, a charge – that demands attention across the many practices that make a corporation.

But purpose has also become the ground upon which battles over corporations' existence, effects, and legitimacy are waged, particularly in the public eye (Patriotta, 2021).[2] One camp in the battles is marked by an adherence to the shareholder value maximization (SVM) thesis: the assertion that firms exist to produce wealth for their shareholders (and are assumed to be *required* to do so by Western corporate law). Belief in SVM is accompanied by a belief that the pursuit of shareholder returns[3] generates better governance practices and organizational success than would be possible without it (Lazonick & O'Sullivan, 2000; Bhagat & Hubbard, 2022). An opposing camp asserts that firms must serve the interests of the many *stakeholders* affected by the firm's activity, both for long-term social and environmental health and because firms' longevity hinges on responsivity to, and productive relationships with, those stakeholding groups. And because employees increasingly want to believe that their daily toil at work is directed toward reasonably moral ends, purpose is where they find significance. From this second stance, then, *purpose* often rhymes with 'ethical' or 'personally meaningful.'

Following Milton Friedman (1970), those in the first camp declare that any imperative beyond increasing profits is both detrimental for firms and exceeds what managers have been trained to do, whereas many in the second camp hold that working toward 'pro-social' purposes like environmental, social, and governance (ESG) goals should – nay, *must* – become a widespread corporate obligation.[4] Another way of saying this is to note that between the two camps there exists a conceptual gulf in the unit of analysis, where some understand 'corporate purpose' to refer to a characteristic or feature of individual firms, whereas others see purpose as a claim about the power of the corporation as an encompassing social institution (Ocasio et al, 2023a). This book provides a tool to understand the struggles over corporate purpose that occurs in that gulf.

A good distillation of the battle's binary opposition can be found in a recent review article on this theme. In it, George et al (2023) divide literature into the same two traditional camps, which they term goal-based and duty-based stances. A *goal-based* approach, often seen in formal statements and management's strategic intent, expresses a firm's objectives for profitable performance. In its focus on the firm's business practices as the reason for its existence, goals-based stances pay little attention to the social antecedents for, and consequences of, corporate action. In contrast, a *duty-based* approach is normative in orientation, suggesting that firms harbour values and have moral responsibilities. These values and responsibilities generally supplant the profit motive and concomitant emphases on shareholder wealth; firms professing a duty-based purpose assert that they exist as an instrument to address societal grand challenges (see Gartenberg & Zenger, 2023). After detailing these two camps, George et al (2023) offer what they see as a rapprochement:

> *Purpose in the for-profit firm captures the essence of an organization's existence by explaining what value it seeks to create for its stakeholders. In doing so, purpose provides a clear definition of the firm's intent, creates the ability for stakeholders to identify with, and be inspired by, the firm's mission, vision, and values, and establishes actionable pathways and an aspirational outcome for the firm's actions.* (p 1847; emphasis in original)

George et al, in other words, attempt to negotiate the divide between the two camps: between purpose as a guide to profitable practice versus purpose as moral action. In their suggestion that it is stakeholders – and not simply shareholders or employees – who need to identify with (and be inspired by) the firm, they align with thinkers who argue that companies can eliminate the binary separating the two camps by simply avoiding talk of financial returns, substituting instead references to outcomes stakeholders value. And while 'value' is left ambiguous in their approach, choosing only one of the camps mentioned earlier is increasingly rejected by managements, as markets reward firms that practice some version of moral responsibility to stakeholders *alongside* the conventional register of wealth creation (Husted & Allen, 2000; Vogel, 2005). Including stakeholder values in a company's purpose will, the story goes, build the sort of strong relationships with those groups that will pay off for the firm in the long run (Henisz, 2023).

The battle these last few paragraphs illustrate is simultaneously general and specific. The sides disagree about the role of the corporation in producing 'the good society' while also making claims on the direction a given company should follow. In other words – and this much may be obvious – arguments about corporate purpose are *contests for control over the identity and trajectory of the firm*. They're about the interests written into the corporation's very being and becoming. In this sense, the battles call upon *authority*, with its attention to claiming legitimacy in shaping (or authoring) firms' decisional practices. Making claims to legitimacy in shaping decision-making is more a matter of contending for legitimate influence than of the imposition of will associated with conventional conceptions of *power*.

In other words, purpose and influence go hand in hand. But, as I'll argue in the chapters to follow, the way firms' strategic managers, as well as our theories of the firm, think about purpose provides an *illusion of control* that blinds them (blinds both the theories and the managers, that is) to the forces of desire shaping authority in corporate practice.

What's the *problem* here?

If 'the problem of the firm is purpose,' what's the issue with writers like George et al and their attempts to transcend the two-camp issue? First, as noted, talk of purpose often references only a corporation's reason for existence. By then turning to stakeholders' interpretations of claims regarding existence, such models of purpose tend to look outward, largely ignoring the everyday operations – what I framed as 'every element of being, and becoming, a firm' – that are essential to understanding the complexity of corporations' practices and the authority flowing through them. Second, as Herbert Simon (1964) noted six decades ago, talking about organizations as *having* or *possessing* purposes involves a reification, an unreflective attribution of agency to a collective. When writers treat purpose as an existential question for the organization, they tend to instinctively consider 'the organization' to be an essence, a substance, an 'it.' The few writers who grapple with this issue tend to reduce firms to conglomerations of individual persons and the interests that drive them, yet have no answer for how agency might emerge from that agglomeration such that 'it' can be considered a distinct entity. Consequently, scholars tend to assume that the externally focused statements of a company's leaders are the values of the firm. Third, efforts like George et al's portray corporate purpose as an ordering device, one that reduces ambiguity and misunderstanding because stakeholders will know what the company desires and will be motivated to align with it (Fisch & Solomon, 2021). In assuming order, observers gloss over the messy complexity of organizing, including the possibility that companies may want many things, even conflicting things, at the same time. (They also ignore the possibility that *stakeholders'* desires are equally messy, complex, and changing.) Fourth, and perhaps most importantly, purpose is framed as *unitary*: there can be only *one* essence, *one* intention, *one* mission, *one* aspirational outcome if stakeholders can be expected to identify with it.

As is probably obvious, I see these assumptions – that purpose is an outward-facing claim regarding existence, that organizations are entities built from persons and their interests, that purpose is a straightforward ordering device, and that firms possess a single purpose – as highly dubious when it comes to complex organizations. Each is interested in what purpose *does* for organizations – what *goods* it brings – without examining what firms *are* and *become* when they organize in the pursuit of purpose. This is the problem created by the question of purpose: attempts to answer it, to transcend the two-camp binary thinking upon which it's based, are accompanied by simplistic models of organizations and organizing practices. Those simplified models impinge upon the imagination we can bring to bear on the problems corporations encounter (as well as the problems they create).

Carrying forth this line of thinking, the astute reader may have noticed that the opening phrase was *not* 'the firm's problem is *its* purpose.' Framing the problem this way would entreat firms (again, typically rendered as uninterrogated entities) and their managers to find a single purpose, understood as a noun, that fuels their action and satisfies their stakeholders. Instead, in proposing that '*the problem of the firm is purpose*,' I'm suggesting something both more abstract and more interesting: that *the* central issue around which organizing occurs is the notion of purpose, and purpose cannot be considered a simple noun. And I'll argue that this condition has become more acute under late capitalism.

As this book will show, corporate purpose can be passion and *raison d'être*, but it can also be a vague evocation, a branding endeavour, a lingering question, a site of struggle, or a cudgel brandished to force compliance. What purpose *is* depends on how it's deployed in practice. Asking '*what corporations want'* is therefore a route to interrogating how purposes emerge and become animated.[5] Purpose, in this sense, is *what firms do*, but that doing is more conflictual and disorderly, more driven by the forces that make them want in particular ways, than our theories currently grasp.

And then, as mentioned a few paragraphs ago, I'll take one further step: I'll show that battles over purpose are really *contests for control*. Because our corporate practices typically afford strategic managers the capacity to articulate the firm's purpose, they believe their decisions *control* the firm. The image of management underlying such a stance is often one of shrewdly guiding the firm across the choppy waters it encounters, with corporate purpose (as frequently embodied by strategic managers) serving as its rudder. I argue that such a metaphor is illusory. It may even be a dangerous *delusion*: not only is decidability about the firm's trajectory contested terrain, but forces well beyond the control of the strategic manager participate in the very *constitution* of the firm and its purpose. Consequently, the very strategic action designed to control the firm via purpose may have sharply ironic – what I'll call *dis/organizational* – consequences.

As the chapters to follow show, far from a simple justification for existence and action, a richer vision of purpose problematizes conceptual foundations: it disrupts what we consider firms to be (taking up ontological problems) and argues that we need new tools for sensemaking (epistemological problems). It implies a radical revision of what we consider 'the firm' to be. The first step in that re-imagining is to understand, richly, the multiplicity of purpose.

The question of multiplicity

The issue implied in both the battle between the two competing camps and attempts to transcend it, along with my claim that purpose exceeds strategic managers' efforts to control it, is the neglect of *multiplicity*. When most people think of corporate purpose – when they ask, 'what do corporations want?' – they generally respond in the singular. As mentioned in the preceding section, firms are typically understood as integrated entities possessing a single overriding goal. Though there may be sub-goals, such secondary objectives should fall neatly in line with the aim of driving profit through a particular line of activity in an integrated and clearly bounded entity recognized as *a* corporation.[6]

An example of this thinking is Collins's (2001) tremendously influential book *Good to Great*. In it, Collins draws on Isaiah Berlin's analogy of the hedgehog and the fox, a tale in which the fox knows many complicated strategies for hunting, whereas the hedgehog knows only one way to navigate the world:

> Foxes pursue many ends at the same time and see the world in all its complexity. They are 'scattered or diffused, moving on many levels,'

says Berlin, never integrating their thinking into one overall concept or unifying vision. Hedgehogs, on the other hand, simplify a complex world into a single organizing idea, a basic principle that guides everything. … For a hedgehog, anything that does not somehow relate to the hedgehog idea holds no relevance. (p 91)

This, of course, is a false dilemma. Pursuing multiple aims need not be 'scattered' or ineffective, nor is a single fully shared aim a necessity for practice. Nor is it the case that articulating a single overriding vision will generate unanimity across the disparate practices that comprise a firm. Hedgehogs, those laser-focused strategists, may well miss the numerous ways their firms exist beyond the production function (see Drucker, 1946). And in typical corporate governance conversations that invoke the two camps mentioned, shareholders (incidentally, not all firms have a share-based ownership model) tend to be portrayed as motivated *only* by wealth – a depiction that runs counter to the recognition that their values are as complex as any other person's[7] (Thompson & Davis, 1997; Brennan, 2006). Corporate purposes therefore can, and perhaps *must*, serve many masters – especially because those masters themselves contain multitudes.

It is not enough, however, to see those many masters as summoning purpose*s* in the plural. This book will go further and argue that purpose is always *multiple*: purpose is many things, assumes different forms, accomplishes myriad goals, addresses varied values, and is the unstable result of numerous influences – *all at once*. This multiplicity is the same for firms; in fact, separating *firm* and *purpose* on this count may be impossible. This book, and the theory it advances, starts by interrogating the assumptions of a singular logic for purpose. What if corporations, even when they're made to *signal* uniformity because of the expectations of stakeholders or a market (shaped, incidentally, by the likes of Collins), are fundamentally *many things at once*? What if we give up on the notion of a single strategic direction, a unitary purpose?

Using these questions as a point of departure, this book makes another move to challenge a taken-for-granted element of the battles over purpose – the one brought up in the critique of the George et al (2023) reviewed earlier. It poses a simple, perhaps even naïve, question: what *are* these things we call corporations that they might be said to possess a *purpose*? And what if the organizations to which we attach purposes aren't merely aggregations of individuals and their interests, but are far more complex, disorderly, protean – *and thus more interesting* – than we've been led to believe? What if the organizations we treat as 'things' are *also* many things at once?

Consider the Catholic church – not exactly a *firm*, but surely a powerful global institution populated by local organizations (and not just houses of worship) around the world. In a conversation in the *New York Times*, journalist Elizabeth Breunig replied to the question, 'what do we mean by the Catholic church?' She replied:

> When we're talking about the Catholic Church in this context we refer to a number of things. The Catholic Church refers to, at times, the hierarchy, the church authorities. It, at times, refers to the laity, everyone who is baptized Catholic and receives the sacraments and is confirmed to the church. And then at times, it refers to the internal logic, the tradition, the rules of the Catholic Church. It takes all of those things to constitute it. (Bruni & Douthat, 2020)

As one considers how and when the church gets deployed in social practice, why it appears, who or what represents it, and to whom the representations happen, one could certainly add many more facets to what Bruenig counts as 'the Catholic church,' including when 'it' becomes bound up in political battles, reproduction debates, sexual abuse scandals, intergroup and ethnic violence, family heritage, or spiritual visions. The point is that any singular response to the question put to Bruenig would fail to address the multiplicity of its manifestations.

If we can't determine unambiguously what the Catholic church *is*, what hope would we have of knowing what it *wants*? Responses to questions such as 'what does the Catholic church *want*?' or 'what is the Catholic church's *purpose*?' thus necessarily imply multiplicity. 'It' wants many things, contrasting things, paradoxical things, things that shift across time and context. The task of figuring out what the church wants has been at the core of conflict within and around the church, in the myriad of practices in which 'the Catholic church' is invoked, for a couple of millennia. And Bruenig's attention to *constitution* is important, for it urges us to reject the presumption of entitativity already mentioned, and instead, to ask how those elements are stitched together in the accomplishment of something recognizable *as* the church – and also how the seams created by the stitching may challenge its smooth practice. (More on that in Chapter 3.)

Thinking of firms and purposes in this register means understanding them as *ontologically* multiple (Mol, 2002). Considering only corporate purpose for the time being, multiplicity is neither about options for alternative views, nor is it the expressions of the varied perspectives individuals bring to bear on what the corporation should do. Instead, ontological multiplicity is about how 'things' materialize differently – how they come into existence and find recognition – as they are implicated in different activities marked by 'assemblages' of objects, people, and discourses (Ehrnström-Fuentes & Böhm, 2023).

Thinking with ontological multiplicity, 'purpose' names a fluid and precarious, yet absolutely essential, component of organizing – one that takes on different hues when deployed in different practices. A coordination device, a legal justification, a collective commitment, a brand, an appeal to stakeholders, a disciplinary cudgel: they *all* are purpose, *all at once*. Accordingly, focusing on an explicitly stated doctrine written into a corporate charter (see Pollman, 2021) may well miss the *operative*, and potentially inadvertent and impeding, logics *performed* by corporate purpose. By way of illustration, in a study of the creation of a military aircraft, Law (2002) demonstrates that the aircraft (the British TSR2) exhibits ontological multiplicity across its many manifestations, but then shows how its 'various versions also interfere with one another and shuffle themselves together to make a single aircraft' (p 3). A key question for this book, then, has to do with the practices that make a firm *appear* singular – and whether the 'shuffling' Law mentions also creates potentials for firms' re-invention.

That's the complexity this book takes up. Be warned: it'll get messy. But also, I hope, provocative.

The stakes

This talk of ontological multiplicity could lead one to think that this book will be yet another esoteric academic exploration of a corporate commonplace – the latest iteration of the tired academic exercise of showing what we thought was real and stable isn't *really* so solid once we understand how it's constructed. Acknowledging that possibility, the urgent question is this: what are the stakes here – why should anyone care about battles over purpose? And why would we need a new conception of the firm to support it?

One answer is that the consequences of the battle mentioned, between advocates of shareholder primacy and stakeholder obligation, are crucial for our shared social future. No book can hope to put the two-camp debate to rest, but a perspective with which to grasp its consequences for firms can offer a useful tool to organization studies scholarship. In other words, understanding what commercial firms want, and *how* they want, is crucial for diagnosing contemporary social ills and steering toward better futures. Corporations – and not merely large and easily identifiable multinational corporations – are among the most influential actors on the planet. Probably the most influential.[8] When encountering any site of influence, it's essential to be able to explain, and perhaps even predict, its action. To do so, we must know what it *wants*. And only when we can grasp what (and how) corporations want can we ask the more pointed and pressing question: *what's worth wanting* in the first place?

Second is that if purpose is multiple, then there can be no single correct or canonical answer to what a given corporation wants. If its wants aren't unitary, we analysts need a framework that allows us to grasp that multiplicity. The conventional answer to questions of corporate wanting is that what a corporation wants is a function of its founder, its senior leadership, or its shareholders: they're generally assumed to *make* the firm desire particular outcomes because those are the things *those groups* want. In such a telling, the corporation is merely a tool, a vessel for the intentions of influential individuals to realize their desires. In other words, in response to the question from the title, what corporations want is often understood to be what particular parties *make* it want.

But we should be under no illusions that the matter is as simple as this. If we put the question to a firm's chief executive, board of directors, or shareholders, we'd be unlikely to get a unitary answer beyond platitudes about profit or some recounting of a mission statement. But if we broadened out to other stakeholders like employees, customers, or members of communities surrounding the firm's operations, we'd likely hear an array of contrasting versions of purpose, not all of them aligned with the first set of voices. If purpose is contested terrain, the interesting and important questions arise when these groups come into contact, and potential conflict, around the path(s) to pursue. Efforts to shape organizational trajectories via assertions of purpose are crucial to understanding the trajectories firms pursue.

A third answer to the question of stakes – the 'so what' question – is that we cannot reconceptualize firms, cannot add richness to the presumption of entitativity, without knowing the character of problems that purpose presents. Complex organizations want in ways that cannot be reduced to the desires of individuals; their wanting exceeds persons' abilities to influence their trajectories. Corporations are more than simply tools to carry humans' yearnings; comprehending their practices requires that we attend to a much wider array of forces brought together in complex practices of organizing.

In the organization studies literature, steering an organization toward its purpose is typically understood as a managerial problem. Capable leaders, often trained at our best business schools, comprehend the economic realities, production trends, and models of human motivation to enable firms to accomplish their aims. Those business schools, however, frame 'the firm' as a coherent entity, a substance that has an obvious existence and unquestioned boundaries. And 'its' singular purpose, in turn, is generally understood as an outgrowth of the 'nature' of a business enterprise that must respond to seemingly objective realities and trends (Mayer, 2021). It is certainly not *wrong* to see the problem of purpose and associated models of firms as the realm of management, especially given the history of the corporate form, but the baggage associated with doing so limits our collective conceptual gaze and re-inscribes the battle discussed previously.

In other words, as Morrison and Mota (2023) argue in another recent model of organizational purpose, our vocabulary regarding purpose is limited by our theories of firms: 'it is very difficult to conceive of meaningful changes to the role of firms within existing theoretical frameworks because, much of the time, those frameworks are built on strong assumptions about what firms are for' (p 203). The point is that the problems we address when conceptualizing purpose are *those our frameworks tell us are addressable*. Unless we reconceptualize the firm, the pursuit of purpose will re-ignite the same divisions it always has. Portraying purpose not merely as an external claim on corporate activity, but as the central problem with which organizing must contend, is the first step in making that reconceptualization possible.

The chapters that follow outline how the problem of purpose is a *communicative* concern, but not in the sense most think about communication. In bringing together thinking on organizational communication, new materialist theorizing, strategic management, and authority, the book presents a substantial re-imagining of the firm, which both situates it firmly within late capitalism and presents a novel vision of these prominent organizational forms.

Illustrating purpose multiplicity

To activate that reconceptualization, I offer two relatively brief cases of firms struggling with the emergence of corporate purpose in the face of multiplicity. Let's begin this at the beginning.

The British East India Company

When thinking about firms, 'the beginning' is often represented by the British East India Company (BEIC), generally understood as the world's first multinational corporation.[9] Starting its life on the last day of 1600 with a charter granted by Queen Elizabeth – this was back when states and monarchs granted charters to support specific remits desirable to the polity – what became known as 'John Company' presents a captivating tale for its mix of commerce, colonialism, and empire.

What was the company's purpose? The BEIC's original aim, at least as articulated by a small group of wealthy London merchants and adventurers who wrote its charter, was to satisfy (and foster, and thus profit from) England's appetite for goods from afar. Over its history, however, that purpose shifted as the BEIC became a colossus, engaging in half the world's international trade in the 18th and 19th centuries (Farrington, 2002). It overtook the market first entered by the Dutch East India Company, founded in 1602, which was the first to disrupt the trade in spices then controlled by Portugal. But when it began, the BEIC's original remit was the Indian subcontinent and surrounding regions, where representatives traded for the spices, tea, sugar, pepper, textiles, and other commodities for which Britons yearned. Though early trade with Indian merchants was relatively genial, the relationship between them became complicated and contentious over time.

Knowing England's longstanding penchant for conquest, it should come as no surprise that the BEIC embodied the moral quandaries associated with British imperialism. As its trade grew in India, the company gradually allowed executives on the ground to engage in private trading alongside the company's business. The ability to control local trading practices and simultaneously bend them to the executive's personal benefit generated impressive wealth for high-level employees stationed abroad, but 'became one of a series of cancers that gnawed at the Company's ethical fibre' (Robins, 2012, p 86). The tension between employee self-interest and the good of the collective was not unique to the world's first real joint stock company, but made the drive for domination over local economies a personal mission that became embedded in the company's routine operations. A second purpose thus emerged as a companion to the purpose articulated in its charter.

One of the company's other cancers, and another source of purpose multiplicity, was its opium trade. Although British consumers became enamored with the Chinese goods like tea, silk, and porcelain made available via the BEIC, Chinese authorities had little interest in British goods. Those authorities went so far as to restrict European trading locations to a single port. Yet the BEIC found a lever in opium, which consumers addictively demanded but which was unquestionably outlawed in China. The company's experience with corruption served the BEIC well, however: produced in India under a monopoly the BEIC won in 1773 (a monopoly that earned the company a tremendous profit margin well into the 1830s), the company smuggled opium to private traders in Canton, where local officials were bribed to ignore the cargo. Chinese authorities sought to extinguish the smuggling, but the British military started an all-out war with China to open the country to traders like the BEIC. John Company eventually extricated itself from the opium trade, but whether this was the result of its leaders' moral conscience or powerful opium competitors is not clear (Blake, 1999). What is well known, however, is the tremendous toll opium addiction took on China (Zheng, 2003) and the enormous benefit the opium trade had on the company's coffers (Robins, 2012). In the wake of two opium wars in the 1800s, England only outlawed its trade in 1907.

Returning to the profiteering of local BEIC authorities stationed in India, London executives at one point attempted to extinguish the practice. But after the 1757 Battle of Plassey (*Palashi*), where the company's own quasi-military forces (which at one point outnumbered the British military) took control of Bengal, there was no stopping the company's incursion. The BEIC's shareholders in England, when polled by governor-general (CEO) Robert Clive, agreed that the battle was essential for the company's continued existence. Because the company's existence, and the colonization that became an outgrowth of its *raison d'être*, was believed by so many shareholders and citizens to be necessary for both personal and national fortunes, the military power that won Bengal also supported the BEIC's continued ambitions in India. The Battle of Plassey was key to securing the company's dominion over trade in the country, but it also generated the conditions that led to the Indian rebellion against British forces a century later. A year after that rebellion (1858), the UK Parliament claimed India for Queen Victoria, effectively ending the BEIC's run in the country and ushering in the British occupation that lasted until 1947. The company survived another 16 years, being officially dissolved in 1874.[10]

This depiction provides a very small part of a very complicated story, one with immense implications for the foundations of modern capitalism – not to mention for the lives colonized by the BEIC's commercial and military forces. Unfolding over nearly three centuries, the BEIC lived far longer than anyone with a 21st-century vantage point could expect. The issue at the core of this tale is not one of longevity, however, but *dis/order*. Specifically, why did a company with ambitions to cultivate commerce and culture – a company that had access to all the resources needed to match its ambitions – find it so difficult to control the practices in which it engaged? Its managerial employees seemed similar to one another in background and aspiration, its financial and military capacities were vast, its partners and competitors were clear; why then did such disorder and accretion of purpose ensue?

One possibility lies in the internal processes of the firm. A key source of the BEIC's influence was its unique financial structure. This is generally regarded as the first joint stock ownership company offering limited liability. The purchase of shares in the company provided the capital necessary to fund the company's excursions, and when boats and men failed to return, when the citizenry of India revolted, and when the company's fortunes reversed, the owners of BEIC stock were only on the hook for the prices of the shares they purchased. This financial arrangement provided the company with an allied purpose in providing returns to investors. It also gave the BEIC an easily identifiable decisional doctrine to guide its trajectory. Because the shares were available on London financial markets as commodities that could be bought and sold, shareholders began to pressure the company's decision-makers to engage in practices that increased the value of those shares. In due course, the company took as one of its purposes the ensuring of shareholders' long-term financial returns. Although it's hardly startling from a 21st-century vantage point, that the first company owned by a broad set of changing shareholders experienced competitions over authority – that shareholders' claims to property were translated into assertions of control over the firm's purpose – was rather surprising to observers at the time.

Anglo American Mining Company

Although the BEIC case is fascinating, one could reasonably argue that it is in no way representative of contemporary firms. So let's consider a case that's a bit more current in both time and topic. This one is the South African mining company Anglo American, the largest private sector employer on the African continent and the third largest mining company in the world (it operates in 65 countries across six continents). The company was founded in Johannesburg in 1917 but moved its headquarters to London in 1999 after a merger. Dinah Rajak's (2011) book *In Good Company* offers a compelling account of how the firm's corporate social responsibility (CSR) initiatives allowed it to accumulate and exercise power because those programs drew on a relatively new logic of authority in the socioeconomic milieu. Rajak notes that trans-national corporations like this 'require constant renewal, need constantly to be remade, seeking not just new sources of legitimacy but new sources of power, new avenues of practice in order to sustain and expand their operations' (p 17). Offering an ability to shift its claims of purpose, CSR provided those sources of legitimacy and power.

In the 1990s, corporations encountered a new force influencing their operations, one grounded in the second camp on purpose mentioned previously. In no small part a response to the dominance of Friedman-esque beliefs in the preeminence of profit, a new moral code of global corporate citizenship emerged, where firms were understood to have 'conscience, culture, DNA, and even heart' (Rajak, 2011, p 36). Logics of a competitive marketplace were still pervasive but began to be accompanied by claims that morality is at the centre of firms' existence – a claim of an overarching purpose. Rajak terms this 'responsible competitiveness,' a hybrid that retains the supremacy of marketplace logics while asserting that what counts as '"value" can be broadened to include sustainability and social welfare, so making social responsibility itself subject to competitive rigours of the market' (p 10). These hybrid logics of CSR were articulated at first globally, by entities like the UN Global Compact, CSR conferences, a network of NGOs, and (to a lesser extent) governments. If corporations were to be moral citizens, they needed to embrace this conception of value and show how their work addressed pressing social problems like global poverty and health disparities.

Such a model of corporate responsibility was taken up enthusiastically by Anglo American in both its pronouncements and its practices. Unsurprisingly, however, CSR was complicated for a large multinational in extractive industries. To illustrate, Rajak relates the company's HIV/AIDS initiatives, noting that HIV prevalence was higher (20–25 per cent of the workforce) in mining than other industries, in part because of the vulnerability of the large number of impoverished migrant workers. In the context of a lack of governmental attention to disease prevention in South Africa, Anglo American executives talked about the need for the company to take its own action on this issue, framing it as a *moral* mission. But there was also an actuarial benefit, since providing anti-retroviral treatments were significantly less expensive than the impairments to worker productivity HIV/AIDS caused. Rajak notes that this quantification of benefit was deemed necessary for the executives in London and their need to satisfy shareholder concerns for profit, suggesting morality may not have been the sole aim.

One way the company controlled the distribution of the HIV/AIDS treatments was to set up, at a large platinum mine in Rustenburg, South Africa, compounds with dormitories designed to prevent the miners – almost exclusively men – from engaging in risky sexual behaviour in the informal settlements surrounding the mine. (Although company housing has been common in many settings, this was new for Anglo American.) The company encouraged workers, even those with families, to live in these dormitories and to reject the informal settlements beyond the fences enclosing the company's property. Workers living in the dormitories enjoyed regular health monitoring and maintenance; 'unclean' and threatening outsiders (such as prostitutes) could also be kept at bay. HIV was, accordingly, portrayed as a threat existing beyond the firm's boundaries, one the company's managers worked to keep outside. The CSR work of HIV/AIDS prevention involved, then, interesting boundary work: the miners' health was claimed as Anglo American's responsibility, and boundary enforcement protected the productive capacity of these resources.

Initiatives like this allowed Anglo American to portray itself as a champion of public health and human rights in locations where those CSR logics were promulgated. Rajak noted that its 'narratives present the company as an engine of growth and industry, an agent of empowerment, and midwife of democracy. … CSR past and present is thus mobilised to create a history which purifies the past and reinvents the company' (p 67). As a mining firm rooted in South Africa, Anglo American's present could not be divorced from its colonial past and its founding in apartheid. CSR aids in purifying the firm, proffering a penance for past sins. Rajak's implication, then, is that this foray into CSR may have been mere 'purpose-washing.'

Another example Rajak provides on this theme is that the company developed 'Empowerment Deals' in response to the post-apartheid government's edict to generate increased market share for Black-owned-and-managed companies. This initiative won the company political capital in South Africa, though it was likely associated with corrupt governmental rent-seeking behaviour that capitalizes on firms' CSR activities exposed by Bayart (2000) and documented, in Tanzania, by Nilsson (2023). Interestingly, Anglo American's portrayal of these deals downplayed their origins as governmental mandates; the firm framed them instead as evidence that the firm was a progressive force, a corporate citizen always committed to South Africans. This argument was contested by black senior managers in Anglo American who accused it of being hollow and disingenuous, but their counterarguments eventually lost purchase in the public eye. Anglo American's branding initiative appeared to win the day.

Perhaps obviously, CSR and empowerment were not explicit parts of the firm's purpose at its founding. At the time of this writing, the company's publicly stated purpose is 're-imagining mining to improve people's lives' (https://www.angloamerican.com/about-us/our-purpose), yet Rajak notes that no evidence of such a pro-social mission was present before that 1990s CSR turn. One can thus question, as Rajak does, the sincerity of the firm's commitment, especially given the need to navigate a complex set of financial and regulatory institutions. But doing so would require that we be able to ascertain the *real* purpose and, thus, to be able to identify precisely where sincerity resides. Were we to embark on such an effort to definitively locate corporate purpose, we would also want to acknowledge that CSR initiatives unfold in fits and starts over time, and what begin as 'empty' promises and tentative commitments can gain purchase later (Christensen et al, 2013). And if we reject simple assertions about organizational essences, we might see firms like Anglo American as exhibiting, and inhabiting, *multiple* purposes, *multiple* ways in which the company might be taken to be 'sincere.' Corporate wanting is, in other words, multiple, shifting, and not easily determinable. Perhaps a better wanting question in this case, then, could be this: what attachments matter when a firm expresses a desire to be a 'good company'?

The lesson of Anglo American is that purpose, as a form of wanting, can mutate as new attachments between the firm and NGOs, communities, governments, workers, and the like to develop. Practices that implicated large multinationals like Anglo American via finance and (inter-)governmental regulation provided a new way to evaluate corporations like this one. Rajak states clearly the changed practices and the new attachments they offered:

> CSR thus provides [trans-national corporations] with a platform to forge alliances with diverse actors in the development arena (including many who previously would have possessed divergent agendas and conflicting ideologies), enabling them to incorporate social challenges and counter-hegemonic voices, and pave the way for development to be reframed according to their interests. (p 62)

The discourse of responsible competitiveness and its injunction for firms to address both local and global problems enabled the extension of Anglo American's boundaries, though these extensions were not always the intentional choices of the company's strategic management. Expansion occurred as 'citizenship' became an expectation of corporate practice, as HIV/AIDS ravaged workers' bodies, as corporate-NGO-government partnerships became expected practices, and as governmental regulations re-shaped ownership (as in the aforementioned Empowerment Deals). Purpose was thus a complex and contingent *practice* of multiplicity not reducible to strategic managers' choices. And purpose was at least as much about the surrounding logics and attachments as it was about managerial action.

The lessons of the cases and the question of authority

The BEIC and Anglo American cases illustrate something important about corporate purpose. As suggested, purpose is neither unitary nor monolithic; it is ontologically *multiple*. Purpose is multiple in the sense that it takes different forms, manifests differently in different practices, and depends on the position of those relating to it at a given moment in a flow of activity. The purpose of these companies surely felt very different to the colonized Indians and the dormitory-dwelling miners than it did to shareholders, British royalty, South African government representatives, or CSR advocates. These groups would have provided sharply contrasting interpretations of what the corporation *wanted*. And the shifting aims to which each of those groups put these firms also shaped the meanings they made of them. Purpose was multiple, too, in its incarnations: it appeared in formal charters, in pronouncements that responded to new social expectations, on the bodies of those representing it and subject to it, and in practices that evinced priorities not always reflected in declarations from the firms' leaders.

Further, in these cases, purpose was not merely the product of human minds. The allure of Indian and Chinese goods, the concealing of valuable metals and gemstones under layers of barely penetrable earth, the addictive quality of opium and tea, generations of oppression of nonwhite bodies, and the menace of a deadly virus *summoned* corporate wanting. Purpose, as the reason(s) for these firms' existence, shifted over time in response to the pursuit of profit, the establishment of boundaries, and the modes of internal operation (including the influence of obstinate shareholders, CSR demands, and unruly bodies and material artifacts). And at least in the case of the BEIC, the spiraling of its purposes beyond any simple control led to the firm's eventual expiration.

Ascertaining a firm's purpose – *what a corporation wants* – is not, therefore, like the fable of the blind men and the elephant, where we are to conclude that each man's limited access to sensorial data could be triangulated were there only a formula (or a person) to bring the observations together. Such a stance would assert that the purpose of the BEIC and Anglo American could be discovered if we could only get all the human sensemakers in a room and find some common ground across them. Ontological multiplicity argues, in

16

contrast, that there is no object, no *real* element to be discovered, that we can call 'the firm' or its sole purpose (Ford & Harding, 2004). The varied renderings of firms and their purposes are not alternative interpretations of one 'true thing,' but are alternative, and potentially oppositional, manifestations unlikely to fit nicely together to form a single image.

Accordingly, statements of purpose purporting to characterize 'the' firm, those claiming that it's possible to identify the one *real* reason a firm exists, are political stories told for partisan aims. One important aim, when purpose is defined by those claiming to speak on behalf of the firm as a whole, is the coordination of activity under a single banner (a form of the aforementioned managerial control). But another can be to solidify the relations of authority that privilege some parties over others in practices that invoke 'the' corporation – where capital flows more to some locations than others. Yet there is no a priori reason to believe that the story of purpose is *only* the one told by strategic managers, since an aim underlying *counter-narratives* can also be to marshal forces for a movement to challenge corporate influence toward social change. How purpose becomes known – how it is operationalized – is thus a hermeneutic matter that involves 'reading' the practices associated with a given corporation and ascertaining what it 'wants' and where it's going. But no single reading can ever be *true*. If strategic managers endeavour to control the being and becoming of the firm by articulating a unitary corporate purpose, they are very likely to meet substantial disappointment. The BEIC and Anglo American cases show a myriad of forces beyond human actors and the multiplicity of materializations of purpose, which suggest that achieving managerial control over corporate identity and trajectory may be at best an illusion.

Another way of saying this is to hold that what the BEIC and Anglo American *wanted* was never singular – but neither were the practices that became identified as the entities 'The British East India Company' and 'Anglo American.' Wanting was always a product of the practices and decisions falling under the mantle of 'the' firm. Those practices and decisions were embedded in actors' reflexive understandings of the firm, selections of insides and outsides, and models of control over operations (and the bodies involved). These elements thus speak to the notion of *authority*.

In the typical Weberian rendering of authority, the concept is attached to a person with a position, knowledge, or magnetism; in the reinterpretation by Follett and Barnard, attention turned to the power of messages to convey orders in the context of an agreeable relationship between leaders and followers. What the cases reveal is that the trajectories of purpose, and thus of these firms, were guided by (a) conceptions of value, here calculated in the register of capital accumulation, and (b) visions of property, both in terms of their assertions of control over elements of the world (including persons) and their beliefs about what can be taken to be 'proper' organizational objectives.

The two cases in this section show that authority is far more informative about organizational purpose and trajectory – and is thus also the site of conflict and contestation – than OS's conventional thinking on the theme. This book, in fact, will pursue this richer conception of authority, going so far as to frame firms as authority *machines* that seek attachments in ways that cultivate purpose multiplicity.

Why a theory of the firm? The stakes, take 2

This book is aimed primarily at scholars of organizations, those who identify with the field called organization studies (OS).[11] This is a broad and interdisciplinary field; despite a few isolated efforts (such as Pirson et al, 2022) it has kept an arms-length distance from theories of the firm. Those theories develop answers to four key questions: *why firms exist, how they operate internally, where their boundaries lie,* and *how they secure profitability (or competitive advantage) in the market.* Theories pursuing these issues tend to be dominated by OS's distant cousins in the fields of strategic management and managerial economics. Indeed, Davis and De Witt (2021) acknowledge the divide between the fields, suggesting that organization theorists are interested in why firms exhibit the forms and behaviours they do, whereas strategic management and economics scholars more narrowly attempt to tie particular features of the firm to its economic performance. Consequently, classics of the OS field are ignored in most theories of the firm, and strategic management and economics thinking has made little inroads on the questions regarding the dynamics and impacts of organizing asked by OS scholars. Because strategic management's explanations for firm performance generally point to either industry categories or firm-specific configurations of resources, theories of the firm generally sidestep attention to the practices that (re)establish firms' existence while also disregarding disputes around performance assessment.

As I note in Chapter 2, theories of the firm weren't intended for OS scholars, particularly not those with a critical bent. They were first imagined by economists, the sort whose models of organization strip away the fascinating complexity of organizing. They were then taken up by strategic management thinkers and legal scholars, many of whom were strongly influenced by economic modes of reasoning. Across these visions of the firm, a particular sort of theory took root: the sort that sees the world as patterned by forces beyond our control, one where the role of theory is to articulate generalizable claims about the relationships between inputs and outputs. These are normative theories, the sort populated by *should* statements and straightforward 'if-then' reasoning aimed at seemingly unambiguous performance outcomes. They're useful when the aim is advancing unequivocal assertions about firm ownership and governance or about how to adjudicate different groups' claims on the firm's assets.

But that, of course, is not the only type of theory. And, to return to the two camps introduced earlier, some suggest that pursuing the zero-sum versions of efficiency proffered by existing theories of the firm (those in the first camp) are fundamentally incompatible with the moral claims of those populating the second camp (see, for example, Ghosal & Moran, 1996).

Scholars who hold complexity, uncertainty, and contradiction as key planks of the world; those who ask *how* rather than *what* questions; and those who ask theory to lead simultaneously to novel insight and creative action tend to find little of value in existing theories of the firm. Those scholars may know about the practical impact, even dominance, of theories of the firm in law, economics, and corporate governance, but then again these theories are involved in a game that doesn't interest them. These are the scholars of *organization* found in many fields; though many of them are drawn to the study of corporations, the questions they ask tend to be about the social consequences underlying firms' contemporary configurations and the consequences of organizing practices.

For these OS scholars, ignoring theories of the firm is a missed opportunity. As the preceding paragraph noted, theories of the firm form the contours of both corporate law and managerial responsibilities (Deakin, 2017); neglecting these vital influences on organizational practice leaves a significant gap in our conceptions of firms as complex and precarious organizations. For instance, the literature on firms as potential moral agents – a key set of issues for those in OS who study CSR, corporate power, and the like – hinges on what we conceive these collectives to be and the legitimacy of the purposes to which they're put (Boatright, 1996; Rhee, 2008; Orts & Smith, 2017). Likewise, research on knowledge, learning, and innovation generally builds on conceptions of internal organizational practice, models of collective performance, and assumptions about boundaries that are driven by theories of the firm. And scholars throughout OS acknowledge that those in positions of authority draw boundaries and configure internal operations in ways that influence work practices and workers' identity formation, privileging some interests over others.

My aim in this book is to reclaim the theory of the firm for the scholars who puzzle over the mysteries of organization – where 'organization' can be both noun and verb. We OS scholars are just as interested in the questions addressed by theories of the firm as are those in economics and strategic management, though we tend to approach them from rather different angles and tend to eschew simple normative claims. Those issues (again, why firms exist, how they operate internally, where their boundaries lie, and how they secure profitability) have long been core to organization theory, even if they're not always stated in these terms. This book provides OS scholars the outline of a framework that can, over time, offer an alternative to the constrained view of existing theories of the firm. Offering perspectives on the four core questions can spur new lines of thinking and provide texture to conversations about firms in the fields of law, economics, and strategic management.

Strictly speaking, then, those who are curious about corporations *qua* organizations don't *need* a theory of the firm. They can examine the four questions without any such theory. But a framework that ties those concerns together, one that provides a logic for thinking through firms' complexities and differences, can help with articulating the value of their work for audiences outside their conventional domains. My hope is that such a framework can induce imagination in how we understand firms as ongoing communication practices, and that the unconventional connections it draws between purpose and authority produce new templates for examining commercial firms.

Preview of the book

Pragmatists would question the question in this book's title. They'd assert that the meaning of this question, as is the case with all questions, is shaped by the objectives to which we put it. Like firms and their purposes, the meaning of the question 'what do corporations want?' is ontologically multiple. One could follow existing theories of the firm in articulating paths toward greater operational efficiency and effectiveness, replicating the claims of the administratively focused research that has a long tradition in the strategic management and economic arms of OS. This move is front and centre in thinking on corporate purpose, where the aim is to enumerate the (positively coded) outcomes a compelling purpose brings, such as infusing work with meaning, providing resources for public accountability, or clarifying strategic direction (Lee et al, 2023; Pratt & Hedden, 2023).

In contrast, I position the theory developed in this book as framing the question in *critical* terms. Existing theories of the firm are not known for being critical-theoretical tools. They're an especially uncomfortable fit with critical projects that understand organizations as political systems and that see the task of scholarship as uncovering unjust exercises of power emanating from deep ideological structures (for overviews of this thinking, see Mumby, 1987 and Alvesson & Deetz, 2006). Yet if 'critical' is today less about ideology critique – a modernist discourse of suspicion that posits sedimented social structures as the source of injustice (Mumby, 1997) – than it is about communicative practice (Fournier & Grey, 2000; Del Fa & Vásquez, 2020); if it's about denaturalizing and decolonizing the status quo with an anti-performative intent in an effort to generate heterotopic and productive alternatives, rather than merely critiquing unjustified exercises of power (Kuhn, 2021; Loacker, 2021); if it's thus about the subtle shift from negative critiques of managerial power toward affirmative and imaginative engagement with alternative organizational futures that encode historical asymmetries in struggles over meaning (Rosiek, 2013); then an unconventional theory of the firm can indeed be critical. In this register, advocating a Communicative Theory of the Firm, as this book does, is less about dislodging existing perspectives on commercial organizations and more about developing tools for imagination that can inspire new questions and, in turn, new futures. Deploying those tools is about both pointing out the unintended consequences of established configurations of corporate wanting and generating alternatives that respond to the exigencies of capitalism's present.

A key argument of the book is that a relatively new development in the operation of capitalism – what I'll call *communicative* capitalism – makes corporations want (that is, makes them pursue purpose) in ways that interfere with a demand for new 'becomings' (the awkward term is meant to signal multiplicity and emergence, as I'll discuss more in Chapter 4). The central point of the book is that the forces of communicative capitalism advance conceptions of purpose that constrain the very aims from which those purposes emanate. A novel tool for imagination is required to enable alternative becomings – and such a tool can be found by understanding communication far differently than OS scholars typically do.

To pursue this argument, Chapter 1 overviews the dramatic shifts in the practices of capitalism that make it revolve around communication practices. I term these affect capture, platformization, and branding, and suggest that new logics of capital accumulation, new demands for purpose multiplicity, and new requisites for examinations of for-profit firms result from these transformations.

Chapter 2 turns to existing theories of these for-profit firms, those that address the four questions posed earlier. Profiling what are called *governance* and *competence* approaches to theories of the firm, the chapter traces their varieties and assesses their adequacy for grasping the problems of purpose under communicative capitalism. (As one might imagine, it finds them lacking.)

Chapter 3 then develops a conceptual framework upon which an alternative may be built. It brings together theory that understands communication to be *constitutive* of organizations and organizing practices with theory drawing on new materialism(s) that portrays all practices as *sociomaterial*. It argues that the intersection of these bodies of thought connect at French philosopher Gilles Deleuze, whose work provides provocative images that induce the sort of imagination necessary to respond to the problem of corporate purpose.

In Chapter 4, I sketch out a distinctly Communicative Theory of the Firm (CTF) based on Chapter 3's framework. (I know this is an awfully long way into a book for the key theoretical contribution to be found, but a good deal of preparatory material is needed before this crucial chapter.) The theory presented there both develops responses to the four theory of the firm questions and proposes a model for analysing firms' wanting. In arguing that wanting, and thus the trajectory a firm follows, is an outgrowth of *decidability*, Chapter 4 presents a construct I call the *authoritative text* as the vehicle to make sense of organizations' purpose(s) in practice. Such a text, I contend in that chapter, is ongoingly produced by *claims to property* and *promises of value*; its production generates practices of *boundarying, branding*, and *binding* for authority machines.

Chapter 5 presents the case of a large airline's attempt to develop (or reclaim) a dynamic customer service capability, but its practices of boundarying made the performance of that capability brittle. Chapter 6 concerns a high-tech startup accelerator that advanced a model of value based around branding for the fledgling ventures it nurtured, one that worked at cross purposes with the model of value the accelerator – as a startup firm itself – practiced. And Chapter 7 is about Certified Benefit Corporations™, a relatively new development in corporate form that attempts to meld people, planet, and profits in a model of corporate purpose. The form of binding fostered by the 'B Corp' platform, though advocating community responsibility, ironically carried the potential for what I call collective atomization as individual firms pursued their wants.

The final chapter, Chapter 8, concludes the book by reiterating the overall argument of the CTF (simplifying it via a set of bullet points) and suggesting possibilities for investigations led by it. Drawing upon the theme of ontological multiplicity and the associated problem of purpose, this closing chapter asserts that the theory developed in the pages between here and there presents a novel way to make sense of *what (and how) corporations want* – one that promises to bear fruit for analysts looking for the sort of critical intervention a communicative new materialism can provide.

Notes

[1] A 2021 survey of 212 large companies, across several industries, by the consulting firm Deloitte found that 44 per cent had executive-level officers focused on the notion of purpose, including Chief Purpose and Chief Sustainability officers (Beery et al, 2022).

[2] Mocsary (2016) sees the issue as recurrent: 'Every few decades, there erupt political and academic debates over the proper nature and purpose of the corporation' (p 1320).

[3] Incidentally, firms rarely pursue (or even conceptualize) *maximization* per se; it's much more frequently simply higher share prices that count as SVM.

[4] A common move in this second camp, however, is a sort of hollow normativism, one that fails to follow the *should* claims of the ESG advocates with answers to the *how* questions that inevitably arise (see Greenfield, 2007). In this second camp, there is no shortage of calls for an overhaul of corporate practices and corporate law, but those calls are accompanied by precious little understanding of the complexities of corporations' wanting.

[5] In framing the question this way, there is the risk of attributing a typically human capability, wanting, to a nonhuman called the corporation, similar to the response that Talcott Parsons encountered when he asserted that social systems have specific needs and that they summon action that responds to them. Critics have argued that Parsons committed an inappropriate anthropomorphism – one that the question 'what do corporations want'

could be accused of reproducing. I'll address this issue more specifically in Chapter 3 with a discussion of new materialisms, where I'll argue for a route to understand wanting as a more-than-human *practice*.

[6] In the case of the Chandlerian (1962) multidivisional firm, each sub-unit can have its own purpose, so long as it contributes to the larger firm's performance and does not encroach on other units' business; this stance merely aggregates those individual purposes.

[7] For those who insist that firms are akin to persons, the lack of interrogation of the multiplicity of human individuals is stunning. Thinkers like Hacking (1995) and Rose (1999) clearly document that personality is a historical project of a range of discursive practices that, over the years, has engaged variously with the likelihood of multiplicity. Yet almost all scholars of organization, particularly those to be discussed in Chapter 2, ignore the possibility of multiplicity.

[8] Davis (2016a, b, c) argues that an emphasis on corporations as powerful entities may increasingly be misguided, as technological developments and new modes of coordination make our existing conceptions of firms outdated. This future may come to pass, but it's not here yet; corporations of all stripes and sizes continue to exert tremendous influence over our collective becomings.

[9] We should be skeptical about attributing too much causal power to 'firsts' like the BEIC. In a 1971 lecture, Foucault, quoting Nietzsche, cautioned, 'History also teaches how to laugh at the solemnities of the origin. The lofty origin is no more than "a metaphysical extension which arises from the belief that things are most precious and essential at the moment of birth"' (1977, p 143). Origins are stories that enable the punctuation of streams of experience, but such punctuations often are the result of sectional interests. Importantly, some historians, like Magnuson (2022) see the origins occurring much earlier, dating as far back as the Roman empire.

[10] In 2004, the BEIC was resurrected when the name 'British East India Company' was purchased and re-incorporated by two British and one Indian entrepreneur. It now consults other firms with sourcing and logistics challenges; on its website, the company outlines a purpose similar to the vision George et al (2023) urge, one that promises both profit and social responsibility – a set of claims that contrast with its predecessor of the same name.

[11] I use this term as a catch-all to encompass many associated conglomerations of thought, some of which have designations associated with professional associations, including organization theory, organization and management theory, organizational behaviour, industrial and organizational psychology, and organizational communication. Understandably, nuance is lost in collapsing these loose affiliations, but the aim here is to address several lines of organization-oriented scholarship not accustomed to thinking in terms of theories of the firm – and then to articulate an alternative.

1

New Forms of Value Generation
Under Communicative Capitalism

Regardless of the era, efforts to come to grips with the capitalism we confront invoke Karl Marx. As well they should. Inspired by Marxist thought, scholars for generations understood organizations as sites not only devoted to the production of goods and services, but also where the reproduction of social order, and the domination that secures it, occurs. Punctuating stories of the firm as an engine of capitalism is the figure of Henry Ford, who (substantially aided by a Detroit-area coal dealer) in 1903 founded the Ford Motor Company. The company introduced several innovations in manufacturing that defined 20th-century capitalism in the Western world, such that the term 'Fordism' has come to refer not merely to the company's production process, but also to the ideology it encompassed.

Most are aware of Ford's use of the Taylorist assembly line, introduced 10 years after the company's founding. Ford's assembly line standardized production, reducing production time of a Model T from 12 hours to 2.5, while also largely eliminating the skills required of workers. It's also become common knowledge that Ford, in 1914, initiated a new approach to wages, paying workers $5 per day (the equivalent of $153, roughly $19 per hour, at the time of this writing). The increased pay, along with a 5-day workweek, were presented as a form of corporate welfare that allowed workers to become consumers of the cars they were building, but it also reduced turnover and forced competitors and associated firms to match the wage to attract and retain employees. Combined, these elements increased productivity, efficiency, and consumption practices all at once (Jessop, 1992).

Somewhat less well-known elements of foundational Fordist practices were its antipathy toward unions and its surveillance of workers. The former point may be unsurprising, but the latter is rarely part of the story. Ford, the man and the company, sought workers with the correct moral fibre; the company thus created a 'Social Department' to investigate whether the men – employees were virtually all men – were engaged in illicit behaviour

24

such as drinking or gambling. The surveillance frequently involved the department's investigators tailing employees after hours, but those who passed these tests were rewarded with profit sharing. Keeping such high-quality workers around the plant for their entire careers was seen as both wise and desirable. The lessons of Fordism, in short, were about production and consumption: standardization, economies of scale, fostering a stable workforce, and the provision of adequate wages.

There's no precision when it comes to determining when or why Fordism fell; societal shifts rarely have simple, or single, explanations. Its decline seemed to begin in the 1960s and 1970s, as Western economies began to transfer the production of goods to countries with relatively smaller economies and lower production costs (including significantly lower wages). Economic Keynesianism receded and neoliberalism advanced; with it financial markets fragmented and nation-state regulation ebbed. Increased attention to services, away from material goods, led to a Western valorization of knowledge-based work. Management of the labour process shifted from bureaucratic command to technological, relational, and ideological forms of control. Identification with labour unions sank, leading to reduced feelings of connection with shared struggles. Individualism and an entrepreneurial ethic emerged as guiding principles not only in the economic realm, but for public life writ large. Consumption patterns gradually changed to smaller groupings, led by pervasive marketing alongside identity-based social movements; production shifted to accommodate flexible demand for more specialized wares. Firms' decision-makers recognized cost benefits to 'fissuring' the workplace by relying on networks of flexible independent contractors (Weil, 2014). Certainly, these shifts do not imply that Fordism vanished; it's that the dominant approach to capital accumulation took on a new cast as Fordism receded. Outlining that new style of capitalism is the aim of this chapter.

The ascendancy of communicative capitalism

What post-Fordism summoned was a new model of value generation. No doubt communicative practice has always been intimately tied to working and organizing; none of the features of the Fordist approach to production and capital accumulation are possible without the flow of meanings accomplished in and through communicative practice. Indeed, as I'll argue more directly in Chapter 3, communication is the very foundation of organizational existence. But only recently have observers argued that communication is fully central to the very fabric of contemporary capitalism. For instance, Moor (2022) argues that in the constitution of money and prices, in the conduct of promotion and marketing, in the circulation of information, and in the promulgation of economic narratives, communication *creates* – and does not merely *represent*, as many assume – economic life. Others, like Mumby (2016, 2019, 2020), argue that the indeterminacy of meaning in the practice of branding reflects a sea change in the capital accumulation process, one that exploits precarious and insecure selves, particularly (though not at all limited to) what is often called 'immaterial' or symbolic labour. Thinkers operating in this vein argue that late capitalism displays a significant and dramatic shift toward communicative practices of meaning emergence as constitutive of capitalist relations and processes of accumulation. We need new conceptual tools for this altered world.

A new 'spirit' of capitalism

Across the social sciences, there is no shortage of observers heralding the dawn of a 'new' version of capitalism. The adjectives signaling substantial shifts in capitalism are many: knowing (Thrift, 2005), surveillance (Zuboff, 2019), informational (Arvidsson & Colleoni, 2012), platform (Srnicek, 2017), financialized (Maia, 2022), and the list goes on. The differences between these versions are important, but the message of the group is that something is afoot, tied to the changes post-Fordism wrought. One of the more exhaustive efforts to account for the changes in capitalism is Boltanski and Chiapello's (2005) *The New Spirit of Capitalism*, which outlines capitalism's transformations as bound up in neoliberalism's veneration of the market as a rational arbiter of worth, alongside its devotion to private enterprise as a tonic for the problems of governance. Boltanski and Chiapello hold that capitalism is a continual shapeshifter, responding to criticisms by embodying new 'spirits' that offer ever-new justifications for its existence. The version we currently inhabit, they say, is built upon the project rather than Fordist bureaucratic structures; it sees capitalism as revolving around short-term activities and the ad hoc networks that spring up to accomplish them. Projectification, as a contemporary version of capitalism, values firms and individuals who maintain mobility through the complexly connected networks that projects activate: we learn that we must work 'never to be short of a project, bereft of an idea, always to have something in mind, in the pipeline, with other people whom one meets out of a desire to do something' (Boltanski & Chiapello, 2005, p 110). The project becomes the mode by which value is attached to subjects and objects (Jensen, 2023).

Boltanski and Chiapello (2005) take the further step of situating projectification squarely in communication. We develop networks through project-based work, and those links – the practice and product of communication – become social capital activated in future projects. The authors note that this version of capitalism also develops in individuals particular sensibilities with respect to their participation in, and availability for, projects and the multiplex connections that are required:

[C]onnexionist man [*sic*] relies on his *communication* skills, his *convivial* temperament, his *open* and *inquiring* mind. ... He possesses a strategy for conducting relationships, a kind of *self-monitoring* that results in an aptitude for producing signs that can *facilitate contacts*. (p 114; emphasis in original)

These, perhaps obviously, are all communicative performances (not merely the first item in that list). But more to the point is that building out the notion of connection-making as key to generating the networks that make projects possible, Boltanski and Chiapello argue that an assortment of objects and mechanisms are constitutively bound up in those connections, including information and communication technologies, informal relations, relations of trust, agreements and alliances, networks of firms, synapses and neurons, and projects themselves (pp 117–18). These 'objects' are not merely tools, but are themselves active participants in the communicative practices that are, or become, projects.

In other words, capitalism has experienced significant changes, and there's something uniquely and deeply communicative (in a constitutive sense) about the present version. Value production has become communicative in ways it never was – or at least never appeared to be – in its previous iterations (Hill, 2015; Fuchs, 2020). Accompanying a broadened attention to the character of value production is a recognition that capital accumulation in the production/consumption process occurs in several varieties. Bourdieu (1986), for instance, argued that capital can be of the conventional *economic* form (financial elements like money), but can also be *social* (networks of connection), *cultural* (skills, habits, and tastes that comprise class) and *symbolic* (resources associated with prestige, status, or recognition). For Bourdieu, there is clearly significant overlap and co-determination across these forms, and they can all be both input to, and outcome of, profit-seeking activity. But the point is that what is deployed, developed, and captured in economic activity is more wide-ranging than typically conceived. Consequently, a foundation has been laid for how an enlarged conception of communication – one that refuses to limit itself to presentational skills in interpersonal contexts or message transmission – might be understood to be the motor of capitalism's contemporary form.

Capitalism's communicative spirit

Were we to entertain the notion that capitalism has become thoroughly communicative in this enlarged sense, what practices could support the claim? Informed by the aforementioned work by Mumby and the claims of the previous section, I see three: affect capture, platformization, and branding.

Affect capture

A first practice is the recognition that, with the rise of the service sector, the encounter between employee and customer supplanted the production process to become the key point of competitive differentiation and, thus, of value delivery. Three decades ago, Hochschild (1983) documented how the emotional connections forged in service work through communicative performances, even if fleeting, were increasingly expected of workers in service-oriented fields, with the typical examples being flight attendants, health care providers, and customer service representatives.[1] What Hochschild found is that not only does the notion of emotional labour provide insight into a wide array of organizing practices, but it also provides a tool to examine how the management of workers' emotions, in the workplace and beyond, sustains the very expectations – highly *gendered* expectations – that make the continued performance of the work possible. And to break from the conventional restricted conception of communication (as message transmission), think of the sensations generated in the service encounter, the subtle moves that control a customer's behaviour, the appropriation of passion in managing, the image-making of everyday office work, and the projections of fear and desire in strategizing – these forms of connection-making and connection-denying via emotional labour are all deeply *communicative* (Korczynzski et al, 2000). And those emotions, though long deemed the domain of personal cognition, have been shown to be more the product of histories of communicative meaning-making than detached in-the-moment stimuli for action (for example, Barrett, 2017). And even more to the point, the management of emotional expressions can serve as resources that confer advantage in group settings, suggesting a form of value that Zhang et al (in press) call *emotional capital*. Emotions and emotional labour, in short, are deeply communicative – and a manifestation of communicative capitalism.

Eva Illouz (2007) takes the argument about the place of emotion a step further in arguing for a tenor to commercial practice she calls *emotional capitalism*. The theorist *par excellence* when it comes to analyses of capitalizing on emotion, Illouz shows how movements in management emerging throughout the 20th century, most of which remain highly influential in the 21st, were preoccupied with how employees' emotional lives could be channelled in the interest of capital. To some extent, the transformation of emotion into capital comes via notions like *emotional intelligence*, which emerged most strongly in the latter parts of that century. Rather than a simple 'objective' feature of a person, emotional intelligence signals membership in a particular class and, in turn, displays that the person in question can control the self, be controlled, and can be deployed for creative and productive ends. Emotional intelligence, for Illouz, is thus an emotional *style*, which 'is crucial to how people acquire networks, both strong and weak, and build what sociologists call social capital, that is, the ways in which personal relationships are converted into forms of capital, such as career advancement or increased wealth' (p 67). Emotions are captured by the firms representing and accumulating capital.

The particular emotional style valued in post-Fordism embodies a distinctively *communicative* ethic, says Illouz. The link here is that the tenor of management under post-Fordism operationalizes communication as a mode of social competence able to meet the emotional needs of others. In complex organizations, persons with these skills are essential:

> Communication has thus become an emotional skill with which to navigate in an environment fraught with uncertainties and conflicting imperatives and with which one can engage in collaboration with others through skills in instilling coordination and recognition. ... Emotional capitalism realigned emotional cultures, making the economic self emotional and emotions more closely harnessed to instrumental action. (Illouz, 2007, p 23)

And it is not merely individuals who are expected to evince these emotional communicative skills. Illouz demonstrates how *organizations* now operate in an emotional register, as she draws upon Hewlett Packard's self-description (or, rather, a unit of the company's depiction) of its culture, which emphasized that HP employees could expect to 'breathe a spirit of communication, a strong spirit of interrelations, where people communicate' (p 22).

Extending this line of thinking, Illouz later argued that *consumption* has become pivotal to contemporary capitalism, though not merely as the final step in the utilization of commodities as in Marxist thought. Instead, what she calls 'consumer capitalism' re-works the relationship between objects/commodities and emotions. She posits three types of relation between objects and emotions in the process of consumption:

> Objects have an emotional-sensorial meaning constructed by a complex network of image-making industries ... objects are consumed in the framework of emotional motivations and intentions that are themselves framed by consumer culture ... finally, at the moment of consumption, these objects help create an emotional atmosphere between two or more people and mediate between their different desires. (Illouz, 2018, p 6)

Previewing my discussion in Chapter 3, Illouz portrays emotions as 'the products of socio-technical assemblages' (p 15) divorced from the interiority of the individual human; they are free-flowing forces at the root of consumption. Though this may sound perplexing, the upshot of her thinking is that objects and emotions are inseparable in consumption, to that point that emotions themselves are converted into consumable commodities. That recognition led Illouz to coin the neologism *emodities*. Not only do consumers seek emotional experiences like holiday resort travel or a temporary immersion in virtual reality *as* commodities, but they now define their very selves in terms of affective atmospheres and emotional possessions (Illouz & Benger Alauf, 2019).

Those experiences are increasingly the target of corporate design, as seen in the rise of the 'experience economy' and the proliferation of Chief Experience Officers ('CXOs') in corporations (Pine & Gilmore, 2011). Firms are now even commissioning their own fragrances to induce employees and customers alike to associate a particular scent, and affective aura, with companies and their 'experience centers' (Brown, 2023). Firms are, moreover, pursuing neuromarketing, which marketers see as operating beneath the level of targets' cognitive or conscious awareness (Morin, 2011). No less sensorial are so-called 'self-care' regimens and corporate wellness programs, which are of a piece with emodities since they individualize emotional responses to workplace stressors while fostering incessant social comparison, which promote the continual consumption of the products associated with a 'wellness' lifestyle. Emotional commodities, emodities, are what we learn to seek and what firms learn to offer. And it is not merely consumers outside a firm who purchase emodities; firms that foster emotional connections with employees and suppliers based on public stances on social issues can bind those actors tightly to the firm and its practices.

As a development in capitalism, affect capture is of course not universal, but the production, management, and capture of emodities presents a new logic for firms' capital accumulation. The centrality of emodities demonstrates how the communicative circulation of meanings prefigures and infiltrates experiences. The capture of emotions, in other words, is thoroughly communicative. Value production, then, is far more affect-driven, and thus communicative, than previously understood. Firms that can capture and capitalize upon emotions enjoy advantages in their markets.

Platformization

A second way we see the economic centrality of communication is in the practice of platformization. Platforms, as articulated by Srnicek (2017), are 'digital infrastructures that enable two or more groups to interact. They therefore position themselves as intermediaries that bring together different users: customers, advertisers, service providers, producers, suppliers, and even physical objects' (p 43). Beyond the interest in electronic connection, platforms are defined by a governance structure, including a set of guidelines for participation or membership, along with rules that foster (or constrain) connection, coordination, and collaboration.

Most frequently, platforms look like internet-based companies organizing an electronic enterprise (such as via an app or a website) where many smaller companies or independent operators offer specific services. Think Uber, Alibaba, Etsy, Amazon, Deliveroo, Zeel, and even Google: each firm provides a set of tools that allow users to build their own products or presence associated with the platform, with rules set by the platform owner. Consumers start with the platform, and then can locate the individual providers (sellers, operators), though they also can be assigned to individual providers based on a matching algorithm. Usually, too, there is cross-subsidization, such that using the overall service is inexpensive (or free) for consumers, with platforms making money through selling advertisements, selling users' data, or taking a portion of each sale. Recent versions of this phenomenon see the platform operators not merely taking a slice of each transaction, but also controlling the providers by constraining their pricing and limiting their ability to participate on other platforms.

A platform needs to attract a critical mass of users to both provide the demand to meet the contractors' supply and to generate the data that allow further economic rents; this attraction of users displays how communicative practice makes platformization possible. And it requires a critical mass of contractors willing to provide the service in question. Consequently, the cultural frames that valorize employment freedom, flexibility, and the technologically new are very much part of the platform scene.

Beyond cultural frames, however, investigations of platform work often foreground artificial intelligence (AI), and the algorithms powering it, as particularly powerful actors in platform work. When scholars isolate algorithms as 'things' coded with intention akin to human versions of agency, they're able to show how algorithms encode longstanding social biases (Rosenblat et al, 2016) and restrict contractors' opportunities for contestation (Vandaele, 2021). These are certainly valuable findings, but they only occasionally question the dominant model of capitalist reality guiding platformization, in which autonomous persons (more or less) willingly engage in contract-bound behaviour coupled to digital infrastructure. The question in much of this literature repeats an old refrain: the issue is control over the worker, where individual humans are losing autonomy as machines gain power.

When we put communication rather than entities (algorithmic or otherwise) centre stage, however, we embrace a vocabulary for making sense of the types and tenor of platformization practices that can free our thinking from the assumption of individual choice-making and organizational domination, even when those choices are delegated to AI. Were one to, for instance, examine the use of reputation systems – those that compile ratings of the supplier by previous customers to influence the results of a matching algorithm – in the conduct of platform work, what would become evident is that linking platform operators and service providers is not simply the connecting of individuals and organizations. Nor is the relationship merely *mediated* by a technological tool. Instead, studying the practices of platform work requires that we reject simple separations between firms, contractors, algorithms, and customers. For instance, though the materiality of 'cables, servers, interfaces, the desk you type at, the way light hits the screen' (Hill, 2021, p 573) are necessary in the production of platformization, these infrastructural elements could be understood as only some of the various participants in complex *practices*. And those complex practices involve desires, data, and values, among other more-than-material forces. If we were able to understand communication as the vehicle for connecting and dis-connecting such elements in practice, we'd start to see that algorithms are bound up with firms, bound up with contracts and contractors, bound up with work, bound up with desires/data/values. And were we to move beyond specific organizing practices to consider the forces that had to be in place to enable a platform-based 'gig economy,' we would further ask about the influence of firms and their private equity funders influencing governments to re-write laws conceptualizing and constraining the rights of contractors (as opposed to employees), delivering open markets for these firms, and providing quite favourable loans (Vallas & Schor, 2020); such influence cannot *not* be communicative.

Communication is thus the name for the practices, longitudinal and shifting as they always are, of algorithms connecting workers, fungible assets, funders, desires, and users into a relationship recognizable as a given platform company. It is contractors on platforms sharing insights on how to position themselves to profit from algorithms that otherwise remain obscure just as much as it is social movements altering the legal status of contractors and shaping the coagulating meanings around them (Laapotti & Raappana, 2022). Communication is also how idle objects (cars, homes, time, computing power) become coded as assets to be sold, such that virtually any property can transform into economic capital.

The business model guiding many of these firms, one that sees the data exhaust produced through the platform exchange as key to the economic logic, is also deeply communicative. That platform firms gather voluminous data on every micro-instance of engagement with their sites is by now well known, as is the practice of employing those data to design interfaces and deliver content to induce ongoing engagement. Understanding how platforms, *as practices themselves*, construct experiences, obscure the production process through information asymmetry, and project images that 'generate attachments that in turn cement political alliances with consumers that can be used to justify or further their practices' (Hill, 2021, p 570) requires an interrogation of communication. The question is about the meanings emerging on and through the flows of datafied subjectivity that (re)make the possibilities for platformization, which simultaneously constitute the firms populating this new logic of capitalism. And it is not merely the recognizable firms, like those already named, that emerge from platformization: as has long been the case in many industries, novel forms of capital accumulation give rise to new intermediary organizations that heretofore hadn't existed. Although platforms are themselves intermediaries, under platformization we see the advent of under-the-radar intermediaries like data (and ranking) aggregators, micro-targeting marketers, demand-side advertising technologists, and brand management gurus; these firms may not be the names we associate with platformization, but they have become essential participants in making the practice both possible and profitable (Sharkey et al, 2023).

The key question, then, is about the accumulation and capture of value from production/consumption processes distributed across an array of participants. Communication is thus how platformization operates, how it *materializes a practice*: from the exchange of messages that coordinate activity between heterogeneous actors, to the meanings flowing and congealing around participants, to the ways digital mediation organizes agency, to explorations of hybrid connection-making. When we broaden our conception of communication, it becomes evident that platformization, as a central mode of contemporary capitalism, is both pervasive and inherently communicative.

Branding

The third demonstration that capitalism has become profoundly communicative (this one longer than the preceding sections because of recent turns in the literature) can be found in the rise of branding as a contemporary logic of socioeconomic life. Branding used to be the province of marketing and advertising, where information about products (and to a lesser extent, services) distinguished those objects, functionally, from competitors. Most accounts point to the influence of Edward Bernays, nephew of Sigmund Freud, as the turning point. Writing in the 1920s, Bernays drew on psychoanalysis and crowd psychology to recognize that consumers sought products not merely to satisfy needs, but to fulfil deep-seated desires. And that turn is key: desires are primary motivations that neither action nor possession can extinguish, so if a product were to be linked to desires (and thus connected with values and detached from functions), unlimited demand could be the result.

That story is now well known. From soap to shoes to political candidates to universities to nations, marketing became much more about selling a desirable lifestyle and image of the self than about the 'objective' features of the product. But three revolutions in branding occurred in the century since Bernays and his ilk re-imagined it. First is an extension throughout the social world: what was to be branded were not simply products and services, but firms, communities, and individuals. The people guiding firms started to see that branding was key to differentiating the organization itself: not merely as a producer of goods, but as a site of value production and an object through which individuals could satisfy desires:

> It was not enough that a company would produce brands while remaining anonymously in the background. Nor was it enough that a firm attached meaning to its output as a mere afterthought. Increasingly, companies realized that they needed to brand their businesses and inject them with meaning as a whole. (Kornberger, 2010, p 14)

Branding, then, wasn't merely about making biscuits, beer, or bassinettes convey a lifestyle (Lury, 2004; de Botton, 2009); it became about creating meanings aligned with desires that induce attachments to the firm as a brand itself.

Tapping into consumer desires to brand a company isn't simply a ploy to sell more products and services (though it is also that). Connecting with the discussion of affect capture, because branding is about desire-based attachment, it has become key to the ways employees and customers alike identify with a firm as an extension of their individual yearnings for social impact (Rhodes, 2022). Desire thus forces firms to 'take a stand' on the potent issues of the day. This requirement to assume positions on social issues to signal to an internal audience was articulated in a US context by conservative political analyst Yuval Levin:

> [There is] a rising generation of employees in white-collar America … (who) enter the world of work expecting their workplace to stand for what they stand for and expecting a company that's not in the business of anything political to express political views, to stand for a kind of political identity when things happen in the country that speaks to their core concerns. Often, these are well-motivated concerns about race, about justice, about other things. Sometimes, they're more radical social views. But whatever they are, you find young workers pressing companies to become more political and to do so on the left. … Michael Jordan's old line that got him in so much trouble, that he doesn't talk about politics because Republicans buy sneakers, too, that's the logic of a lot of corporate America at the end of the day. And they just don't want to be in these fights. But increasingly, the logic looks a little different to them. Some of

their customers want them to be in the fight and to have something to say, whether it's about Black Lives Matter or whether it's about the big issue of the day. And a lot of the workers want them to. (Klein, 2021)

Levin may have been overstating the case a bit. But only a bit. A 2022 poll found distinctions on this count by age and political persuasion, at least in the US context: younger respondents (18–29 years old) were much more likely than their older (60+) counterparts to say that corporations should take a public stance on current events (59 per cent to 43 per cent); the split was 75 per cent to 18 per cent when comparing political left-and right-wingers. Further, 71 per cent of those youngsters would change jobs to work at an organization that made a positive impact on the world, compared to only 32 per cent of the old-timers (Gallup, 2022). Moreover, in line with Levin's point, when corporate leaders take political stances, it's perceived by employees and prospective members as 'authentic leadership' that makes the firm a more desirable place to work (Kärreman & Rylander, 2008; Appels, 2023; Wright, 2023). The upshot here is that taking a stand on vexing social issues is a key part of corporate branding and an expression of what firms (are urged to) want.

Under communicative capitalism, firms have good reason to speak purpose and brand in the same breath – and even to see them as identical. Little wonder, then, that public relations professionals now see it as their task to manage relationships between corporations and publics, less than promoting particular products and activities (Ledingham & Bruning, 2000). It also increases attributions of brand value (Pope & Kim, 2022), though observers note the persistent echoes of "woke washing": signalling faux social bravery through superficial messaging (Sobande, 2019). Clearly, branding has become about much more than presenting a desirable image to an audience. It's about the crafting and cleansing of the individual and social soul, presenting firms – particularly, as Levin says, white-collar firms – as tools in a putatively righteous battle for a certain type of social change. And though Levin presents this as being driven by a new generation of workers and consumers who prod corporate executives to represent company stances on contentious issues (which of course assumes that 'the company' is both determinate and has a single 'stance'), the plethora of consulting firms devoted to helping companies navigate these demands suggests a more complex communicative practice, one dispersed across sites and temporalities.

The second turn in branding is an extension in its targets, one that should be no surprise given the link to desire and value: branding individuals themselves. 'Personal branding' has become an industry unto itself, one that is about every individual's responsibility to project meanings about identity to provoke emotional responses and persuade audiences of the person's worth. Broad cultural attention to personal branding is usually dated to Peters's (1997) magazine article *The Brand Called You*, which argued that competitions in the employment and entrepreneurial marketplaces could be won by the development of narratives that create simple and lasting impressions in the minds of others. It is not simply that the person becomes a product; relationships as well as selves become marketable assets in a world beset by branding.

The personal branding 'movement' picked up significant steam with the advent of social media. Adept use of these new tools allows messages to circulate in ways previously inconceivable, and wider audiences meant more opportunities for impact beyond the personal relationship. Hence the rise of social media influencers, a form of celebrity that offers the dream of widespread admiration alongside financial profit (Vasconcelos & Rua, 2021). That profit comes as company brands align themselves with particular influencers and their personal brands, and also when persons leverage their personal brands into selling themselves within or beyond a firm, because a personal brand promises to increase one's value in the marketplace and raise one's profile in the pursuit of projects. It is interesting, too, that, *anti*-branding activity can ironically serve as a person's brand: entrepreneurs market 'anti-brand' brands to consumers hoping to craft an alternative claim to lifestyle – one that evades conventional corporate branding via consumption, of course (Rodrigues et al, 2021). Social media amplifies possibilities for connection while also (to hearken back to Illouz) fostering communicative-emotive styles valued by the audiences in relationships mediated by these media. Branding has become a logic for mediation and impact in the world, a recognition that meaning-making practice aligned with viral flows of feeling and the inspiration of images is the mode by which collective 'choice' proceeds (Ashcraft, 2022). It is no stretch, therefore, to see branding as a logic guiding large swathes of social life.

The third branding move is a shift in its site. If, as mentioned, branding is not reducible to advertising and public relations messages, where does it occur? Under both Fordism and much post-Fordism, the production and consumption of value were distinct activities: production of value occurred in the factory (or some version thereof where a good was manufactured), and consumption depleted the value when the good was used (perhaps in the home). The contemporary practice of branding, however, is about 'prosumption,'[2] where production and consumption are often coterminous and distributed among many participants – including those not employed by the firm (Ritzer & Jurgenson, 2010). Brands are now produced in a 'social factory' (Mumby, 2020). The purchase of emotional experience occurs also when consumers are drawn to *brand communities*, where consumers form collectives through their connections with brands and branded products (De Kosnik, 2013), those who contribute 'free labour' via content contributions (for example customer ratings, game play, or personal posts) to social media or the aforementioned platforms (Terranova, 2000), or those who engage in commons-based peer production like open-source software development. In many cases, 'community' is a misnomer, as most aficionados of Apple products, Doc Martens shoes, or Peloton workout equipment experience no interdependence and never interact beyond following the brand on social media.

Brand communities offer firms the opportunity to accumulate capital based on prosumers' labour. For instance, in Land and Taylor's (2010) study of the apparel company Ethico, the firm's marketing material made commercial use of employees' recreational activity outside working hours, blurring the line between workplace and private lives. And community members beyond those employed by a firm are framed as useful sources of continuously updated socio-cultural knowledge:

> [C]o-creation represents a dialogical model that no longer privileges the company's vision of production ... co-creation instead aspires to build ambiences that foster contingency, experimentation, and playfulness among consumers. From this perspective, customers are configured as uniquely skilled workers who, for the production of value-in-use to occur, must be given full rein to articulate their inimitable requirements and share their knowledge. (Zwick et al, 2008, p 166)

A logical question is whether this provision of free labour constitutes exploitation, regardless of whether prosumers claim to be willing participants or whether they're aware that their digital exhaust becomes a source of company profit (Andrejevic, 2013). Given the focus of this section, however, the more pressing issue is whether the articulation of the brand escapes the control of companies' marketing and advertising arms because of prosumers' participation. It is when these prosumers' co-creative labour alters a company's brand that questions arise for the theory of the firm. Although marketers suggest that adroit storytelling and consumer engagement enlists prosumers into alignment (Argenti, 2022), managers might rightly be concerned that the polyphony of voices participating in branding turns into a cacophony (Schmeltz & Kjeldsen, 2022). Cacophonous influence can wrest control of what might normally be seen as a firm's property – *its* brand – by those who seek to subvert, re-articulate, or augment the meanings of the brands, who often consider it equally *theirs*. In Derridean terms, the text escapes its authors – or, better, *attracts* and *accumulates* authors who vie with one another for authorship.

Given these three extensions to the practice of branding, one could be forgiven for confusion regarding just what a *brand* is. I find Arvidsson and Peitersen's (2013, p 32) conception useful:

> Today a brand is much more than a mere symbol of a product, created by a designated marketing division. Rather, brands are better understood as something akin to a common 'ethos' that is able to cohere consumers, employees, and other stakeholders around a common 'enterprise,' be this the reproduction of the particular 'feel' associated with a consumer brand or the co-construction of the common sense of purpose that defines a corporate brand.

The brand, here, is a narrative that ties various participants together in some version of a common pursuit, which simultaneously provides for that pursuit a sense of positive distinctiveness and conception of value. A *purpose*. It is about an ineffable sense of attraction or repulsion to the atmosphere associated with a firm – a manifestation of the aforementioned desire. In other words, the practice of branding forms organizations that orient to their surroundings in ways that foster claims to value production. Those claims to value production revolve around attention and attachment, primary vehicles for accumulation under communicative capitalism.

Conclusion

This section presented three manifestations of a new capitalist spirit, one I've labelled *communicative capitalism*. In any discussion of communicative capitalism, one concluding point is vital: Jodi Dean was here first. As a political scientist Dean's interest was less in understanding organizational practices and more in how new developments in social media altered political economy. She noted that our participation in democracy tends not to be about engaging in dialogue with others, especially those different from oneself, but is instead about sending messages into a system in ways that signal allegiance with one 'side' or another. Those messages may be considered by their senders to be democratic contributions, but:

> The message is simply part of a circulating data stream. Its particular content is irrelevant. Who receives it is irrelevant. That it need be responded to is irrelevant. The only thing that is relevant is circulation, the addition to the pool ... the more opinions or comments that are out there, the less of an impact any one given one [*sic*] might make (and the more shock, spectacle, or newness is necessary for a contribution to register or have an impact). (Dean, 2005, p 58)

The enactment of circulation not only undermines democracy – it's evidence of a new form of production. For Dean and others in this line of thought (a line that began, incidentally, with Galbraith and Habermas), the power exercised by owners of media firms dominates production to such an extent that it can be considered a neo-feudalism where the many (users, contractors) are compelled to serve the interests of the few (owners of platformed media enterprises). The fact that the drive to foster circulation and the experience of polarization has only intensified in the two decades since Dean's early statement on the topic is testament to the value of her thinking.

To say that capitalism has become communicative in no way suggests that the conventional actors in the capitalist drama of production and consumption – assets like land, resources, and machinery, along with labour power residing in bodies and the rise of financialization – are suddenly irrelevant. Instead, the argument of communicative capitalism is that the tenor of capitalism is shifting: assets are becoming ever more intangible and tied to production/consumption practices that extend well beyond the workplace. Positions in the relations of production accrue meanings that require transcending stark divisions between commodities and other putative entities. And communication manifests emotional styles that generate the social capital that has always been at least as important as the material. Added together, these suggest that capitalism has assumed a new form ... a new *spirit*.

What, then, is the thread connecting the three manifestations? What makes this a *new* spirit of capitalism? Simply put, the difference lies in the circulation of communicative practices that produce individuals and firms who/that embrace precarity and fluidity in their wanting. What capital is considered to be, where decision-making power resides, and how images are (trans)formed, are all situated in communicative practice – and nowhere else. Persons and organizations become individuated devices for the many forms of capital attraction and accumulation via the continual production of image – an individuation that dissolves distinctions between production and consumption and creates new potentials for control. Because value now *follows* image, participants in production/consumption become protean, their wanting a response to the ceaseless communicative circulation. Control thus becomes the continuous assessment of image's adequacy, enforced by data-based algorithms and enabled by the assertion of beneficent corporate purposes; as Deleuze (1992) observes, 'We are taught that corporations have a soul, which is the most terrifying news in the world' (p 6).

Toward responsive theory

The developments in the preceding section are not unfamiliar territory. Indeed, writers have been addressing the consequences of post-Fordism for years, and the phenomena generating communicative capitalism have received a good deal of scholarly attention. Yet in OS, communication's central role in firms' existence, as well as in capitalism, has been poorly recognized because it is not calculable in dominant practices, particularly those of finance and accounting: 'the types of communicative processes standing behind the production of innovation, brand, and flexibility cut across discrete tasks and functions, thus making them less easy to divide according to the principles of cost accounting' (Arvidsson & Peitersen, 2013, p 37). Aside from a need to expand the conceptual vocabulary of accounting, what does communicative capitalism summon from those of us trying to make sense of firms operating in its midst? How should theorists interested in understanding *what corporations want* respond?

Conceptual considerations

A first call that communicative capitalism issues to OS is a challenge to the boundaries regarding who and what generates organization. The preceding section showed that when prosumers engage in branding activity, we need to re-imagine where firms' boundaries lie. Beyond that, the attention to nonhuman actors, like the algorithms and physical assets bound up in platformization, are undeniably participants in organizing. Although some in the field hold on to visions of organizations that see them as conglomerations of individual persons alone, or merely the products of coordinated human action, or perhaps as systems guided by human strategizing, communicative capitalism shows that materiality cannot be relegated to the control of human intention. As we acknowledge that brands escape marketers' control, as we recognize the centrality of algorithmic governance in the process of capital accumulation, as we see emotions as exceeding human bodies, as commentators herald workplace trends that will soon be pervasive, as we absorb the allure of big data and AI, and as we grasp the consequences of ceaseless meaning circulation, we gradually appreciate that our conceptions of organizations require a thoroughgoing attention to the more–than–human.

Second, and related, communicative capitalism calls upon scholars to abandon efforts to think of organizations as stable and moored entities. Both inside and outside the academy, we often reify firms to simplify a complex landscape, but we know, at least at some level, that we're referring to continually recreated practices with unclear boundaries and variable trajectories. A rejection of the unquestioning assignment of entitativity like this is far from new; it has been part of conceptual critiques for decades (Weick, 1979; Phillips, 1992; Petit, 2017). It has become common to acknowledge that organizations are better understood as fluid practices available for conceptualization and depiction as entities by situated actors for particular aims (see Cruz & Sodeke, 2021). And if the problem of purpose, as introduced in the preceding chapter, is its ontological multiplicity, it becomes necessary to understand the forces that endeavour to make corporations want – to channel organizations' fluidity – in one direction or another as political projects.

Yet the majority of the OS field has continued to use organizations of all sorts, along with seemingly fixed characteristics of them, as its basic units of analysis. Thus, a third conceptual consideration is this: if organizations (including firms) are practices rather than entities, the *practice itself* must be the unit of analysis (Nicolini, 2012). Starting with practice would mark a stark onto-epistemological shift that would threaten many of our existing theory-method complexes. When it comes to communicative capitalism, the challenge is to develop a conception of organization stable enough to support the assignment and promotion of characteristics like value and, at the same time, flexible enough to account for its multiplicity of enactments across sites not controllable by those who think themselves in charge. How, then, to account for the firm as simultaneously chimera and actuality?

That's the challenge this book takes on. It argues that communicative capitalism has transformed both organizing practices and firms; it shows that the questions we're led to ask by existing theories of the firm inhibit insight into these communicative processes. It argues that the shifts in capitalism present to corporations a new conception of *authority*, a conception connected not with persons or positions, but with the multiplicity of forces that shape firms' identities and trajectories, their being and becoming. Communicative capitalism makes them *want* differently than ever before. And that new conception of authority requires a conceptual apparatus capable of both explaining how this force participates in organizing practices and offering novel insights on its consequences.

Countering correspondence

Any effort to develop new theory should be guided by the aim of avoiding dead ends. The most important is the ontological and epistemological illusion that theory addressing communicative capitalism should mirror everyday observations of affect capture, practices of platformization, and logics of branding. A correspondence model of truth (and not the re-working of correspondence thinking undertaken by philosophical pragmatists) unfortunately continues to dominate the OS field, leading analysts to develop theory-method complexes that purport to align with the external 'reality' they attempt to map. An adherence to correspondence thinking leads to a focus on measurement tools, data adequacy, and criteria of our models' comprehensiveness and parsimony. Though we may question the breadth and depth of economic changes, we typically refuse to imagine that the phenomena presented to us are anything other than a relatively objective reality. Theories are presented as rational conclusions drawn from reliable and valid observations of a putatively external world.

The subjectivity of objectivity, the reality-defining character of language and culture, and the non-scientific constitution of scientific facts should have shaken our faith in a correspondence model of truth by now (see Rorty, 1979). Yet our theories, our depictions of spirits of capitalism – including the rendering of communicative capitalism supplied earlier – are *stories*. Both merely and fully stories. But inventive approaches to storytelling (and storified marshaling of data) can challenge our very thinking about reality, whether those approaches come in terms of 'turns' in the field, intra-field challenges to paradigmatic thinking, or the place of nonhumans in producing the modern world.

Nevertheless, the correspondence model of truth continues its influence across academic fields. Analyses seeking to break with it would be wise to use as a criterion of quality theoretical novelty: that which generates new vistas on working and organizing occluded from those inhabiting dominant stories. That's what this book seeks, and it's also how the field can productively engage with the continually shifting sands of capitalism.

To do so, though, an alternative point of entry is needed. The next chapter lays out a rationale for expanding prevailing thinking on the theory of the firm.

Notes

[1]   Of course, it is not merely in the encounter between customer and employee where emotion labour occurs; it unfolds in all types of work, whenever there are interactions that involve expectations for deportment (that'd imply almost every sort of work and workplace).

[2]   This is also a term that applies to the simultaneous production and consumption of energy, by (for instance) those with solar panels who use the power for their own homes while also sending some electricity back to the electrical grid. The attention here, perhaps obviously, is instead on the branding connotation of the term.

2

Why an Alternative Theory
of the Firm?

The previous chapter argued that our present era is marked by communicative capitalism. The three practices presented there, emanating from the precarity and meaning indeterminacy observers note, are increasingly the logics through which firms operate and capital accumulation occurs. The question with which Chapter 1 concluded was how scholars might investigate how a firm's purpose – the corporation's wanting – is fashioned under this spirit of capitalism. A corollary question for OS thinkers is to wonder how well our theorizing prepares us to make sense of these changes. Undoubtedly, scholars can produce interesting studies of affect capture, platformization, and branding without theorizing the firm, but because such theories are onto–epistemological fundaments that guide claims of consequentiality, it's necessary to consider whether existing theories of the firm allow the sort of reconceptualization needed to enhance OS's capacity to produce novel and useful stances on the multiplicity of purpose.

This chapter, accordingly, will start with theories that serve as the central vehicles for providing coherence for central questions of firms. It will introduce governance and competence approaches to the firm, with special attention to those stances' shortcomings when it comes to the problem of purpose under communicative capitalism. It will conclude with the requisites an alternative would need to incorporate.

Here at the outset, I'll acknowledge that this presentation is necessarily succinct. A good deal of the complexity of sophisticated theories developed over decades is filtered out in an effort to access their conceptual cores and their relevance for this book's guiding question: *what do corporations want?*

The key intellectual target at which this book aims is the theory of the firm. What unites the many theories of the commercial enterprise is a desire to provide answers to four fundamental and enduring questions that occupy the thinking of the economics and strategic management scholars who dominate this domain: *why firms exist, how they operate internally, where their boundaries lie*, and *how they secure profitability (or competitive advantage) in the market*. Before any alternative theory can be imagined, however, we need to know the existing territory, which is characterized by two broad camps: governance and competence approaches.[1]

Governance approaches

Theories of the firm generally mark 1937 as the year of their birth, when economist Ronald Coase pondered the reason for the very existence of firms. He started with a simple observation: if firms are mechanisms that produce goods and services based on the activity of the people inside them, there seems to be no necessary distinction between firms and the operations of independent producers in an open market. In economists' ideal world, information circulates freely throughout markets, so the people populating them have no obstacles coordinating the buying and selling – and setting the prices and wages – that comprise production. Of course, Coase (1937, 1960, 1988) knew that information flows in markets are far from perfect and people are flawed information-processors; he thus recognized that markets can exhibit high transaction costs, and firms' centralized planning and control can reduce those costs. What Coase assumed, then, was that the distinction between firms and markets was, at base, a *choice* that turned on the promise of efficiency promised by centralization. Firms, in other words, are responses to efficiency problems, because their centralized planning creates specialization, eliminates duplication of effort, and prevents producers' self-interests from impairing the productivity needs of the larger enterprise.

Obviously, this is an idealized (and limiting) vision of the firm. But its image of a centralized coordination mechanism for governing the activities of independent producers (employees), along with the firm/market distinction upon which it rests, became the template for thinking about the logic underlying the firm's existence. Two lines of thinking stem from Coase's foundation: transaction cost economics and Agency Theory.

Transaction cost economics

Theorizing that engaged with Coase's question didn't take off for several decades, when Alchian and Demsetz (1972) used his framing to explore contracting within and beyond the firm. Since Coase's vision is concerned with production, individuals (for him, persons as well as firms) can be understood as contractors involved in agreements about the provision of their products and services. Alchian and Demsetz saw the challenges of information sharing as falling under the mantle of the contract and held that, because of actors' bounded rationality, inability to predict the future, and opportunism, contracts are inevitably *incomplete*. Firms, they argued, are better than markets at limiting the costs of those incompleteness problems and the costs they produce. Contracts, for Alchian and Demsetz, are the *ex ante* elements of organization, since they're in place before coordinated action occurs; governance practices are the *ex post* actions that address the coordination problems – the costs – that contracts' incompleteness cannot address.

The model based on these costs came to be called *transaction cost economics* (TCE) and was usually defined as the product of inefficient information transmission between people within a firm. These costs include problems of conveying information up and down the hierarchy, information overload at the top, slow decision-making, and the inability to access information adequate to determine prices. In the decades following Alchian and Demsetz's framing of the root issue as one of contracting, the trio of Grossman, Hart, and Moore (Grossman & Hart, 1986; Hart & Moore, 1990) developed a property rights approach that showed how ownership (and thus governance) of the assets involved in production can reduce transaction costs. This is because it is the *firm* that owns assets rather than the contractor/employee – and, they argued, control follows asset ownership, so the firm can determine contractors' action and thus reduce costs. Oliver Williamson (1988) echoed the Grossman-Hart-Moore logic, arguing that firms internalize, and then integrate, production assets in service both of transaction cost efficiency and because asset ownership provides a compelling claim on the surpluses of production. Yet expecting dramatic reductions in transaction costs would ignore the related challenges introduced by the bureaucracy that would arise alongside centralized control; the challenges of bureaucracy, Williamson reasoned, counteract the transaction cost savings of centralized control.

What TCE thinkers have shown is that centralization provides benefits in terms of transaction costs, contracting, and ownership clams, but that these benefits dwindle as firms grow large and bureaucratic. In an important sense, then, TCE thinkers began to recognize the need to theorize the complex practice of organization, though they have rarely ventured very far in that direction.

Agency Theory

A second governance approach also draws inspiration from an almost century-old insight: Berle and Means' (1932) recognition that firms separate ownership (*principals*, like shareholders, who putatively own the firm) from control (*agents*, like employees, who carry out principals' aims). The employment contract both tacitly and explicitly compels agents to generate benefits for principals, but these groups' divergent interests created what Berle and Means termed *agency costs*. The notion has three elements. One is the *agency problem*: under industrial capitalism, principals were rarely at the site of production to ensure that agents were working on their behalf, so those principals could not assess whether agents were fulfilling their obligations (both opportunism and asymmetric information prevent principals from getting a full view of what agents are up to). A second component of agency costs is *risk sharing*, which refers to the principal and the agent operating with different preferences for risk, including bodily risk to the employee. And, finally, the third element is *agent attention*: when agents serve the interests of many principals at the same time, as is the case with firms characterized by distributed ownership (and increasingly so under platformization and fissured firms), how actors allocate their attention and choose among conflicting activities requires explanation.

As was the case with TCE, the theory that developed in response to the recognition of agency costs focused on contracts. Agency Theory argues that contracts including incentives (such as performance-based wages, including equity in the firm, profit sharing) align agents' interests with those of principal(s). Continuing to portray individuals as providers of productive capacities who participate freely in economic exchange (Williamson, 2002), firms then become '*legal fictions which serve as a nexus for a set of contracting relationships among individuals*' (Jensen & Meckling, 1976, p 311; emphasis in original). Firms exist because that nexus of contracts is denser and more controllable than those in the market, and also because the legal apparatus allows the firm (as entity) to both own assets and to position itself as the lone common party in all employment contracts (owing to Western corporate law traditions). The firm, as a set of contracts, implies 'a system of property rights that defines a set of principal–agent relations and divides up claims to assets and residual cash flow' (Fligstein & Freeland, 1995, p 26). And in that Western corporate law, shareholders' (owners') claims on assets come *after* creditors if performance goes awry; those principals thus have a strong financial interest in motivating the agents in the company to secure high levels of performance, particularly the sorts of performance that will raise share prices (at least in publicly traded companies). And the logic has been extended to the question of competing firm purposes, where the claims stakeholders make on firms can be sold by firms (in products and/or share prices) at a point higher than the cost to honour those implicit contracts (Cornell & Shapiro, 2021).

Critique of governance approaches

Governance approaches have shaped how we think about strategy, management, and firms' legal status. Yet despite Williamson's concern for bureaucracy as a challenge to cost reduction, scholars in this tradition remain relatively uninterested in the conduct of firms' operations: as Arrow (1999) argues, they render the firm a 'black box' and peer inside it only to grasp how to govern contracts in ways that will control individuals' conduct.

The Carnegie school's *behavioural theory of the firm* argued this point in suggesting that firms are devices for making decisions in a market economy and for managing coalitions toward a shared goal (Cyert & March, 1963); yet in their economistic frame, the trajectory of governance approaches led them to ignore how the firm is also a complex organization beyond the managerial need to provide incentives to induce cooperation (Holmström & Milgrom, 1991; Parkinson, 2003). Consequently, the Carnegie School, like TCE and Agency Theory, render transactions and contracts basically the same in character (Cowling & Sugden, 1998), constraining their ability to address how innovation and competitive advantage occur (Foss, 1999), how complex and covert forms of power shape organizing (Kuhn, 2008), and why cooperation frequently arises in the midst of competition (Ghosal & Moran, 1996). Although Davis and Kim (2017) see the nexus of contracts view as aligned with the decentralization of the contemporary corporate landscape, if the firm is merely a nexus of contracts, the conviction that this nexus holds responsibilities beyond principals and agents is, according to Jensen and Meckling (1976, p 311), 'seriously misleading' and thus generally disregarded.

These theories are also limited in their grasp of the shifting character of capitalism. As Foss and Linder (2019) note, the increased dispersion of information, along with the pressing societal drive for CSR as a central plank of firms' existence – what the preceding chapter might denote as platformization and branding – are challenges to economic theories of the firm. Foss and Linder, however, see those challenges as addressable from within the logic of governance approaches as long as scholars recognize the need to foreground both team-based production and the centrality of implicit or relational contracts between firms and their stakeholders.

I argue otherwise: a communicative logic of capitalism does not merely alter the location or tenor of contractual power, but fundamentally re-imagines both what firms are taken to be and how they operate. The image of the firm as an efficient transaction system marked off from – and able to enter into implicit and explicit contracts with – actors beyond its boundaries, an image that sees individual humans (or collectives of them) as the primary contracting parties, misses the complexity of organizing outlined in the preceding chapter. If the firm and its purpose are ontologically multiple, its instantiations cannot be limited to contractor coordination. Governance theories are unable to conceive of firms as complex and nebulous practices and are consequently unable to imagine the forces making purpose a cornerstone of understanding their practices and prospects.

Competence/capability approaches

Governance approaches, says Heugens (2005), tend to address 'why' questions about firms' formation and production choices. A second body of work asks 'how' questions, explaining the creation of firm-level outcomes from lower-level resources and routines. In pursuing issues such as these, the firm becomes more organization than economic entity, and the explanatory devices are the creation and protection of unique production competencies that can provide sustainable competitive advantage. The particular attention in most of these theories is with firms' production choices: 'Firms must not only decide whether to integrate or outsource to protect values: they must also consider whether to invest in intangibles, to bundle products, to offer complements, how to segment the market and what value propositions to put to the customer' (Pitelis & Teece, 2009, p 6). Importantly, with respect to that quote, competence approaches acknowledge that it is not abstract 'firms' that decide, but the strategic managers to whom responsibility for firms' futures is affixed (indeed, one of the problems confronting this view is that equating strategic managers and 'the' firm is rarely interrogated). There are three main variants of this approach.

The resource-based view

The resource-based view of the firm (RBV) takes the focus on strategic managers seriously, understanding them as possessing insight into the firm's outside and inside that determine how it will compete in the marketplace and how it will structure its internal resources (Wernerfelt, 1984). The model of the firm here is novel: it is a bundle of resources, and those resources are to be controlled by management in an effort to generate competencies that are 'VRIN' (Valuable, Rare, Inimitable, and Non-substitutable; as I note in Chapter 5, this was later amended to 'VRIO' to highlight the importance of Organizational properties that fostered competencies). And differences across firms' marketplace success are chalked up to how well management cultivates and protects those resources (Barney, 1991).

What are the resources prized by managers? Resources, in the RBV, fall into tangible and intangible categories: elements like financial capital, production capabilities, location, legal codes, and a positive brand reputation. Led by Edith Penrose's (1959) insight about the sources of firm growth, over the past few decades RBV thinking has been interested in one particular intangible: knowledge. Arguing that conventional resource-based thinking misses the keys to competitive advantage in the 'information society,' the *knowledge-based theory of the firm* has become a significant RBV offshoot. Knowledge assets like intellectual property or personal expertise, say this stance's champions, are difficult to imitate, challenging to transfer to new environments, strongly associated with individual knowers, and are socially complex. Firms, in turn, are more fully understood to be *organizations*, social systems where individuals externalize and integrate their specialist knowledge to produce collective competencies. The task of management under a knowledge-based theory is coordinating individuals' activity through creating rules, sequencing tasks, establishing routines, fostering interpersonal relations, and encouraging group decision making (Grant, 1996). Moreover, management is tasked with creating an integrated culture (with collectively shared identities, symbols, and rules), which is believed to reduce the costs of coordination, learning, and communication.[2] In the RBV and its knowledge-based extension, then, firms are unique collections of resources that, if guided well, undergo continual refinement. That refinement increases assets and hones production capabilities to meet the strategic directions mapped out by management.

Dynamic capabilities

An alternative (yet complementary) view suggests that the key to competitive advantage is the firm-specific and organizationally embedded ability to adapt resources in the development of new processes and products. For scholars in this tradition, dynamic capabilities are a 'firm's ability to integrate, build, and reconfigure internal and external competences to address rapidly changing environments' (Teece et al, 1997, p 516). A firm's capabilities enable it to both enhance the productivity of its *other* resources and create advantageous positions in markets. The mere acquisition of resources like new production technologies, for instance, may not alter a firm's competitive position if the organization is internally unfit to capitalize on them, so the managerial arrangement of resources into activity is the key (Dosi et al, 2008; Spender, 2014).

The dynamic capabilities view thus focuses on organizing processes, often captured under the notion of *routines* (Nelson & Winter, 1982), which can be managed in the creation of capabilities. In contrast to the RBV and the aforementioned governance approaches, this perspective considers organizational change to be a crucial component in obtaining and protecting competitive advantage. The modes of change include reconfiguring existing resources, leveraging a process by transferring it from one part of a system to another, learning new processes (or refinement to existing ones) through exploration and exploitation, and creatively integrating existing resources into novel configurations. In contrast to governance approaches, this theory identifies firms' internal operations as key contributors to competitive advantage. Yet the dynamic capabilities view retains attention to managerial power, seeing managers as the sites of decision-making in the creation and utilization of collective capabilities, as articulated by Winter (2003): '*An organizational capability is a high-level routine (or collection of routines) that, together with its implementing input flows, confers upon an organization's management a set of decision options for producing significant outputs of a particular type*' (p 991; emphasis in original.)

This vision places on managers' shoulders the responsibility to nurture and refresh malleable capabilities that keep the firm nimble enough to adjust to market changes. There are two important points here. First, variations in firms' dynamic capabilities produce differences in production costs; such cost differentials influence managements' make or buy decisions – and hence firms' boundaries (in other words, though firms' *capabilities* are typically built internally; *resources* can be bought in the market). Second, the theory's attention to firm-level adaptation appeals to strategy scholars who see markets as experiencing radical and transformative changes to which firms must adapt, especially those subject to internet-based digital networks.

The attention-based view

A recent entrant into the theory of the firm conversation is the attention-based view (ABV), first articulated by William Ocasio. An outgrowth of the aforementioned Carnegie School and its vision of firms as information processing systems, the ABV was founded with a desire to explain strategic decision-making in firms that poorly resembled the sort of large, multidivisional, and vertically integrated organizations described by Alfred Chandler (1962). Organizational attention – a firm-level, rather than individual, construct – was portrayed as producing a firm's strategic vision and, consequently, its allocation of resources.

The important question was, and remains, how organizational attention arises and becomes focused on particular ends. With its grounding in the aforementioned Carnegie School's behavioural theory of the firm, the view began with a fairly straightforward conception of information processing, one that placed the forces that structure cognition in the foreground. The ABV thus examined how firms guide and direct the attention of their members (and particularly their strategic managers), both in terms of internal processes and events in the firm's environment. Crucially, Ocasio (1997) argued that 'the firm's rules, resources, and social relationships regulate and control the distribution and allocation of issues, answers, and decision-makers into specific activities, communications, and procedures' (p 188). It was a model of distributed cognition, one that found several mechanisms influencing information processing, including environmental stimuli, cultural and institutional processes, communication channels, and procedural rules (including participation).

Over its history, the ABV has gradually engaged more directly with communication processes (Ocasio et al, 2018). Its early adherence to cognitive and information processing thinking drew on almost no work treating communication as a practice that generates social realities, preventing the ABV from engaging with theory that frames organizations as complex communicative endeavours (as betrayed by its early – but continued – use of the transmission-oriented term communication*S* in the previous quote). Its original lack of awareness of directly relevant communication scholarship is emblematic of the general obliviousness many MOS scholars exhibit to work even slightly outside their preferred domain. Obliviousness is not merely a fault of this stance or its authors, however; indeed, a similar unawareness is visited upon the ABV itself, which has been largely ignored by central strategic management texts, such as Roberts (2004), Spender (2014), Golsorkhi et al (2015), Baars and Spicer (2017) and Grant (2019).

Critique of competence approaches

Competence approaches have engaged in a good deal of internal criticism over the decades of their existence, from questioning the conceptualizations of resources to claims that VRIN/O resources are neither necessary nor sufficient for creating sustained competitive advantage (Freiling, 2004; Moldaschl & Fischer, 2004; Kraaijenbrink et al, 2010). Some, moreover, see the logic of the stance, particularly the RBV, as tautological and thus not a theory *per se* (Priem & Butler, 2001a, b; see Barney & Clark, 2007, for a response). Registering such concerns is essential for the development of this line of theorizing, but I'd like to move in a slightly different direction: assessing whether competence approaches are up to the task of addressing the problem of purpose under communicative capitalism.

Not surprisingly, I think they're limited in a few important ways. First is that, as strategic theories of the firm, they seek to explain how competitive advantage is generated. That's to be expected. But in so doing, they tend to ignore competing logics of corporate purpose, those that might broaden the aims of the firm and enable an exploration of the many motivations characterizing principals and the shifting demands of publics (and markets) for social responsibility. Freeman et al (2021) argue that, as currently formulated, competence approaches like the RBV do nothing to challenge dominant visions of shareholder primacy and, in turn, they lack comprehension of how sustainability (in the attention to sustainable competitive advantage) necessarily invokes *equitable* relationships with an array of stakeholders. Although the competence stance's focus would place the onus for navigating the multiplicity of purpose squarely on managers who may be ill-equipped to do so, broadening the capacity to address multiple logics of valuation is necessary to accommodate the complex landscapes in which strategists find themselves (Hitt et al, 2021).

A second concern is the black-boxing of the organization, a charge also levelled against governance approaches. Despite Heugens's claim about competence questions that opened this section, Miller and Shamsie (1996) accuse the RBV (in particular) of disregarding thorny 'where, when, and how' questions about the links between resources, management, and firm performance. The concern, then, is that the conception of organization in this theory of the firm is not up to the explanatory task it's undertaking. The notion that firms are collections of resources and routines guided by managers and their resources of attention strips away the complex organizing practices associated with those where, when, and how questions, as well as the capacity to track changes (including purpose drift) over time.

The ABV's encounter with communication theory represents a useful illustration of how this narrowing of organizational phenomena might be avoided. Its authors have begun to recognize the limitations of the Carnegie informational approach and understand that communication processes influence organizational attention. In so doing, the ABV now notes that (a) the communication shaping decisions occurs well beyond the conventional intra-organizational channels, (b) communicative practices supply the frames that guide the logic(s) of decision-making, (c) managers' communicative performances can alter organization members' sensemaking about choices, and (d) the very site of decision-making is the ongoing stream of talk and text that constitutes organization (Ocasio et al, 2018). These moves have led the ABV toward useful reconceptualizations of dynamic capabilities (see Ocasio et al, 2023b).

While this expansion is welcome, the ABV demonstrates some continued occlusions that hamper its ability to address the sort of questions this book pursues. First, the ABV's focus remains situated directly on decision-makers, with the assumption that decisions are individual and group selections, and that those decisions *are* firm behaviour. If a theory of the firm is to address the intersections of growth and purpose, its conceptual framework must not understand the firm as an entity moved solely by internal processes (even when the firm is no longer a Chandlerian object), but as a complex field of practice involving numerous connections that disrupt the notion of stable boundaries and identities. Second, the ABV situates communication in the behaviours and cognitions of persons alone, a move that fits with familiar lay assumptions about communication. Though it's a common, even culturally dominant, view (Axley, 1996), it prevents the possibility that determining the strategic direction and purpose(s) of a firm are the result of more than the human elements of the communicative scene. Some of those elements may not be represented discursively by managers; a few candidate nonhuman elements were offered in the BEIC and Anglo American examples presented in the Introduction (though the identification of factors like these is always an empirical question). In other words, the ABV's retention of cognition as a frame impedes a thorough exploration of the power and complexity of communication. Taken together, these two points suggest that the ABV's unit of analysis may be inadequate to grasp the fluidity of contemporary firms and the contemporaneous multiplicity of purposes they exhibit – neither of which can be reduced to the explicit choices strategic managers make.

The ABV is not the only competence-based view that has recognized a need to engage with organizing processes. Barney and Clark (2007) recognize that the RBV's conception of the firm as an entity – where the firm itself is the unit of analysis – lacks dynamism in that 'the resources and capabilities that give a firm competitive advantage are relatively fixed in nature' (p 259). Recently, authors engaging with the emerging Strategy-as-Practice stream of thinking have worked to infuse competence approaches with an understanding of practice that eliminates conventional levels-based distinctions (between the macro level of the environment/market, the meso level of the firm, and the micro level of organizing activity). Regnér (2015) shows how research examining the details of routines and coordination activities – the everyday *doing* of organizing that (re)makes strategy – can help answer those pressing where, when, and how questions. Although this research has expanded in the decade since Regnér's review (see Kohtamäki et al, 2022), it generally retains the adherence to managerial power as articulating the purpose and trajectory of the firm. And because the theory has an insubstantial explanation for how firms operate, it also lacks an account of why (and how) firms emerge *as* firms in the first place – which, as mentioned in the Introduction, is a cornerstone of theories of the firm.

Criteria for an alternative theory of the firm

Both governance and capabilities approaches understand firms to be the products of managerial control; they thus tend to be more interested in structuring contracts, assets, resources, and relationships, and comparatively less interested in how the firm can be bound up in complex, generative, and consequential relationships that shape its existence and trajectory. Their lack of compelling responses to the questions raised in each critique section earlier suggests that they are generally incapable of addressing the problems of firm purpose under communicative capitalism. Their inability stems from the fact that they're uninterested in the ways firms are constituted – and continually so – in their interactions with the multitude of participants, human and nonhuman, they encounter in their organizing practices. If purpose becomes many things based on the actions of a myriad of more-than-human actors, reducing purpose to what strategic managers want severely impedes theorizing.

The preceding chapter concluded with three 'conceptual considerations' for theory responsive to communicative capitalism: attending to the more-than-human, grasping organizations' fluidity, and advancing practice as the key unit of analysis. The question at this point then is this: if the governance and competence approaches are unsuitable to the challenges of the multiplicity of firm purpose and the logics of communicative capitalism, of what must a theory of the firm consist for it to be able to provide satisfactory responses? Building upon those three conceptual considerations, I'd argue for four criteria an alternative theory of the firm should pursue.

First, the communicative character of contemporary capitalism calls for a theory of the firm with communication at its conceptual core. What is needed is a move from a *representational* to a *constitutive* conception of communication. The typical rendering of communication among theories of the firm is as messaging activity that occurs inside, or emanates from, pre-existing organizational forms. In those portrayals, communication represents the interests or intentions of the persons or firms who/that devise and transmit it. Alternatively, communication in the TCE represents a transaction cost, since communication is understood merely as the vehicle to convey information, a vision haunted by the impossibility of delivering precisely the sender's intent into the cognitive apparatus of the receiver (Peters, 1999). Representational thinking is message-oriented, suggesting that messages conveyed well will exert the desired influence on intra- and extra-organizational audiences.

The shortcomings of such a stance should be obvious, but a representational view continues to mark a good deal of OS scholarship. A *constitutive* stance, in sharp contrast, sees communication as the practice of (re)creating and transforming multiple and temporally fluctuating meanings. Yet 'meaning,' at the core of a communicative stance, evades simple determination: it is found neither in the messages actors exchange nor in their individual minds, but in the *practices* in which they participate. And as signalled, practices are populated by more than merely human participants; they involve a heterogeneous mix of that which we typically consider the material domain (artifacts, objects, sites, bodies) constitutively entangled with – even ontologically *inseparable from* – symbol-using humans. Communication, viewed *as* practice, centres meaning generation while attending to the forces that an array of participants generates.

It's important to recognize that what constitutive communication scholars mean by meaning is not merely the province of human cognition, nor does it exist solely in the linguistic/symbolic domain. Instead, communication names the practice 'whereby human and non-human agencies interpenetrate ideation and materiality toward meanings that are tangible and axial to organizational existence' (Ashcraft et al, 2009, p 42). Communication constitutes meanings, and meanings constitute realities. This does not mean that those realities, and thus also firms, are *reducible to* meanings, but insists that the productivity of meaning always retains a seat at the explanatory table. It is communication's performativity – its capacity to exceed the utterance to bring realities into being – that produces its constitutive impact (Loxley, 2007; Gond et al, 2015).

A constitutive stance sets the stage for an alternative story of organization, one that frames communication as not merely one of several things that happens inside a pre-established container called 'a' firm, and instead as the *practice* that brings organization to life (Kuhn et al, 2017). Framed as a practice, communication is not simply a process (a flow rather than a series of discrete acts) but exceeds processual thinking in suggesting that communication is dis/ordered activity directed toward multiple simultaneous ends, proceeding through the multi-agentic generation of historically situated significances that bind various (non)human participants to that practice while also articulating a trajectory for its own future as linked with other practices. Seen in terms of practice, then, communication is comprised of doings and sayings aimed at a teleo-affective outcomes (Schatzki, 2006). The practice of communication is the site for the interpenetration of human and nonhuman participants in the production of activity (Czarniawska, 2008; Ashcraft et al, 2009), where coherence and harmony – which may well be inventions of observers as much as unassailable depictions of activity – are not necessary for a practice to proceed (Cooper, 1986; Weick, 1995).

A second criterion is a need to re-imagine agency, one of the key themes of all social theory. What constitutive communication thinking allows is nothing less than a wholesale rejection of the individualism and humanism marking most models of organization (and theories of the firm). Individualism and humanism accompanied the discursive and interpretive turns in the OS field, leading most analysts to seat agency – defined as choice and difference-making capacities – largely in the human person. The symbolic activity in which that person engages was, as a corollary, understood to be a device that represented (again with the representational register) the person's putatively pre-existing intentions.

Given the ontological questions communicative capitalism asks regarding firms, along with the assertion that practices always involve more-than-human participants, it should come as no surprise that constitutive communication thinking rejects the restriction of agency to individual humans. As theorists of agency sought a corrective to the dominance of the symbolic frame in the late 1990s and early 2000s (a movement that continues apace today), they did not seek to merely swing a conceptual pendulum more toward the material, but to transcend the dualism altogether (Emirbayer, 1997). So constitutive communication theory does not merely argue that material entities possess agency just as people do; it argues that *all* action is the result of a conglomeration of forces being brought together in the pursuit of some end: 'It is not quite right, then, to say that either humans or nonhumans "have" or "possess" agency; rather, a capacity to act is the product of the marshaling of multiple elements of an assemblage in the performative and relational generation of action' (Kuhn & Burk, 2014, p 154).

In other words, the problem occurs when analysts suggest that circumscribed 'things' called humans or nonhumans have an autonomous existence and are the wellspring of action. Questions of agency, however, are not about determining the capacities of entities in the abstract but are about tracing the ensemble of forces that produce practices. Agency is re-imagined as a hybrid, heterogeneous, and distributed *accomplishment* (see Brummans, 2018). Returning to the centring of practice from the first criterion, Schatzki (2001) notes that 'the status of human beings as "subjects" (and "agents") is bound to practices. Practices, in sum, displace mind as the central phenomenon in human life' (p 11).

A third criterion, and one that is a direct offshoot of this conception of agency, is to deploy a concept capable of addressing the shifting trajectory of purpose (as well as changes to a firm's practices). If we take trajectory to be a firm's unfolding over time and space, and if that unfolding is the contingent and temporary result of struggles over meaning, we're engaging with a question of authority. As noted, existing theories of the firm situate authority squarely in strategic managers, but the need to attend to the more-than-human should guide consideration of a wider range of participants. And because the notion of authority is etymologically tied to writing and inscription – as in *author* and *authorship* – authority leads an analyst toward the many participants in a practice vying to write a firm's past, present, and future. Authority then can encourage a consideration of what the firm is taken (and hoped) to be by its many stakeholders and influencers, and how they compete to write the narrative that will guide its future. Authority, in other words, can be a route to grasping the shifting multiplicity of purpose.

A final criterion is a consideration of dis/organization (the '/' indicates that organization and disorganization are implied in one another yet often rendered conceptually distinct). Given the fluidity of organization and organizing presented at the end of Chapter 1, a theory of the firm must be able to 'see' order and disorder not as poles on a scale but as mutually implicated visions of practice. Although *dis*order and *dis*organization have long been recognized in organization studies, they've generally been understood to be *problems*: deviations from the typical and desirable states of affairs and, thus, need to be eliminated in practice or pushed outside the analyst's conceptual apparatus (Martin, 1992). And this makes sense given the conventional frame: if organizing is the work of a set of cognizing persons (those typically understood to be agents), failures to produce reasoned and systematic action would imply deficits in those persons' abilities. Situating organizing in communication, however, displays that the meanings emerging in communication always exceed the intentions of participants, such that communicative practice can *never* be reduced to individuals' desires.

Accounts of dis/organization show firms to be far messier than the visions of coherent and integrated order marking theories of the firm (Vásquez et al, 2016; Kuhn, 2022). They hold that order and disorder are *simultaneous* products of the complex and conflicted practice of communication. Accordingly, *choosing* to attend to the accomplishment of smooth coordination and control, or treating those as unacknowledged background conditions for the study of other phenomena, ignores the richness afforded by interrogating organizing's inevitable tensions, paradoxes, slippages, confusions, and contradictions (Cooper, 1986; Plotnikof et al, 2022). Being able to understand and anticipate those tensions is not about generating a 'fuller' picture of the firm to comport with some external 'reality' (returning to last chapter's point about correspondence theorizing) but is instead about producing insight-generating explanations of how firms and their wanting(s) unfold.

A theory that uses these four criteria as a guide will be better positioned to explain how corporate purpose becomes multiple and how firms operate under communicative capitalism. Building on these criteria, the next chapter lays a conceptual foundation for a distinctly *communicative* theory of the firm. It begins with thinking that frames communicative practice as constitutive of organization, then brings this work together with social theory that transcends conventional epistemological and ontological divisions in presenting a vision of the world as assemblage. The chapter to follow that one (Chapter 4) then pursues distinctly communicative answers to the four theory of the firm questions highlighted here.

Notes

[1]   These are mere snapshots for the sake of understanding the assumptions, claims, and shortcomings of these approaches; for more detailed examinations, see Williamson (1999), Roberts (2004), Petrin (2013), and Singer (2019).

[2]   As mentioned previously (and which will be elaborated in Chapter 3), coordination and learning are deeply communicative; separating these elements here shows the conceptual reduction of communication to messaging.

3

Assembling an Analytical Apparatus: CCO Encounters Deleuzian New Materialism

The preceding chapter presented the two dominant approaches to theorizing the firm and outlined why they're inadequate to grasp the problems of purpose under communicative capitalism. As suggested there, the key shortcoming is their limited (and limiting) models of organizing and communicating in a world where conceptions of value are the result of a wide array of forces and participants bound up in complex practices. This chapter is the first step in developing an alternative. Building on the requisites for an organization theory responsive to the shift toward communicative capitalism from the end of Chapter 1 as well as the conceptual blind spots noted in Chapter 2, it starts with efforts to build a body of organizational theory explicitly devoted to centring communication processes.

Before beginning, a note about communication is necessary. As is the case in most vibrant academic enterprises, those who foreground communication – as simultaneously phenomenon and mode of explanation – in OS are a varied bunch. Although I identify with the discipline called communication, it's important to note that even among those who earn their PhDs in the field and who are employed in academic departments bearing that name,[1] there is tremendous heterogeneity in what the term connotes. Scholars locate in communication theory responses to the most vexing and persistent problems of philosophy, including selfhood, morality, and intersubjectivity (Grossberg, 1982; Radford, 2005). Undergraduate textbooks on communication theory routinely recount the history of shifting models, from those portraying communication as a linear *act* of message transmission to a complex *process* of meaning emergence, and then to the proliferation of present-day intellectual projects drawing from those stances. As one piece of evidence of this heterogeneity, one collection, nearly two decades old, presents no less than 27 mostly distinct conceptions of communication across its chapters (Shepherd et al, 2006). The upshot is that, although there are significant shifts away from simplistic transmission models, we should expect neither a canonical nor unassailable conception of communication, in this book or anywhere else.

The task, therefore, is to seek neither conceptual purity nor harmony; instead, it is to articulate what a given conception of communication can *accomplish* with respect to a particular aim. If the ambition is to develop an account of the firm that can develop insights into purpose under communicative capitalism, a novel conception of the firm and its organizing practices is what we need. Thinking on the communicative constitution of organization provides just that inspiration. After presenting that body of theory, I augment it via an encounter with new materialist thinking, particularly the assemblage-based theory associated with French philosopher Gilles Deleuze. The latter half of the chapter uses Deleuzian work to prepare the ground for the distinctive theory of the firm articulated in Chapter 4.

Communication as constitutive of organization

In the 1990s, a body of theorizing picked up on some of the currents moving OS. As mentioned in preceding chapters, a move away from the field's historical bias toward organizational entitativity was afoot since the 1970s, congealing in 'turns' linguistic, interpretive, cultural, discursive, and practice-based (Ashcraft et al, 2009). Though there are important distinctions between these, they signal a move from a *representational* to a *constitutive* conception of communication, as discussed in the preceding chapter. Representational thinking is message-oriented, suggesting that messages, if conveyed or transmitted well, will influence intra- and extra-organizational audiences. In a *constitutive* stance, communication becomes the practice of (re)creating and transforming multiple and temporally fluctuating meanings (Putnam & Boys, 2006). Yet meaning evades simple determination: it is found neither in the messages actors exchange nor in their individual minds, but in the practices in which they participate. And, as also mentioned in that preceding chapter, those actors are not merely human, because practices involve a heterogeneous mix of that which we typically consider the material domain (artifacts, objects, sites, bodies) constitutively entangled with symbol-using people (Reckwitz, 2002). Thus, to repeat the stance produced in Chapter 2, viewing communication as a constitutive practice means seeing it as dis/ordered activity directed toward multiple simultaneous ends, proceeding through the multi-agentic generation of historically situated significances that bind various (non)human participants to that practice while also articulating a trajectory for its own future as linked with other relevant practices. There's a lot going on there, and this chapter will unpack those elements. Or at least try.

In communication studies, getting to this point involved a shift from studying the transmission of messages through vertical and horizontal channels, or examining the (in)formal networks inside organizations, to instead examining how organizations themselves are systems of meaning. Although some of this work took 'the' organization as a question (rather than a given) and turned to communication to explain its ongoing (re)creation, it nevertheless shifted understandings of the ontological status of discourse, language, and communication. No longer merely an epiphenomenon – the surface-level manifestation of deeper, and ontologically prior, structures – communication-related action became the very ground for organization (Fairhurst & Putnam, 2004; Kuhn & Putnam, 2014). To state the matter (too) simply, communicative questions move from 'did the information get through?' to 'what is being (trans)formed in the doing of this practice?' The latter question invites questions about the consequences of meaning creation (as well as its destruction).

Tilling the intellectual soil was a project unfolding over decades, such that no single point of origin for the body of thought that became known as 'Communication as Constitutive of Organization' (CCO) exists. But there are points of punctuation. One is an article by Taylor and colleagues[2] (1996) that, drawing on speech act and narrative theorists, situated the emergence of organization in a dialectic between conversations and texts and then displayed how the products of this dialectic become distanciated (separated and distributed from their initial conditions) to create the elements we come to recognize as organizational. A few years later, McPhee and Zaug (2000) built upon Anthony Giddens's version of structuration theory to suggest that it is the intersecting influence of four interdependent communication flows – activity coordination, membership negotiation, self-structuring, and institutional positioning – that generates organizations.[3] And over a decade after that, Schoeneborn (2011) took inspiration from the autopoietic systems theorizing of Niklas Luhmann to portray organizations as self-organizing systems that operate based on circulating messages' informational content, their form and purpose, and the understandings they generate within a system. Schoeneborn argued for a focus on decisions as the phenomena through which systems produce the logics of their past, present, and future action. These three punctuating articles gave birth to three distinct lines of scholarship gathered under the mantle of CCO. Over the course of its three decades of life – just a baby, in terms of histories of ideas – CCO has moved from occupying a small niche in an oft-neglected corner of a field to an interdisciplinary and multinational enterprise. The body of thought has seen a fourth and more recent punctuation: the publication of a *Handbook of the Communicative Constitution of Organization* (Basque et al, 2022), an effort to concretize CCO's contribution and lay the groundwork for its future development.

Noting moments of punctuation isn't terribly informative regarding the claims and contributions of an entire body of thought, however – especially one with divergent lines of thought and considerable intra-perspective heterogeneity. And reviewing that entire body of thought is well beyond what this short chapter can accomplish, especially since there are other very good introductions available elsewhere (for example, see Ashcraft et al, 2009; Cooren et al, 2011; Brummans et al, 2014; Boivin et al, 2017; Schoeneborn et al, 2019). Yet providing a few key premises will provide some flesh for the bones.

First, *CCO scholarship focuses squarely on communicative practices as they unfold over time and space*, rejecting the assertion that communication can be captured in terms of isolated messages or even episodes populated by message exchange. Communication is a *practice* rather than a series of discrete acts, and our terminology should reflect the intellectual commitment:

> Unfortunately, referring to the study of communication*s* is a widespread illiteracy in our field. Abstract conceptual nouns that refer to ideas, processes, or conditions cannot be pluralized by adding an 's' or 'es.' To attempt to do so ... while it may appear to make sense, changes the basic meaning. Consider that those who study radio, television, and press do not necessarily study radios, televisions, and presses; students of journalism are not students of journalisms, scholars engage in scholarship, not scholarships; biologists study life, not lives; medical students study medicine in general, and medicines only occasionally; nutritionists study nutrition, not nutritions; attorneys study justice, not justices. ... Theorists of communication may occasionally analyze specific messages, or communications, but that is not the name of their field of study. (Cronkhite, 1984, p 473)

Because it confuses the allegiances of the intellectual field, referring to 'communications,' even to conjure sets of messages, must be eradicated. Communication is a meaning- and connection-generating practice not reducible to messaging or information processing. Nominalization, creating a noun from a process, distracts from the necessary attention to the *accomplishing* of the practice.

Keeping with the constitutive principle mentioned, examining communication practices as they occur longitudinally allows us to look *at*, rather than *through*, communication to locate organizing. In other words, communication is the site in which organization is manifest (one must look *at* that site to observe organization); it is not merely the handmaidenly vehicle for its appearance (which can be looked *through* to see organization). Communication is a practice pregnant with potential coordination and control dynamics, the very stuff of organizing, as a direct outgrowth of the constitutive principle mentioned earlier. It thus always involves multiple influences, is always performative, and is always situated in streams of past/present/future action.

A second CCO premise, one connected to the claim of multiple influences, is that *meanings are the provisional accomplishments of many participants*. This means that any given participant's intentions for securing a given meaning from communicative practice inevitably runs up against the will, intentions, and/or action trajectories of a phalanx of others. The 'participants' language here signals something important: a refusal to restrict meaning-making to the actions of persons alone. Meaning is produced in performances involving both humans and nonhumans; as mentioned in Chapter 2 and on which I'll expand, agency is always 'more-than-human.' Even when communication looks like, for instance, a simple customer service exchange in a retail environment, much more is likely to be going on: the organizational loyalties one (or both) persons brings to the conversation, the policies and norms upon which they draw, the spatial setting that shapes interactional possibilities, the materially and historically coded expectations of the other, the script guiding the episode, the marketing promises coursing through the encounter, the legal codes underwriting the firm's stance on intellectual property and customer rights, the artifacts that inform each's moves, the computer codes written into the retail software (and its potential constraints on local decision-making), the bodily sensations and positioning of the interactants, the material lineage of the products ... and the list could go on. Customer service interactions tend to appear simple because analysts ignore the complexities of situations and render them ground as opposed to the interactional figure (Kuhn & Jackson, 2008), but bracketing off the material and discursive contributors carries costs.

Those costs include an inability to explain unexpected divergences and the inevitable improvisation in organizing. Being able to anticipate breakdowns and confusions, along with the resources upon which participants draw to act in response, are key to explaining how organizing unfolds. And relegating nonhuman elements to either the situational background or to tools at the disposal of humans robs them of their capacities to act recalcitrantly or enigmatically (Bennett, 2010; Hodder, 2012).

Moreover, were we to ignore the influence of an array of participants, we'd sacrifice the insight gained from tracing processes of *ventriloquism*, the innovative CCO approaches by Cooren (2012, 2016), Cooren and Sandler (2014), and Nathues et al (2021) depicting all organizing as produced by a multiplicity of agencies. If we take any statement produced by a person involved in organizational activity, the metaphor of ventriloquism urges analysts to think of what might be making that person – as would be the case with a ventriloquist's dummy – produce the messages she does. In ventriloquism, it is another person (the ventriloquist) moving the dummy's mouth while supplying the words; in an organizational context, that which speaks through the dummy is not limited to only another person's words (nor another *person*); they include 'policies and organizations, but also languages, accents, ideologies, speech communities, rules, norms, values, identities, statuses, etc.' (Cooren, 2012: 5). And ventriloquism goes a step further to suggest that it is not only ventriloquial forces making people-as-dummies speak in particular ways, but simultaneously that each person is a ventriloquist mobilizing several participants to make them 'speak' to advance particular aims. Thus, even if we're looking at individual persons and their statements, ventriloquism holds that we're always dummies and ventriloquists at the same time (Meier & Carroll, 2023; Wright et al, 2023). The implication is that agency is far more complex than a focus on individual humans can provide (and becomes even more interesting when we imagine that actors *beyond* humans can also speak – and speak through us). I'll extend this thinking in the section to follow, but the point is that, from this CCO stance, organizing always involves many (non)human participants bound up in complicated practice-based relations.

A third premise, a direct outgrowth of the second, asserts that *the interplay of order and disorder is intrinsic to communicative practice*. If there are many participants involved in organizing and communicating, and if those participants vary in their interests, capacities, and trajectories of action, it would be naïve at best to believe that orderly action would be the normal state of affairs. It is a commonplace of communication inquiry that meanings are always 'up for grabs' in a couple of important senses. One is that the presence of many participants vying for influence over the meanings produced in our interdependent action implies that straight lines between intention and meaning are unlikely. Second, and related, is that the meanings and conception of collective orderliness are 'up for grabs' among and across those multiple participants, suggesting that meanings are always contingent and provisional.

This plank presents another reason to question the assumption of, or at least the desire for, order in organizing. Most people think of communication as a straightforward act of sharing meaning between persons, with the corollary that those who share meanings will produce seamless coordination and control. In CCO thinking, communication is unavoidably ambiguous and nonlinear, and the excesses of meaning suggest that indeterminacy inevitably reigns. In communication, 'meanings are simultaneously opened (i.e., disordering) and closed (i.e., ordering)' (Vásquez et al, 2016, p 630). Consequently, *dis/organization*, a term denoting the mutual *dependence* of order and disorder, is omnipresent if we only know how to look (Cooper, 1986; Karikari, 2023). Framing dis/organization as the normal state of affairs is key to understanding tensions, paradoxes, and contradictions as constituted by communication (Putnam et al, 2016). It's also key to investigating how everyday elements of organizing, like texts and technologies, provoke practices exhibiting coherence and dispersion – simultaneously (see Vásquez et al, 2022). The two enactments of this third premise display that dis/organization is not a failure of communication, but its normal state.

Finally, *CCO thinking exploits the ambiguity of the word 'organization'*. For some lines of work, organization is a noun, such that the explanatory aim is to show how communication 'scales up' from a micro-level practice to create more encompassing macro-level organizations, as actors with some version of collective identity themselves, which emerge from an interlocking network of communication processes (Taylor, 2009, 2011). Others conceive of organization as a verb (organiz*ing*) and show how communication practice is the site of the coordination and control that comprises organizing, whether that practice occurs under the banner of formal organizations, in social movements, or independent of strong centripetal influences. And one relatively recent branch of CCO thinking moves a step further, to explore organization as an adjective: *organizationality*. From this perspective, investigators consider how communication generates more or less coordinated practices that exhibit varying degrees of the characteristics often associated with organizations. Because organizing is about fluidity, as noted in the preceding chapter, we should not expect all its instances to coagulate into the sorts of structured forms seen in organization theory (Ahrne & Brunsson, 2011[4]). Instead, we should be able to recognize temporary, partial, and hidden practices as presenting some features of organization, even if they lack *all* such features, as can be seen in terrorist networks (Stohl and Stohl, 2011; Bean & Buikema, 2015), co-working spaces (Blagoev et al, 2019), hacktivist collectives (Dobusch & Schoeneborn, 2015), and bicycle-commuting and–jumping communities (Wilhoit & Kisselburgh, 2015; Smith, 2024).

An important outcome of this fourth premise is a rejection of organizations as possessing unquestioned boundaries that enclose activity. Even before the acronym 'CCO' was coined, communication scholars railed against the commonplace belief that communication refers to discrete acts or information flows that occur inside the metaphorical container called 'the' organization (Putnam et al, 1996). But it persists in OS, as seen in Turco's (2016) *The Conversational Firm*, which argues that companies can leverage the power of networked social media to transform communication inside the firm by amplifying conversation and employee voice. For CCO scholars, however, communication is far too complex to be limited to locations either internal or external; the physical setting of its observable episodes are not limits on the sources or trajectories of its meaning creation. In other words, that which we consider to be organizational boundaries cannot be casually assumed, for they are emergent and precarious products of communicative practice that shift depending on the exigencies the practice encounters. The power of prosumers, mentioned in Chapter 1, is but one case in point; the lesson of ventriloquism makes the point more stridently, suggesting that participants often give voice to interests distant from any given encounter but which certainly participate in organizational constitution.

We've arrived at an inflection point, where CCO theorizing must engage with a body of thought not conventionally associated with communicative thinking. I'll lay out the challenge and then present a possible path (one I'll quickly reject). In the next section, it'll take a few pages to arrive at the intellectual connection, but I'll be arguing for the necessity of engaging with a body of thought called *new materialism(s)* if CCO thinking is to develop novel theorizations of the firm under communicative capitalism.

New materialism(s) and CCO theorizing

The preceding section situated the constitutive move in communication studies as a reaction to the poverty of transmissional and representational versions of communication. Those views have for the most part been abandoned by communication scholars but are very much alive in theories of the firm, the OS field, and popular culture. Situating communication as active and generative, as the primary force of world-making, promises to 'rescue the field from an epiphenomenal fate wherein communication shrivels into mere transmission, a passive vehicle for expressing what already exists' (Ashcraft, 2021, p 572). In other words, a constitutive view of communication is necessary to answer onto-epistemological questions about how organizations come to exist, how organizing proceeds, and how purpose becomes inserted into organizational practice. But there's a potential cost to that rescue mission. Specifically, as it emphasizes symbolic and human meaning-making, constitutive theorizing (re-)engages with the idealist thinking associated with constructionism, phenomenology, and hermeneutics; in so doing, it runs the risk of re-enacting the longstanding symbolic/material dualism that has for so long plagued OS scholarship (see Orlikowski & Scott, 2008).

Constitutive communication thinking has thus brought us to a Scylla and Charybdis moment. Allow me to explain. Communication defined as discursive meaning-making is in peril of being swallowed by the symbolic and human, for if meanings are only made from symbols and only about what matters to human choice-making, we lose the ability to say anything of value about the *non*human domain, other than acknowledging that humans *use* material in their action. We are led to overlook cases when the more-than-human is recalcitrant or enigmatic, when it exceeds or violates our expectations of its pliability.

The paired danger is the risk of engulfing communication. Some scholars turn away from symbolism to re-define communication as *any* linking, relating, or connecting of *any* two or more elements. Wise (2011), for instance, sees communication occurring whenever forms and substances are brought into relation, which suggests that 'communication' can be the name for any time two entities get linked through a third entity, even if humans have no part in it.[5] When communication refers to all forms of connection-making, regardless of whether symbolic meanings lead to their accomplishment, *every* act of existence becomes potentially communicative. The tiresome 'if it's everything, it's nothing' trope crops up, as does the fear of providing distinctive analytical devices for investigating the practice of organization. I will delve further into this concern, but the question here is about how to address the relation, or lack of it, between meaning and the nuance necessary to provide analytical purchase on organizing practice.

Hybridizing agency

Underlying these seemingly dichotomous alternatives – the focus on either symbolic/human meaning or the assertion that all connecting counts as communication – is a desire to identify the participants making social practice possible. This is, as noted in this and in the preceding chapter, a question of agency. And although most lay visions of organizing see humans as the only agents capable of producing and responding to meaning, communicative perspectives reject the implication that *non*humans occupy a meaning*less* world.[6] The obvious invitation, then, is to take up the ways nonhumans create and inhabit a form of meaning in their own trajectories of action.

A broadened conception of agency would lead us to consider, for instance, AI that seems to 'desire' particular actions and connections, even those that escape the will of the programmers who coded it (Swanepoel, 2021). We'd start to consider whether nonhumans do things typically considered reserved for humans, such as developing culture and accented symbol use that's now seen in birds, honeybees, primates, and cetaceans like whales and dolphins (Aplin, 2019; Whitehead et al, 2021; Bakker, 2022).[7] When we recognize the relationships between animals' environments and their behaviours, we might see those relationships as displaying meanings and networked cognition, as well as narrative, that escape our human categories.[8] We might also be astounded by the perplexingly uncategorizable fungi, which not only are essential to life on the planet but which seem to have problem-solving and messaging (perhaps communication) capacities previously thought to belong only to organisms with brains (Sheldrake, 2020). We also might then align with

Wheeler (2014), who argues that human language, often considered the foundation of agency, 'is just the most recent evolutionary part of a vast global web of semiosis encompassing all living things' (p 71).

These examples of nonhuman meaning and thinking are all versions of the agency question: who or what can be said to be an agent? This is a common question in contemporary social science, *but it's a dead end* – another dichotomous devil and the deep blue sea. It's not a bad idea to reject humans' status as the only makers of meaning, and it's undoubtedly wise to follow such a refusal with questions about what meaning is, where it's to be found, and how it motivates action. It's also valuable to dissolve the differences between humans and nonhumans, whether that be via examples such as those in the preceding paragraph, or a cyborgian recognition that we humans are more-than-human: 'Things can be alive and people can be machines ... we might add to Bruno Latour's saying "Things are people too" the corollary: "People are things too." Saint Augustine said it well: "We, however, who enjoy and use other things, are things ourselves."' (Peters, 2015, p 89).

So perhaps our thing-ness should encourage us to think about the many planes of meaning moving humans, just as the alternative renderings of meaning move *non*humans.

The problem, however, is that when we seek to affix agency and meaning-making to individual entities, be they human or nonhuman, we're getting further from the analytical moves that deepen our understandings of organization. If organization is both noun and verb, and if communicative capitalism is a set of practices rather than a monolith, our theoretical apparatus must offer the nuance to comprehend their complexities. Seeing agency as seated *in* uninterrogated entities, *in* substances, won't cut it.[9]

What is needed, instead, is a vision of agency that builds on the second premise of CCO mentioned earlier, one that considers action to always be the product of *hybrid* agency realized in practice (Brummans, 2018). A recognition of hybridity is not about supplementing the human with attention to (separate) nonhuman entities; it involves a full transcendence of the dualism discussed earlier. It is also a rejection of 'human' and 'nonhuman' as stable, taken-for-granted categories. In organizing, humans cannot be considered the autonomous font of action because all capacities are produced in combination with an aggregation of other agencies. Practice, in turn, refers to how various agencies emerge and combine (as well as conflict) in the production of action.

Hybridizing agency is a radical break with most conventional models of agency and practice. It is also not the way we scholars and practitioners typically tell the story of organization. Our narratives are full of persons and firms (and firms are often likened to persons) as heroes and villains who make choices, build coalitions, manage others, and sell visions. Hybridity says, in contrast, that we are all the product of *multiple* agencies (Cooren, 2018), such that our humanness is simultaneously *non*humanness, and that the agencies producing organizational action are necessarily multiple and shifting. (The resonance with ontological multiplicity is probably obvious here, and I attend more explicitly to it in the following section.) Delving into this question to see how this hybrid conception of agency transcends dualism will require a foray into new materialist thinking.

Two tenets of the new materialism(s)

Although theory and research in the 'new materialist' vein (also known as the 'ontological turn' in social theory and 'co-production' in Science and Technology Studies) has made numerous appearances in OS, the moves it makes and the assumptive ground upon which it is established is foreign to many, so a bit of introductory work is in order. And while I've just called new materialist thought an 'it,' there exist several distinct approaches and emerging themes (as is the case for any growing research area), necessitating the clunky term 'new materialisms' (Coole & Frost, 2010) to describe its many strands – hence the parenthetical 's' in this section's heading. After a relatively brief overview of two key tenets, I present a particular line of new materialist thought that, in conjunction with CCO, will underwrite the alternative theory of the firm this book articulates.

An ontological break

Traditionally, materialist thought evinces a concern for deep structures, classes, and macro-level forces, often drawing a direct line back to Marx's historical materialism. The idealist thought that emerged in response (including constructionism and poststructuralism) argued against traditional materialism's reductionist thinking and argued instead for the need to examine discourse and language in detailed accounts of social process. Into this opposition – the dualism I mentioned – stepped new materialist thought, which rejects any models of a swinging pendulum or a happy medium and instead seeks to fundamentally re-describe (and re-imagine) the world.

New materialisms' re-description begins with a point made previously: that thinking in terms of entities and substances as agents with an independent existence is an ontological dead end. Given ontological multiplicity, all 'things' are all multiple and hybrid, and only come into existence as (re)produced in practice (see also Bencherki & Elmholdt, 2022). The apparent stability of persons, organizations, and technologies is the result of them being regularly re-enacted in similar ways in similar practices, where boundary creation is key. Pellizzioni (2015) puts it well:

> [H]ierarchies, identities and dualisms are replaced with fluid, contingent, emergent entities: networks, relations, performances, materializations,

assemblages, human-nonhuman or organic-inorganic hybrids. This means that binary oppositions do not pre-exist but are produced in action. Space and time themselves are no longer assumed as ontological givens, but are regarded as resulting from relational processes. (p 73)

A good example of this thinking, one that makes explicit connection with the claim of multiplicity, is de Laet and Mol's (2000) examination of the Zimbabwe Bush Pump Type B. It is a technology designed to pump water from the ground but, as is the case with most technologies, 'it' is ontologically multiple. Its existence, de Laet and Mol show, is *fluid* in that in its entanglement with various forms of life, the bush pump becomes different 'things.' It can be a source of water, yes, but it is also a site of community development due to the need for shared effort in drilling and pumping; it is part of a national infrastructure plan as a government promise of potable water that can also reduce social divisions; in its hygienic design, it can be a sanitation device and source of health security; it is an impetus for a potential shift in governmental policy focus from communities to extended families; it is a technological accomplishment celebrated by development activists for which its inventor relinquishes credit. 'It' is many things, all at once, shifting fluidly with the practice(s) in which it is bound up. And its potentials for *becoming-other* are always present. Thus, rejecting the notion that a bush pump, or any other entity, is a *substance*, new materialisms assert that such substantialist thinking urges unhelpful questions; the world is comprised of *relations*, all the way down.

The relationality point (the anti-substantialist point) leads directly to what has become known as a flat, or monist, ontology. A flat ontology refuses to privilege one form of agency, or one sort of participant, over others. Often associated with Latour's (2005) thinking on Actor-Network Theory but broadly shared by new materialisms, a flat ontology argues that the world is not made up of the workings of structures at macro and micro levels of analysis, nor is it the product of natural/cultural or material/symbolic connections. Instead, it is the specific conjunction of agencies in any given practice that produces the real. The real is *done*, not *discovered*. This results in a rejection of a search for the realist's generative mechanisms, deep structures, and basic assumptions (Heracleous & Barrett, 2001; Mutch et al, 2006).

Not too long ago, a couple of colleagues and I wrote about the implications of a flat ontology:

[T]he hope of finding *underlying* explanatory properties or mechanisms begins to fade. No wizard hides behind the curtain, and no pearls of essence lay buried at the bottom of the ocean. To be clear, the claim is not simply that we can never finally know these truths; the claim is that they are not 'out there' at all. Only vectors of ordinary practice can explain the relations in which we find ourselves. (Kuhn et al, 2017, p 33; emphasis in original)

It also means that structures, ideologies, and systems can do no explanatory work; the world is produced in events that cascade upon one another (Ganesh & Wang, 2015; Fox & Alldred, 2017). Key to a flat ontology, then, is that our units of analysis must not be persons, firms, technologies, structures, or even any features of these putatively substantive entities. The unit of analysis, as mentioned in both Chapters 1 and 2, must be *the practice itself* – the complex and messy site of becomings, characterized by hybrid agency and ontological fluidity.

From matter to materializing

As should be evident at this point, new materialisms represent not a fetishizing of the material, nor a claim for material agency (Pickering, 1995), but a fundamental rejection of the very categories 'social' and 'material.' The English language does us no favours here, but the portmanteau *sociomateriality* (Orlikowski, 2007; Orlikowski & Scott, 2008) is an effort to recognize the ontological inseparability – *not* entanglement, which implies separate strands – of what are often rendered as distinct substances in conventional theorizing (a practice that is, incidentally, a type of accomplishing itself). Accordingly, if people are simultaneously things, there can be no sharp distinction between the human and nonhuman, nor between the symbolic and material. In slight contrast, or maybe clarification, with what I've written, 'the material' is not a category of entity that can act in congruence with or recalcitrance from the human but is always–already vibrantly bound up in, and emergent from, practice (Bennett, 2010).

The task in OS, then, is not to look for examples of how nonhuman things act independently of humans. The crucial analytical move, argues Cooren (2020), is to trace how particular participants in organizing are made to exist and made to matter – how they are *materialized* – in and through communication. A brand, for instance, is made to exist through the images associated with it, the objects that exemplify it, and the lifestyles that appropriate it; all of these are deployments in practice. A firm may come to exist through the depictions of its spokespersons, the buildings that become the sites of its operations, and the activity carried out in its name – but, again, the focus must remain on the practices in which 'the firm' arises and is made to matter. For Cooren, anytime one seeks to define mattering, the key task is 'to identify *through what or whom* this thing or person presents, embodies, materializes itself/himself or herself' (p 11; emphasis in original). His stance suggests that 'materializing' is not simply the domain of conventionally material elements like artifacts, bodies, or buildings, but that it can occur any time one participant mediates or passes another participant to a third, as when an algorithm presents a byzantine set of ranking metrics to rideshare drivers.

Crucially, materialization can never be anything but *incomplete*, in that any materialization offers only one facet of the practice; the multiplicity of linked practices necessarily escapes any analyst's awareness. Cooren (2020) notes that texts like a firm's strategic plan can materialize in many ways: as senior managers begin discussing the need for such a statement, engage in facilitated conversations about its contents, discuss avenues for inserting their units' preferences into the document, and defend it to lower-level employees. And after a document representing a strategy is created, should it be ignored in subsequent practice, it will not materialize in the sense of guiding future organizing (it will not matter). The upshot is that 'a strategic plan thus has, by definition, *different degrees of materialization*, which means that its materiality will always be *relative, finite*, and somehow *incomplete*' (p 13; emphasis in original). A new materialist orientation to organization, then, forces us to attend to the unfolding of materialization over time, recognizing both that the participants who/that mediate its existence and generate its inevitable multiplicity as 'organization' must be made legible to the researcher.

Thus, one of the tasks confronting us researchers is – to return to the stance on the military aircraft studied by Law (2002) and mentioned in the Introduction – to explain how organizational *singularity* is performed or accomplished alongside, or perhaps in opposition to, ontological multiplicity. Such 'how' questions are ultimately empirical, but the challenge is to develop an analytical apparatus adequate to the task. In the next chapter, I nominate what I'll call the *authoritative text* as just that sort of device.

Conclusion

The tenets of new materialisms are broad depictions of onto-epistemological commitments and, as such, remain relatively abstract with respect to guiding investigations of practice. A recognition of a hybridity in agencies in a flattened ontological plane, participants' fluid multiplicity, and the contingencies of materializing are provocative (and, I hope, evocative) departures from business as usual, but they provide meagre conceptual scaffolding for empirical investigations. What is needed is something akin to a framework, a vision for the coming together of these forces, especially in the context and conduct of organization. Fortunately, the work of Gilles Deleuze and his collaborator Félix Guattari, along with those who have interpreted their thinking and built upon the foundation they laid, provide the basics for articulating such a framework.

Communicatively constituting the assemblage

The iconoclast French philosopher Gilles Deleuze (1925–1995) has experienced a gradual and uneven reception in OS. Writing primarily between the late 1960s and the early 1990s (with a few works trickling out after his death), his thinking on difference and immanence took hold in philosophical and humanistic circles in the first decade of the 21st century. Those scholars clearly saw something of value, since Deleuzian thinking (which includes his collaborative work with Guattari) has seen a dramatic uptick across fields, including OS, in the past decade[10] (Gehman et al, 2022). Although the reasons for this are many, my aim here is not in displaying popularity to justify bandwagon-jumping, but to suggest that Deleuzian thought is slowly capturing the imagination of a wide array of OS thinkers. This section will not review his entire oeuvre, nor will it explain all the ways writers find his work generative. Instead, it will focus on concepts that meet the CCO claims discussed earlier in the development of a framework for an alternative theory of the firm.

Difference and the virtual

Deleuze is often understood as a philosopher of *difference*. Building on Spinoza and Bergson, Deleuze critiques the history of philosophy as being consumed with identity – specifically, with identifying particular phenomena or things, creating categories that distinguish them from other phenomena/things, enumerating their prevalence, and documenting what they do. Foregrounding identity in this way neuters difference by rendering it outside the conceptual scheme, rendering it *not* the phenomenon/thing of interest. A similar recognition characterized Martin's (1992) depiction of an integrationist view of organizational culture, the one characterized by a belief in relative consensus across culture's many manifestations; those holding such a position consider disagreements, confusions, ambiguities, and the like to be *non*-culture, and thus not the phenomenon in which they're interested.

An ontological orientation to difference, however, escapes and denies the logic of identity. Deleuze's interest is not in showing how one entity differs from another, for that would further entrench a logic of identity as the establishment of 'things.' Nor is it with communication rendered as representation, which presents a false hope for setting 'the thing' apart from the world. Instead, difference is always the potentiality of new becomings, and it is the task of philosophy to create concepts and foster interactions that make these becomings possible (Linstead & Thanem, 2007). In a discussion closely related to the rejection of correspondence thinking mentioned in Chapter 1, Deleuze argues that the analyst should seek not to devise better ways to *represent* difference, but instead should deploy novel concepts to discover and invent new ways of living *through* difference (Deleuze & Guattari, 1983).

The key potentiality in Deleuzian thinking aligns with Ovid's opening line of the *Metamorphoses*: 'I speak of forms changed into new bodies.' The aim for the Deleuzian interest in becomings is to acknowledge the materialized, embodied form of assemblage while simultaneously examining those forms' virtual potentialities for always becoming anew. This potentiality is not merely about processes flowing beneath a surface, but about the *capacities of those forms' multiplicities*. Becoming new bodies, new sites of agency.

Centring difference is not to suggest that bodies, identities, routines, organizations, and the like don't exist, but to acknowledge that, as May (2005) explains, 'difference is the overflowing character of things themselves, their inability to be wrestled into categories of representation' (p 82). That overflow comes via the repetition of practice, in which difference continually inserts itself into (what we conceive to be) the entity. Difference is thus always *virtual*, a potentiality immanent to every phenomenon/thing. Immanent difference accompanies the practices in which it is enmeshed as a force filled with possibility. Virtuality is not the potential plans for the future inside the heads of a firm's strategic managers; virtuality occurs because 'multiple forces (e.g., random events, saying and doings of distributed actors both powerful and weak, overflows and misfires) can lead to shifts in agencements, which in turn change the power of actors to speak and act' (Garud & Gehman, 2019, p 682).

The interesting move here is Deleuze's assertion that what a thing like an organization becomes – whether the virtual difference participates in its iterative becoming, whether its possibility of becoming-other is actualized – is a product of the relationships between problems and solutions the phenomenon/thing is *made to face*. (We should be hearing the echo of the 'what do corporations want' question.) Deleuze (1995) suggests that the lion's share of our living consists in answering simple problems with determinable solutions: closed-ended questions that imply stable identities for the phenomenon/thing and which, in turn, reject the immanent potentiality of the virtual. Whether we're thinking with bodies, identities, routines, or organizations, stable representations of phenomena/things relegate difference beyond the ontological boundary.

When we instead refuse definitive vectors of solutions and problems, when we devise and articulate problems that evade undemanding determination, new approaches to being and becoming surface. Not only do an array of solutions to provocative problems emerge, but a multiplicity of difference-infused conceptions of phenomena/things can inspire new ways of living. It is in this latter conception of difference and possibility that I find the value of both CCO and new materialisms: the capacity to pry open taken-for-granted matrices of problems and solutions by posing vexing ontological questions.

Assemblage and agency

The image of the social most commonly associated with Deleuze and Guattari is that of an *assemblage*, a constantly shifting swarm of forces and sociomaterial elements that hang together as both source and site of action. The assemblage both provides a template for making sense of the many participants in practice and provides a route to grasp the immanent difference mentioned in the preceding section, since the continually trembling assemblage of participants provides ever-new potentials for new practice becomings (Thanem & Linstead, 2006; DeLanda, 2016; Gherardi, 2016).

First, a brief note regarding what assemblage thinking is *not*. The image of *an* assemblage refers, at its most basic, to the notion that elements combine to create a whole of some sort that expresses, or manifests, an identity and claims a territory (it's relevant to note, however, that Deleuze and Guattari provide several distinct, though somewhat overlapping, definitions throughout their work). Such a view conjures up visions of a *system* or a *network* characterized by boundaries and discernable internal and external processes. Deleuze and Guattari, however, distance themselves from the register of systems and network theorizing as OS scholars have articulated it. As suggested, the participants in an assemblage are not independent entities wrangled into a 'system' based on some notion of interdependence. Nor is the image one of networks that can be assessed by density, size, node centrality, and the like. It is only in the swarm of things, actions, passions, and signs that the participants take on particular identities, and only when the swarm is made to pursue a particular path that it becomes an 'it' as well. (Again, intimations of the 'what do corporations want' question appear.)

For Deleuze and Guattari (1987), assemblage is noun *and* verb: both the doing of practice and the constitution of an agent. Simultaneously. The French term used by Deleuze and Guattari, *agencement* (included in the quote from Garud and Gehman) conveys more than the English term *assemblage*, in the former's connotation of 'articulating, arranging, disposing, and setting' (Cochoy et al, 2016, p 3). *Agencement* is thus both about arranging and acting *through* that arrangement (Phillips, 2006). So, though the common English use of assemblage loses something in translation, and though it is often deployed by authors without grasping the Deleuzian heritage, for ease of use I'll stick with it. My hope is that there has now been enough writing employing the term assemblage to prevent its interpretive reduction to a mere collection of things (Wise, 2011). In short, assemblage signifies the assortment of forces (capacities of practices-becoming-things, actions, passions, and signs, but also qualities, desires, potentials, and regimes of truth) that need to be assembled for action to occur, with the associated acknowledgement that assemblages' contents and configurations differ across the varied practices they produce (Çalişkan & Callon, 2010).

Assemblages are practices made of practices; they are not networks of entities. Although moment-in-time snapshots (nominalization) can enable us to discern the participants manifesting them – a move possibly necessary for analysis (Leonardi, 2013) – researchers must not lose sight of the focus on practice as the animating force (as verbs). To return to the point made previously about difference and the virtual, assemblages rendered as nouns can be considered entities, *forms* encasing the personhood seen in a good deal of writing on corporate governance (with all the embodied etymological baggage 'corporate' brings).

Assemblages are, moreover, unlikely to be the result of intentional action of humans, or at least not fully so; they develop 'in a kind of chaotic network of habitual and non-habitual connections, always in flux, always reassembling in different ways' (Potts, 2004, p 19). And, importantly, we know nothing about an assemblage until we see what it can *do*. Once again, the value of assemblage is in thinking practice.

Territorialization via coding and connection

And what assemblages do is establish territories by coding themselves and making connections. Territorialization refers to laying claim to domains of activity in space and time, which positions the assemblage with respect to its surround (the encompassing assemblages). At the same time, however, the assemblage may – indeed will – *de*territorialize by encountering events that alter practices, relations, and identities. Assemblages encompass passions, actions, signs, and objects that connect with one another to characterize its practice, and which simultaneously connect with practices in the broader array. Connection-making can also engender de-territorialization via new connections that challenge the existing doings of the assemblage.

Connections, in turn, are the result of *coding*. The notion of coding provides Deleuze and Guattari the ability to discuss the practices and devices by which an assemblage comes to take on an identity as a whole. For social scientists, and communication scholars in particular, 'code' usually conjures up the merely symbolic: coding is often taken to be the province of language and cognition, as in 'A means B' or 'X is an instance of Y.' But Deleuzian thinking uses the template of a genetic code, one that shapes reproduction – but does not determine it, and in fact is the site of rampant unpredictability (Barad, 2012). Codes operate via inscriptions written, both literally and figuratively, on flows (of capital, labour, meaning, affect, etc.) to render them operational, recognizable, sensible. For instance, Kurie (2018) documents how the Hershey chocolate company rode the wave of CSR in the first decade of the 2000s by recalling its founder's (that'd be Milton Snavely Hershey: 1857–1945) commitment to citizenship and education. As a figure, the founder became a coding device useful for determining a stance on CSR that guided the making and breaking of connections in a social surround ambivalent about the company's economic might. Coding thus touched on flows of commitment, place, memory, and brand in the emergence of the company's varying CSR stance.

The key mode of coding when thinking organizationally is communication.[11] The coding in communication drives the production of local (molecular) action and representations of the whole (molar), and assemblages evince a constant and inevitable interplay between the two. The code also underwrites attachment-making, such that codes do not merely outline the reproduction or derivation of the organism (*filiation*, as seen in the Hershey case), but also the creation of unexpected *alliances* with other assemblages. A key question for coding, then, is the character of the connections induced by a code, along with how an assemblage 'becomes other' as a result of those complex and shifting relations. The creation of filiation and alliances (re)produces the assemblage and guides its trajectory.

An important metaphor Deleuze and Guattari deploy to illustrate territorialization-via-coding is that of a *machine*: not a mechanical object but a *practice* that desires connections with other machines.[12] The value of thinking in terms of machines as the image of assemblage, says Mease (2021), is that 'we accentuate connection, or the "plugging" of one machine into another, as the critical event in constitution' (p 237). Moreover, even when serving a particular purpose, immanent differences are always possible for every machine, suggesting possibilities for additional relations and new functions (becoming-other). The important point is that, for Deleuze, machines *are* their connections, and they *want* ever-new connections. (Again, a connection with the 'what do corporations want' question.)

For Deleuze and Guattari, the machine metaphor provides a version of a flat ontology, one in which the connections of the machinic assemblage *are* the spirit of capitalism. Capitalism (along with patriarchy, neoliberalism, and the like) thus does not work from the top down but is the ongoing product of practice. And though I mentioned that Deleuze and Guattari eschew conventional systems theorizing, they appropriate it to suggest that an engagement with a flattened ontology does not preclude talk about larger systems; they enjoin us to see that what we treat as a unified whole 'is so because it implies a constellation of juxtaposed, imbricated, ordered subsystems' (Deleuze & Guattari, 1987, p 21). Power thus is not the structuring or hegemonic force of an ideology, but the capacity to make (im)possible particular relations in the assemblage/machine and to link them with (or isolate them from) other layered and dispersed practices (Nicolini, 2016). In short, then, machines are *practices* (not objects, not technical mechanism) that desire connections with other practices, and in that connection-making the assemblage can become a new practice, a new sort of machine.[13] Machine, in the hands of Deleuze, is more engine than contraption.

Arborescent and rhizomatic organizing

One of Deleuze and Guattari's key analytical devices is the distinction between arboreal and rhizomatic assemblages. Arborescent assemblages are like trees, with direct lines of influence between roots, trunks, branches, and leaves. It is a model of territorialization based on centralization and hierarchy; as a botanical metaphor for the ordering of an assemblage, it displays efforts to reduce complexity through forms of coding that treat elements homogeneously and direct activity into determinable channels. Identities and interests are fixed and essentialized (Gehman et al, 2022). Think bureaucracies or the Catholic church. The theories of the firm introduced in the preceding chapter, with their focus on strategic managers' control and the production of systematicity in the pursuit of profitability, are thoroughly ensconced in arborescent thinking.

Rhizomes, in contrast, are plants with complex structures in which roots, leaves, and stems can sprout from any point of the plant. There is no stem, and their genetic codes do not determine their shape or their growth through space (May, 2005). In making a connection to organization, Gehman et al note that rhizomatic assemblages constantly rupture and (re)establish connections – as machines, assemblages *are* the connections they desire. Continual re-connecting leads to constant flux in the relations among assemblage elements. Rhizomes pursue multiple aims, embody ambiguous identities, and have fluid boundaries.

Rhizomatic assemblages, then, are not unities or monoliths; they are the incarnation of multiplicity. They can become collectives with the capacity for agency, even though they negate conventional notions of organization. To conventional OS thinking, including theories of the firm, rhizomatic thinking may seem like a strange and irrelevant stance, despite the increasing supply of studies displaying evidence of rhizomatic organizing practice (such as Hsu, 2022; Góral, 2023). It could be painted as the sort of philosophical obliviousness to 'reality' that many scholars in strategic management and organizational economics staunchly oppose. The aim in using Deleuzian new materialist thought is, however, less about accurately capturing some current reality (recall the break with correspondence thinking mentioned earlier) and instead employing tools for imagination that urge us to concoct generative alternatives to everyday practice. And if those tools can generate novel engagements with the problem of firms' purpose and the question of corporate wanting, all the better.

But ... why?

The issue left out of the typical presentation of assemblage thinking is a basic ontological question, the sort of question theories of the firm and CCO thinking force us to ask. The question is this: *why do assemblages form in the first place*? It's one thing to see assemblages everywhere, to assert that they make connections and establish territories, to note that force/desire makes them hang together, and to depict the world '*as an assemblage of assemblages*' (DeLanda, 2016, p 37; emphasis in original).[14] Yet it's quite another to provide an answer to the question of why a particular assemblage exists at all.

Returning to the notion of hybridity introduced earlier, one response is that all action involves multiple agencies for its conduct. Although the conventional academic gaze leads us to understand working and organizing as outcomes of individualized, psychologized processes, Deleuzian new materialism argues that agency is always dispersed across many participants (Painter-Morland, 2011), a claim that aligns with CCO's notion of hybrid agency. To the extent that (an) assemblage is an effort to enumerate connected agencies, the answer to the 'why' question is that the existence of assemblages is *required* for any given practice to be carried out. In capitalism, communicative or otherwise, firms are necessary devices to organize passions, actions, signs, and objects into a practice that perpetuates capital attraction and accumulation. Examining this 'why' question is vital, because if, following DeLanda, *firms* are to be considered assemblages situated in more encompassing assemblages, then answering the first theory of the firm question (why do firms exist?) implies attention to the necessity of the forces across an assemblage that can marshal and direct its practice. I turn more explicitly to this question in the next chapter.

Conclusion of assemblage and agency thinking

The upshot of assemblage/machinic thinking is that organizations are not to be understood as stable structures. But neither should they be approached as *shifting* structures populated with durable people, policies, and routines that unfreeze, change, and then refreeze. Both those approaches evince substantialism, but if we are to foreground sociomaterial practice, 'researchers should treat organizations as machines made up of machines, made up of machines, made up of … force' (Mease, 2021, pp 240–1. Ellipsis in original). Force, here, refers to the capacity to affect and be affected, making the analyst's task one of understanding how any particular logic of practice moves through an assemblage, activating and creating (or disabling) connections. Meaning, in turn, cannot be reduced to what is in one's head (nor the average of a collective's cognitive constructs), nor is it in the semiotic domain of signs; meaning is found in the aims of the practices that form on the desiring force that makes an assemblage hang together.

Attracting attachments

New materialism(s) makes practice the unit of analysis, and the Deleuzian stance outlined previously argues that the assemblage *is* practice. The notion of assemblages/machines directs our attention to their attachments, their relations, which are key to making any particular practice (im)possible. A slight framing tweak is to consider those connections to be *attachments*, with the terminological shift highlighting (inter)dependence in the development of the assemblage's identity.[15] Attachments index additions of *property*, possessive relations (Kjellberg, 2017) that conjure up what the assemblage can call its own (what it holds on to), or what is configured as an element of its being by being attached to other participants. Seeking to attach consumers and their money to a given product reflects the assemblage's capacities, as would the creation of a partnership that allowed the assemblage to attach to new production practices, markets, or an organizational culture associated with beliefs of superiority. Attaching elements to one another *(re)produces* the very assemblage.

There are two key questions with respect to attachments: *how are they formed*, and *what consequences do new attachments/detachments create for the assemblage's practice?* On the former question, Michel Callon (2017) provides a useful vocabulary. Discussing the creation of markets – a particular type of assemblage – Callon suggests three generic devices for generating attachments: listening, co-production, and addiction. (Though each of these operates with the notion of a human seller and consumer in his presentation, it's not much of a stretch to move to the sociomaterial domain, as I'll discuss further in Chapter 4.) First, *listening* devices tell consumers that they *need* a particular good or service, operating with a form of dialogue where attachment is not simply the result of a persuasive marketing message but 'listening' to the desires of consumers by tracking contagion, connecting with opinion leaders, and inducing the free and authentic labour of trusted members of targets' social networks (Mellett, 2017; Lo, 2022). When consumers feel heard, when they see connections between engagement and representation in the product or service, they are more likely to attach to a firm through identification. As mentioned in Chapter 1's discussion of communicative capitalism, these attachments can have unintended consequences with respect to control over a company's brand, so those exercising influence over the assemblage via listening may seek to manage the existence and intensity of the relationship.

Callon's second form of attachment, an outgrowth of the first, is *co-production*, where consumers are invited into the process of design, production, and branding (as also discussed in Chapter 1). Attaching consumers is not merely about the production of goods, however. Callon explains by citing Gerlitz's (2017) study of the cosmetic brand Dove, which:

[R]elies on a multitude of stakeholders, working with women's groups, organising forums and projects, and animating a vast movement that questions standards of beauty – particularly those spread by the media – thereby becoming able to involve itself in the development of new practices and new meanings. ... The brand attaches; and one is attached to the brand. It is a collective force that performs the opening of goods and encourages their maximal meshing with the ethical, political, or cultural concerns that simultaneously transform them. (Callon, 2017, p 188)

The implication here is that the assemblage is *comprised of* attachments between stakeholders, the firm-as-producer, a branded lifestyle, and conceptions of bodies (along with many more participants). Though one could understand Dove's stance as a cynical marketing ploy engineered by opportunistic marketers (as is often associated with greenwashing and other forms of CSR), the point is that the practices revolving around and invoking 'Dove'– the interconnected marketing campaigns, the movements for body positivity, the academic critiques, the online conversations re-imagining beauty standards – are the result of a complex set of meaning-full attachments. The brand is ontologically multiple.

Callon's final version of attachment is *addiction*, where attached consumers are made to attach themselves to an assemblage in ways that escape those consumers' control. Callon discusses the configuration of casinos, cigarettes with menthol capsules, and engineered food products as devices calculated to addict consumers. Another example, gamification, has become pervasive under communicative capitalism, not merely in retailing or gambling, but as a mode of both management and consumption themselves (Cochoy et al, 2016; Savignac, 2016). If one were to broaden the notion of addiction to include desires alongside compulsions and obsessions, we might see the ways that other forms of value-generation create the dependencies suggested in the addiction mode: when firms reduce ambiguity by developing the capacity of foresight (Flyverbom & Garsten, 2021; Fergnani, 2022), when identifications with a firm represent personal morality (Costas & Kärreman, 2013), when architectural spaces cultivate aesthetic forms of affect that participate in the creation of cultivation of community (Blok, 2015), or when workplace design endeavours to capture all facets of the worker (Fleming, 2012), there is evidence of firms making the attachments with participants addictive, as desires become needs.

The need to look beyond human intentionality and meaning-making to understand attachments is paramount for not only the new materialist version of CCO discussed in this chapter, but also for communicative capitalism. It is not the case that social media algorithms, for instance, summon attachments by their mere existence; it is only as algorithms are made to matter in being bound up with an array of other elements in capital-accumulative practice that they attach persons, moods, capital, and data to the assemblages through which their practice occurs. Moreover, if, as Deleuze and Guattari argue, assemblages establish territories by making attachments, and if the virtual is an ever-present source of difference, then we should expect shifts in assemblages' operations and trajectories as they grow by accretion. To the extent that assemblages continue to align with the communicative spirit of capitalism even as they grow suggests that their practices are infused by communicative logics of value, and thus that those logics are also central players in the practice of assemblage. We should also expect messes and misfires; as McFall et al (2017) argue, the complexity of attachment (and also *de*tachment) is full of 'uncertainty, guesswork, sentiment, luck, mystery, and failure' (p 10), just as is emblematic of CCO thinking's attention to dis/organization.

The analytical challenge Callon issues is to understand the configurations that make practices – particularly those associated with value production and appropriation under communicative capitalism – possible without focusing on the entities populating of the configuration as distinct agents. As is the case with both CCO and new materialisms, assemblage thinking presents a challenging figure/ground exercise, one that confronts the substantialism of our taken-for-granted perceptual schemas – a necessary exercise if we are to break with the correspondence and entity-based thinking that dominates theories of the firm.

Conclusion

The vocabulary of Deleuze and Guattari, along with CCO thinkers, is both unfamiliar and abstract to the ears/eyes of many OS scholars. We should ask, then, whether there is anything of value in this body of thought. I see a few benefits with respect to re-imagining the firm under communicative capitalism. First is the framing of communicative capitalism not as a domineering ideology or master narrative *determining* firms' activity, but as a set of forces distributed through the practices constituting assemblages. This enjoins scholars to examine practices from the inside, a stance that also can evince novel points of intervention. A second advantage of joining CCO and Deleuzian theorizing is an insistence on problematizing boundaries and, in turn, influence. No firm is an island unto itself, and the thinking presented in this chapter helps analysts see that 'the firm' is a punctuation in a complex array of practices. The turn toward attachment offers a route to understand how new trajectories can result from novel connections, without the implied agency of a pre-existing firm finding new entities to fold into its system of stakeholder alliances. If communicative capitalism highlights interdependence as key to understanding firms, the thinking outlined in this chapter can help us recognize forms of attachment as generating both the firm and its mode of value generation. A third contribution, a direct outgrowth of reconceptualizing influence over the assemblage's becoming, is Deleuzian thinking's capacity to revitalize the study of authority. In the image of the machine, that which pushes the assemblage to one or another trajectory cannot be simply a person or even a group of them (for example, the assumption of the power of strategic management). Authority too is a force, *not a feature attached to a person*, and the call for OS scholars is to clarify its contours and develop routes to trace its influence. I offer a response to each of these issues while building on the work in this chapter in outlining a Communicative Theory of the Firm in Chapter 4.

Notes

1. Earning a PhD from, or being employed by, an academic unit called 'communication' certainly doesn't give one unassailable credentials. This isn't the place for a consideration of disciplinarity, but I'm generally more interested in projects pursuing novel visions of communicating and organizing, regardless of authors' employment affiliation, than in enforcing claims to ownership over terms (see Kuhn, 2017a, for an explanation of this stance). Nevertheless, it's dispiriting that many of those writing about communication in organization studies seem blithely unaware of the existence of an entire field devoted to its study.

2. Taylor was working on these themes before this article, of course. He published a book in French in 1988, *Une organization n'est qu'un tissue de communication: Essais theoriques*, and then another in English in 1993, *Rethinking the Theory of Organizational Communication*. The piece that introduced his thinking on the organization-communication relationship, however, was this 1996 one.

3. That McPhee and Zaug article, incidentally, was where the term 'Communicative Constitution of Organizations' was coined.

4. Ahrne and Brunsson argue that 'complete' organizations are those that make decisions about membership, hierarchy, rules, monitoring compliance, and sanctions, and they hold that there can be many good reasons why partial organizations never become complete, and even recognize that remaining partial can bestow organizing advantages.

5. It's relevant to note that the vast majority of studies employing such a conception of communication retain a focus on phenomena in which humans have a central role. Peters (2015) marks an important, and excellent, departure, but there are very few examinations in communication studies of communication that look past the human.

6. Meaning is not simply the symbolic sense of reference and significance upon which humans operate – but then again – paraphrasing Turing, if a thing doesn't reason like us (and there's little evidence that we understand the vast diversity in human reasoning), does that mean it doesn't *think*?

7. See Mercado III (2021) for a skeptical review of the debate on the cultural foundations of whale songs and their changes.

8. Some scholars work to make fine-grained, and often highly dubious, distinctions between humans. Race has always been an issue in such divisions, particularly as racist thinkers have performed mental and statistical gymnastics to sustain the belief that persons of colour are somehow lower persons (Jackson, 2017). For instance, in 1864, British geologist William King, inspecting Neanderthal skulls, thought that the protruding brow made these ancestors look more like skulls found among Africans and Australian Aboriginals; as Mooallem (2017) writes, 'extrapolating from his low opinion of what he called these "savage" races, he explained that the Neanderthal's skull alone was proof of its moral "darkness" and stupidity.'

9. Paul Rekret (2018) challenges new materialist thinking on this count, arguing that its insistence that the dualism between matter and mind, or between material and the social/discursive, is precisely what needs to be explained in this body of thought. He argues, further, that neglecting the source(s) of separation blunts the ethical and political claims this body of thought can offer empirical projects.

10. Google's Ngram viewer displays the increased attention to (or at least referencing of) Deleuze over time between 1990 and 2019, the most recent data available at the time of this writing (Figure 3.1):

Figure 3.1: Google Ngram viewer of appearance of 'Deleuze' in books published between 1990 and 2019

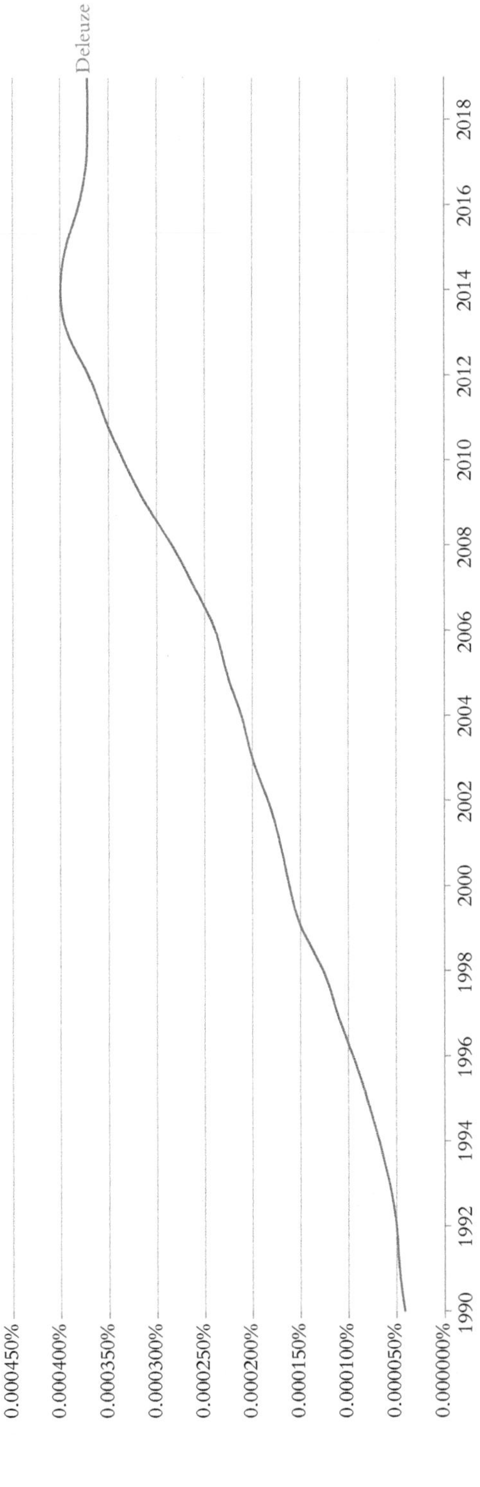

Source: Google Ngram

[11] Often rendered as *language* in the Deleuzian literature (see DeLanda, 2016), the (re) production of social organization – which is never merely social – is not restricted to the symbols and syntax often associated with the linguistic, but is better understood as complexly coordinated meaning processes, hence my substitution of communication here.

[12] Deleuze and Guattari (1987, p 399) express it thus: 'assemblages are passional, they are compositions of desire. Desire has nothing to do with a natural or spontaneous determination; there is no desire but assembling, assembled, desire.'

[13] There are, of course, important critiques of Deleuze and Guattari's thought. For instance, some argue that the drive toward identity instability and re-invention, whether of an individual or a larger assemblage, has no mooring, no direction toward which it should be directed. Best and Kellner (1991), for instance, see this as evidence that the work has 'uncritically accepted the modernist ethos of incessant self-transformation, becoming, and psychic instability ... it is not clear that this position radically breaks from capitalist and consumerist behavior' (p 107). There is not on offer any normative stance, no route to producing new forms of social organization that will be more morally redeemable than current configurations. Because desiring-machines are the focus, and desire 'is revolutionary in its own right' (Deleuze & Guattari, 1983, p 116), it would seem that there is no need for justice-oriented projects that marshal assemblages' energies. Others have likewise considered this question, and I take up one route toward addressing it in the book's final chapter.

[14] There is evidence in Deleuze and Guattari (1987, p 352) that lower-level assemblages that are relatively tightly knit should be understood as *strata*. Strata are the product of distinction-making in assemblages; my interest is less in the production of such distinctions than in the agency associated with creation and action of those assemblages. Consequently, this book will retain the notion of assemblage in its conceptual framework for understanding firms.

[15] And thus not any sort of conjuring of 'attachment theory' in terms of psychological and evolutionary thinking about the person's relations with others.

4

A Communicative Theory
of the Firm

This chapter makes a crucial link between Chapter 2's consideration of the shortcomings of existing theories of the firm and Chapter 3's vision of organizations – and the world – as communicatively buzzing assemblages of objects, actions, signs, and passions. In sketching the contours of a Communicative Theory of the Firm (CTF), my hope is to provide a new option for understanding the firm, an option that will prove analytically novel and empirically fruitful.

In Chapter 2 I described how existing theories frame firms as nexuses of contracts, sites that maximize task efficiency, systems that manage productive resources, decision-making units, or vectors of attention. The blend of CCO theory and new materialism presented in Chapter 3 argued for a new direction, one that portrays firms as *machines*, a term to denote assemblages' action, not a mechanized system. In advancing the ontological claim that communication *is* organization, CCO thinking performs a couple of useful re-orientations. Its attention to the *doing* of organization suggests that communication is the site where the coordination and control associated with order are produced; yet communication likewise is where *dis*order and its corollaries ambiguity, paradox, uncertainty, and confusion emerge. And despite the common association of communication with discourse, neither communication nor organization are ever conducted in the symbolic register alone. Communication and organization are thoroughly sociomaterial, such that agencies, spaces, artifacts, and forces become ontologically inseparable in the eventful practices that (re)constitute organization. This framing summoned an engagement with new materialist theorizing, and Chapter 3 worked through Deleuze and Guattari's thinking to extend CCO thinking. The notions of difference, virtuality, assemblage, and territorializing were the elements drawn out in that chapter, and which will be sources of inspiration for the developments of the present discussion.

As acknowledged in Chapter 3, the terminologies of CCO and Deleuzian new materialism(s) are, to many, unfamiliar and even esoteric. In places, their language can appear intentionally inscrutable. There are good reasons for this, mostly having to do with carving out novel approaches to knowing that contain ontological challenges to existing theorizing – which, therefore, can't be contained in an existing vernacular. If language is performative, efforts to break from conventional modes of thoughts and action necessarily require new language games. Accordingly, my aim in this chapter is to transcend the lexicon and show the value of thinking anew with respect not merely to re-imagining organization, but to the theory of the firm. The sections to follow show how the CTF answers those four theory of the firm issues, starting with why firms exist.

Why do firms exist?

The first issue with which any theory of the firm must grapple is why firms exist in the first place. Existing theories of the firm respond in the register of efficiency: either market *in*efficiencies create opportunities for firms to realize economic rents or creating a firm is a vehicle for control over contracts or resources that creates production and coordination efficiencies when compared to independent suppliers operating in a market. Either way, firms owe their existence to their capacity to operate in a way that minimizes costs relative to other arrangements.

In contrast, a theory of the firm rooted in communication theorizing portrays the matter differently. Rather than understanding markets as objective entities that exist as points of contrast with firms, the stance offered here begins with the logic of capital accumulation characterizing the encompassing assemblage. As noted earlier, capitalism's spirit continually transforms and adapts in relation to the contingencies of space, time, and activity (Boltanski & Chiapello, 2005). The confluence of CCO and new materialism understands these spirits not as overarching ideologies, not as deterministic structures, but as logics of capital accumulation suffusing and linking practices. In other words, capitalism (in its many varieties) names an approach to valuing things, actions, passions, and signs that infuses an assemblage and enables connections across broader assemblages.

The communicative response to the first theory of the firm question is this: *firms exist because capitalism requires them.* Certainly, capitalism – communicative and otherwise – *could* exist were independent contractors to coordinate with other holders of specific assets; this is the background potentiality against which economic theories of the firm are established. And the proliferation of intermediary organizations making a platform enterprise possible, as noted in Chapter 1, suggest that a network of many such contractors could be a viable model. But capitalism in its contemporary guise needs *firms*, and not merely because they provide legal configurations that shield participants from liability. Under communicative capitalism specifically, firms provide (a) a common identity to which attachments can be made, and (b) a site for the enactment of authority that concentrates and amplifies the forces of the assemblage.

Building upon the term introduced in the preceding chapter, a firm is an *authority machine* set in motion by the configuration of the assemblage. To unpack this claim, consider the example of Chinese fast-fashion company Shein. The business model of Shein (originally named ZZKKO, but its online presence appeared as 'She Inside' in 2011; its parent, the privately held Zoetop Business Company, later shortened it to Shein[1]) is to use a near-ubiquitous online presence to sell very inexpensive fashionable clothing and accessories – and to deliver them quickly to any part of the world. Shein's practice relies on several sub-practices. First is the coordination of thousands of suppliers – small, distributed garment manufacturers scattered throughout China, primarily in Guangzhou province. Shein capitalized on opportunity with these manufacturers when Amazon's clothing operation, which also relied on these small garment operations, began to receive criticism for counterfeit and dangerous Chinese products and for providing fake product reviews. The manufacturers objected to Amazon's policies and the fees it charged for warehousing and order fulfilment. As Amazon pulled away, Shein entered by recruiting these operations to its own platform (Matsakis et al, 2021).

Shein's algorithms are deployed to determine what products to manufacture, which triggers orders from a network of suppliers. Importantly, the direct-to-customer model relies on relationships with global shipping and postal systems that ensure quick and inexpensive delivery. In one respect, then, 'Shein' is a point of contact and coordination; as a network's nodal point, it induces and manages connections with suppliers. The relations with suppliers formally outside the firm relies on a vision of Shein as simply the nexus of contracts – a platform. (As noted in Chapter 1, there are also data and review aggregators, along with advertising technology firms, that populate the assemblage and make Shein possible.) This much, at least, is a common practice among apparel manufacturers, and activists level the same accusations of labour exploitation against Shein as they do against other 'fast fashion' firms. But this is only a first pass at how the firm is defined by its authority relations.

A second practice is somewhat more interesting. The process of developing a platform to coordinate suppliers, as mentioned in the preceding paragraph, is an algorithmically driven engagement with reams of data culled from the internet's data exhaust. It is not merely customers' purchases on the Shein site; interaction with the site is gamified to generate far more data than otherwise possible:

Shein grew by bringing traits of China's gamified e-commerce market to the rest of the world. Online shopping in the country has evolved into a form of entertainment, featuring livestreamers, flash sales, and enticing pop-ups that compel consumers to scroll through the newest products ... including a points system that rewards shoppers for making purchases, leaving reviews, and playing minigames. (Matsakis et al, 2021)

Those data are also the result of consumers' engagement with what appears on social media, such as Pinterest boards, Instagram stories, and fashion influencers' TikTok videos. Shein's data operation scours the internet for the objects of desire – desire as indexed by manifestations on those social media – and using those data to order similar items to be quickly produced by the supplier network (often in small batches at first, and quite often violating standards of intellectual property [Nguyen, 2021]). Frequently, those orders are fully algorithmic: it is the algorithm processing data that indicates the need for an order of a new item, along with the necessary pricing on the sales site. After initial coding, humans are not involved in those moves. And the constant addition of new products appearing daily on the site – by one estimate, over 6,000 items daily (Jones, 2021) – lures addicted customers to return over and over (Teeling, 2021).

This second process – deciding what to manufacture – is closely related to a third, Shein's model of branding. Some of the firm's branding efforts are also directed by algorithm, targeting Generation Z consumers and, in particular, women. Among that target market are also plus-size women, represented nearly as frequently as the slender bodies conventionally associated with fashion. On social media, Shein advertising is omnipresent, and it is populated by the requisite celebrity promoters. Yet, as indicated in Chapter 2, the brand is produced just as much by 'prosumers' who produce unboxing and 'haul' videos as by campaigns funded by Shein's coffers. Those fashion bloggers operate on their own, but Shein also cultivates them with an invitation to be a 'Sheingal':

#SHEINgals rule the world, and you can too! We are looking for fierce fashionistas to rock their top SHEIN finds across social media! #SHEINgals can try our new styles in exchange for showing off their favorite looks on Instagram and YouTube.
  We are so excited for your [*sic*] to join the #SHEINgal family!
  xoxo

(https://us.shein.com/Fashion-Blogger-a-475.html)

Those Sheingals sometimes are given the opportunity to move from the online shopping and product recommendation world to an in-person experience: although the company is primarily an online purveyor of direct shipments to customers, its occasional pop-up shops draw fanatical crowds and long queues, and Sheingals get preferred access (Testa, 2022).

Shein's novel business model is one that fits squarely in the communicative capitalism outlined in Chapter 1. As one observer noted, 'Shein operates less like a traditional clothing company and more like a tech startup, with powerful internal management software, and a nimble advertising and social media apparatus layered on top' (Kazis, 2022). Statements like this evoke an important question: what *IS* Shein? Does 'Shein' refer to the brand, the algorithm(s), the legal entity, the handful of employees whose paycheck lists the company's name, or the network of supplier contracting relationships? None or all of these?

This is, obviously, an ontological question: beyond a simple statement that Shein exists to link customer desires for fast fashion with a host of suppliers, is there a single answer to the 'why firms exist' question in this case? The answer, of course, is that conceptualizations of Shein, like any firm, depend on what we want the answer to do for us (and thus back to that pragmatist move from the Introduction). The illustration shows that accumulation and distribution of capital in the assemblage *requires* firms like Shein to perform such linking roles, but *how* they do so – and *whether* the firms monetize elements like data, free labour, and interchangeable supplier relationships – differs markedly across the type of assemblage and the desires animating it.

So, if the statement about the reason for firms' existence holds, how does communicative capitalism *require* Shein? Obviously, it doesn't require this *particular* firm. But the propagation of communicative capitalism necessitates the existence of firms that foment and cater to desire (for fashion's self-displays and bored scrolling-shopping); that cultivate and exploit data; that generate addictive brands; that manage local-global tensions in product access and delivery; and that provide a point of contact for a veritable army of garment-makers, fashion bloggers, and algorithms. As the quote comparing Shein to a tech startup indicates, these elements are observable in many other firms; Shein is somewhat unique in that it conjoins so many features associated with communicative capitalism.

From the perspective of the CTF, 'Shein' refers to the nodal point in the assemblage that organizes disparate participants in practice. It does so by amassing and attaching participants to one another in the service of *authority*. I'll discuss authority in more detail in the next section, but the point here is that authority in the CTF is not about any *person's* influence. It is, instead, a matter of shaping the trajectory of an assemblage's becoming, a force that materializes in the emergence of something akin to a collective identity. A firm harnesses the elements of an assemblage into agentic practices that become coded as coordinated profit-oriented commercial action; in the

Shein case, these participants include platformization of small garment manufacturers, algorithms, data, gendered consumer desire, branding, shipping, cheap materials, low-wage labour, and prosumption. The firm is a site for cultivating attachments, for stitching together relations between these participants in the conduct of action.

The firm is, in short, an *authority machine*, where (as noted in Chapter 3) 'machine' is a reference not to a mechanical device but to a practice that seeks attachments. Terminological caution is warranted here, since machine metaphors have a long history in OS. Largely associated with the era of Fordism and the thinking of Frederick Winslow Taylor, the belief in a set of discrete interlocked elements operating in the service of a single overarching goal has also characterized versions of systems thinking, along with other modes of functionalist thought, over time (Cornelissen & Kafouros, 2008). This is not the machine metaphor Deleuze and Guattari were imagining. Deleuze and Guattari deployed the notion of the machine to conjure up the energy generated by the assemblage in the accomplishment of a particular practice, not the cold rationality and precise synchronization implied in common usage.

The adjective *authority* refers to the territorializing aptitude of the assemblage-machine, its capacity to make particular attachments (im)possible in the shaping of the assemblage's trajectory. Firms are useful because they centralize decidability in a given nodal point in ways that benefit the forces associated with communicative capitalism that flow through the assemblage. In this sense, firms simultaneously organize, and are organized by, the assemblages from which they spring.

The next section works through the functions performed by the machinic capacities for attachment-making, but the primary claim to remember at this point is that the firm itself is an agentic assemblage operating in a more encompassing assemblage; it acquires its agency from the relations and forces it nurtures. The creation of brands, manufacture of desire, algorithmic exploitation of data, and marshalling of small manufacturers and intermediaries are all unimaginable without firms (like Shein) to engage in the practices of assembly and capital attraction.

Coding as a firm part I: how firms operate

The second theory of the firm question concerns organizing practices. When the image of the firm is a nexus of contracts, a site of transactional efficiency, a decisional entity, a bundle of resources, or a mechanism for the focusing of attention, theories of the firm describe how organizing unfolds – and by extension also *pre*scribe the managerial tactics that flow from that vision. In pursuing an alternative stance, the CTF takes what might be seen as a circuitous path. It begins by aligning with last chapter's theorizing on boundaries in dissolving any simple internal/external distinction between firm and environment. In other words, we shouldn't go looking for a bounded *thing* 'inside' of which operations occur.

To suggest that firms are clearly bounded systems with unquestioned insides and outsides invokes the long-assailed container metaphor, an image that oversimplifies organizational existence and ignores boundaries' complexity. Arguing instead that what we take to be *an* organization is always a shifting assemblage of many participants contingently bound together in communicative practice, the CTF re-directs attention to the linked set of practices that invoke, but are not limited to, the entity known as 'the' firm. The previous section made clear that there is no simple answer to the question of precisely what *the* firm is; conceptions depend on what we want the notion to accomplish for us. The firm, like its purpose, is ontologically multiple, suggesting that a depiction of firms' operations must explore the practices of authority machines.

Framing firms as authority machines that organize assemblages means that the first conceptual move must be to clarify what is meant by 'authority'. The next subsection endeavours to do just that.

Authority in the authority machine

Authority is a key notion in social thought generally (Lincoln, 1994; Furedi, 2013) as well as in organization studies' history specifically (Gilman, 1962). Most writers, even those of more recent vintage, diverge very little from Weber's (1978) tripartite division of its bases: rational–legal, traditional, and charismatic (others reframe these as positional, expertise, and personal). The resources of authority, in the common account, become invested in a position that, or a person who, induces in subordinates both voluntary compliance and suspension of judgment; in turn, an individual able to create these effects is said to *have* or *be an* authority (Grimes, 1978). Authority is about possessing (or being seen to possess) the 'right to the last word' (Simon, 1997, p 182) in decision-making practices (Kahn & Kram, 1994; Aghion & Tirole, 1997).

For many in the organization studies field, however, *power* has become the term of choice to address influence in and around organizations, pointing to the domination of ideologies as carried by particular organizational actors (such as managers, boards of directors). Yet few distinguish between the terms power and authority, and frequently use them interchangeably and (seemingly) unreflectively. For those who differentiate, the power–authority distinction hinges on *consensual* acceptance of an influence attempt (Bennis et al, 1958; Huising, 2015), which is usually seen as the result of a mutual commitment to the organization or relationship. There has been little conceptual advance beyond the Follett/Barnard acceptance model (Barnard,

1938; Follett, 1940), in which the axial issue is the relationship between superiors and subordinates in an organizational context that leads those subordinates to accept the boss's orders.

This book isn't going to be able to straighten out that state of affairs. Given the authority-power distinction, however, why do CCO scholars (such as Taylor & Van Every, 2014) opt for the former? Stated simply, they see in authority a connection with creation, production, and accomplishment in a manner akin to writing or inscribing interests onto some collective. For CCO scholars, authority is not merely personal/positional power made acceptable to underlings, but references *decidability in the authoring (writing) of the organization's trajectory*. The negotiation between conflicting interests is key to grasping the problem of purpose in organizing.

Therefore, in keeping with the figure-ground reversal communication theorizing encourages, CCO theorizing urges analysts to switch from thinking of authority as a characteristic of a person/position and to instead imagine it as a *force* manifest in communication. Were we to move in this direction, we'd see the authority underlying decidability not as a person's possession but as an accomplishment situated *in practice* (Dawson & Bencherki, 2022). For instance, Bourgoin et al (2020, p 1138), drawing on Actor-Network Theory, portray authority as 'the process by which an actor contributes to shaping a situation in such a way that it orients collective actions. This shaping is relational and implies the aligning of various actants.'[2] For them, authority emerges from interaction to shape situations, particularly when those situations involve the need for a decision (and, at some level, all action implies decidability). Although it would be possible to accuse this sort of communicative stance of merely pushing the conception of agency from persons to abstract and poorly defined ciphers called 'situations,' Bourgoin et al's commitment to seeing situations as ongoingly constituted outcomes of the weaving of relations offers a novel perspective on authority, one that denies that authority can be a possession of any actor. Instead, they show it to be the *doing* of interactional claims on present and future activity. In this way, Bourgoin et al provide a useful point of departure for a communicative conception of authority.

Returning to the discussion from the previous chapter, the CCO/ Deleuzian new materialist amalgam exposes authority as the *force ordering an assemblage*. Yet identifying 'force' is unsatisfying, since authority often becomes associated with particular actors – individual and collective, but it can also be appended to elements like artifacts (Brummans, 2007) – populating situations. How is it, then, that authority becomes affixed to some participants and not others? And how might that capacity to shape a situation shift across an assemblage over time? Because authority is an accomplishment achieved in practice, the CTF nominates two components to producing it: promises of value and claims to property.

Promises of value

Sennett (1980) noticed that the English root of authority, 'author,' signalled productive potential. He also indicated that the word's Latin root, *auctor*, reveals that 'authority can give guarantees to others about the lasting value of what he [*sic*] does' (pp 18–19). In other words, bestowing decidability upon a given participant, or locating decidability in a given position, depends in part on that participant's pledge to produce a valued outcome for other participants inhabiting the assemblage (though it's rarely stated as an explicit pledge, of course). This could be the case for the guidance of a founder infusing a firm with entrepreneurial energy, an algorithm's ability to quickly process capacious data to make rapid and adaptive choices, the capacity of a well-connected member of a community to exploit her social capital, a platform operator's (such as Shein) assurance to suppliers that financial rewards will come their way if they follow its directives, or a firm with a positive reputation assuming a central role in an inter-organizational partnership as it appeals to a public. The point is that other participants in an assemblage are likely to position decidability (and thus the capacity to shape the decisional situation) as running through the actors who/that can offer prospective value.

Because purpose is multiple, the register of value – what is to be valorized – depends on the game being played. There are cases in which operational efficiency is the aim, others where a particular form of expertise is necessary for problem-solving, some in which aesthetic goods reign supreme, and others where the potential to direct *other* participants' activity is prized. In many firms, the value calculus is delegated to the market, with profit/loss, earnings per share, and assessments of the net present value of future earnings comprising the 'form of life' through which decisions are taken. Although communicative capitalism complicates simple value assessments by reminding us of symbolic and social capital, its proponents generally present those as merely means to a familiar end: the attraction and accumulation of economic/financial capital.

Regardless of the details of that calculus, there would appear to be two primary, and overlapping, routes (there are undoubtedly more) by which participants in an assemblage advance promises of value.

Prophecy

First is *prophecy*, the ability to predict the future. Prophecy includes the force of expertise, since one implicit claim of expertise is that practices will deliver positive results if only decision-making is delegated to those experts (see Treem, 2012; Kuhn & Rennstam, 2016). But prophecy is also about anticipating future events and circumstances that bear on organizational practices, such as in narratives that provide a plot for technological development or adaptation to environmental change (Jacobs et al, 2013). Flyverbom and Garsten (2021) provide useful insight into several approaches to anticipation, including indicative snapshots of performance, prognostic correlations that visualize the need to alter behaviour, and phantasmagoric fictions supplied by third parties to summon new forms of strategic planning from the firm.

Underlying the value of prophecy is an assertion that organizations' primary decisional problem is uncertainty, such that employing devices to manage the tension uncertainty brings is a necessary ground for productive activity. Beckert (2021) is explicit in this regard, arguing that the very logic guiding any firm's activity is the way it manages uncertainty. He suggests that instead of strategic visions and principles, compelling imagined futures are what are actually offered by strategic planning, capital budgeting, and technological projections. Irrespective of the implied motivation for firms' efforts to predict the future (managing uncertainty, securing influence, developing a brand, and so on), the upshot of this thinking is that authority in, and of, the assemblage is a result of drawing together a variety of elements to proffer persuasive and visionary assurances that value will result from situating decidability in one practice site rather than another.

Analysts typically think of both the authors and beneficiaries of the prediction devices mentioned here to be firms' managements, such that anticipating the future has become an expected part of strategizers' roles. Yet the source of prophesying is not affixed to a single organizational actor (moreover, as argued in the last chapter, no agent is ever singular); instead, shaping the trajectory of an assemblage via prognostication can come from any of an array of (non)human participants. What is important is to recognize the relational character of the promise, since it is the *connection* among participants, roles, devices, practices, intuitions, and predictions that acts; in a word, prognostication is thus always a thoroughly *communicative accomplishment*.

Gravity

A second path toward promises of value is *gravity*. Simply put, in an assemblage of participants and practices, the capacity to attract attachments to a particular nodal point – to 'weigh down' a plane in the assemblage, to deploy another metaphor – can be a source of authority. Indeed, as suggested in the preceding chapter, attracting attachments is how any machine, including an authority machine, works.

The notion of gravity expresses magnitude and weight, an attraction based on mass and energy. In OS, gravity assumes several guises. Among those who might see assemblages in network terms, a participant's centrality, along with its capacity to fill structural holes, can be an index of gravity.

This was evident when Scott and Lane (2000) described the place of a firm in its stakeholder network as influenced by its identity and image. Though clearly not assuming the ontological stance undergirding the CTF, Scott and Lane argued that centrality in interorganizational networks allows firms' decision-makers to selectively manage stakeholders and to moderate their influence. Other authors note that political connections, such as those between firms and governments, attract both economic and intellectual capital and, consequently, produce the decisions associated with firm-level innovation (Tsai et al, 2019). A participant's capacity to foster connections, to induce new political attachments for other components of the assemblage, is a potential source of value. And for participants to realize this value, simply occupying a position isn't sufficient: for authority to be operational in shaping an assemblage's trajectory, actors need to display their potential for gravity by proffering narratives of their attachments' potency and significance (Alvesson & Robertson, 2006; Golant & Sillince, 2007). In other words, participants need to be visible in their displays of value to attract authority (Leonardi & Treem, 2020).

A key basis of gravitational pull is the brand. In the OS literature, the link between branding and attraction has often operated through the human resources function, since 'strong' company brands attract more job applicants and induce fiercer employee identification than others, including firms with strong reputations for CSR performance (Luce et al, 2001; Pfister, 2020). When firms develop an identifiable and appealing brand, they engender attachments from other firms, consumers, and employees. And when we switch the focus from links between presumed *entities* to attachments across *practices*, the gravitational force becomes clearer. Critical analyses of the workplace show how the allure of putatively ethical branding practices can, perhaps ironically, be associated with invasive forms of control over work practices and the proliferation of the prosumption practices, accompanied by potential metric manipulation to bolster claims of responsibility (Arvidsson, 2005; Kuhn & Deetz, 2008).

Network and brand-based thinking presents something of a chicken/egg problem, since the genesis of alliances, brands, and collective identity is murky at best (Gulati & Gargiulo, 1999). Yet the more interesting questions are likely to arrive in the form of temporal dynamics: how do prophecy and gravity in the assemblage re-configure relations of decidability over time? Answering questions like this requires a communicative sensibility, one where analysts understand claims to value as practices themselves that incite assemblage participants to position a given participant (or nodal point) as the site through which some set of decisions flow. Consequently, changes in relations of authority can occur when the mode and criteria of value shift over time or when participants conclude that promises have failed to yield the outcomes assured.

Claims to property

A second basis for situating decidability is establishing ownership, as an assertion that it is 'proper' for a given participant to guide the firm's trajectory based on control of property (Bencherki & Bourgoin, 2019). Often, such a claim can depend on one's position in a firm, as when a corporation's majority share owner (or owner of 'better' shares in a dual class share structure) signals a willingness to flex its muscles to deter competition over decisions. But it could also reference a domain beyond the firm, as was the case with the BEIC mentioned in the Introduction, when the British government grew weary of financially backing the firm and exercised its property rights over its future. In such cases, authority is obviously not merely 'in' the possessor of the ownership stake; it also depends on invoking some mode of decision-making as legitimate, determinable assessments of asset possession, and the validity of distinctions in the power accorded to particular types of property. Models of property show up in corporate form and logics of firm practice.

Corporate form

Ownership of property, at least in Western social and legal thinking, provides its possessor with use capacity. Property is usually imagined as an asset, a commodity that its owner can consume, sell, exchange, rent, modify, or even demolish (Pistor, 2019).[3] Even when the conception is broadened to include elements not conventionally understood in objectual terms like ideas, knowledge, trademarks, and processes, property rights secure assets, and therefore appear necessary to claim in the name of the firm. And claims are always relational. Not only do the claims require some interdependence between potentially conflicting parties, but they also imply some relation to social codes such as organizational policies and corporate law, both of which are resources, and also *moral* codes, onto which influential actors have inscribed their interests while preventing others from doing the same. Claims to property are, therefore, always bound up in assemblages of participants and practices.

A key contributor to property claims is the firm's legal structure. Although much of this book has used the generic 'corporation' for the legal status of the firm, there are important differences across forms,[4] and many differences across countries' legal statutes for those forms. There are many options for the form of the firm – Luyckx et al (2022) present cooperatives, state-owned enterprises, democracies, stakeholder firms, social enterprises, and a sharing economy model as alternatives – but by far the most common is the charter given by the nation-state (and, as seen in the Introduction's BEIC illustration, formerly the monarch) to act as a single collective, a corporate entity, in pursuing specific (and limited) aims understood to benefit the larger whole.

Over time, nation-states erased many limits on those objectives, enabling corporations to move from specific to general purposes. As the code in the dominant US location[5] now holds:

> It shall be sufficient to state, either alone or with other businesses or purposes, that the purpose of the corporation is to engage in any lawful act or activity for which corporations may be organized under the General Corporation Law of Delaware, and by such statement all lawful acts and activities shall be within the purposes of the corporation. (Delaware Code, 2019–2020, Title 8, §102)

Incorporating under statutes such as this generally underwrites firms' 'thirdness': their status as a legal party owning assets distinct from their principals and agents, to protect against those actors expropriating corporate assets for personal use (which certainly happens regularly – but runs counter to the spirit of the law). Corporate thirdness also presents several long-acknowledged claims regarding property, including limited liability, magnification of voice, centralization of control, principal-centric capital flows, continuity of operations, and succession in property claims. The central property claim, however, revolves around a seemingly determinate object: corporations can issue ownership shares, or stock,[6] and those who own those objects are encoded as principals. Coding an assemblage participant as a principal provides the capacity to weigh in on decision-making and to receive a portion of firm outcomes (and, unsurprisingly, more shares = more influence). Coding principals as owners also allows them to participate in asset lock-in: possessors of economic capital in the form of shares can sell those shares to others, but the capital originally exchanged for the share cannot be removed from the firm regardless of the shareholder's intent; that capital becomes the property of the corporation (Ciepley, 2013).

Grandori (2022) notes that shareholders should not, strictly speaking, be called *owners*: in Western corporate law, they own not the assets of the firm but, instead, merely own claims on the economic rewards from the firm's activity (Roman law's *fructus*; see this chapter's note 3). Nevertheless, the shareholder-owner equivalence persists, even among scholars of organization. And despite great diversity in the rights associated with shares in contemporary corporate practice (such as dual-class models, along with the recognition that equity investment often has other paths to influence), the advantage of a share-based approach to authority in corporate firms is that it offers what appears to be an unambiguous approach to where decidability resides. Returning to the BEIC example that opened this book, the very notion that corporations can be divided into shares that signal ownership is a historical artifact, one undergirding the claim that the corporation is the property of some participants in the assemblage more than others. Such assertions of property have consequences not merely for internal firm practices but extend well beyond: as Werner (2015) shows in a scathing critique of corporate law, the assertion of corporate ownership has a long history of spreading Whiteness and distributing corporate benefit to a small segment of (White) people. Claims to property are, in short, deeply communicative, accomplished over significant spans of time with the formidable resources of legal-code-shaping assemblages.

Moreover, highlighting the complicated negotiations that mark claims to property, consider the principal-agent model introduced in Chapter 2. The Berle and Means (1932) model implies that agents (managers) are to act at the behest of principals (owners/shareholders), such that agents are to be transparent operators while principals can remain opaque. But principals' opacity can also present an opportunity to those very agents, at least in firms where these two parties are distanced: in the absence of evidence regarding their desires, management can impute or ascribe demands that serve those *managers'* sectional interests. This is another route to claim property: to assert the right to act on behalf of those who are opaque and do not speak on their own, ventriloquizing them in the direction of firm practice in a register preferable to a particular set of participants.

An alternative to the standard corporate form is the private limited company. In the US, this form is the Limited Liability Company, or LLC, but very similar codes exist around the world. This form is relatively young: although progress of LLC law unfolded slowly across the US, it was in force in all of the states only at the beginning of 1997. In that short span of time, the LLC became one of the dominant forms of legal coding because it combines characteristics of the corporation with those of a partnership. The *members* – not shareholders – of an LLC are connected by a transferable 'membership interest,' which provides a share of the firm's profits and voting rights. Moreover, the code provides them limited liability, while also allowing dissolution of the firm at members' will (Ribstein, 2003). Further, LLCs avoid the double taxation that accompanies a corporation (taxing both corporate earnings and shareholders' dividends), providing an attractive option for capital accumulation.

A third – but by no means final – approach to incorporation is the Benefit Corporation (also known as the public benefit corporation and the *société à mission* in France). One of the newest forms available, the 'B Corp™' will be the subject of Chapter 7 but, for now, the important element of this form of legal structuring, is that it enforces a firm-level responsibility to social and environmental causes alongside the drive for profit (Moroz et al, 2018; Segrestin et al, 2021). It is thus a corporation, but one that strives to preclude from its operations and governance an exclusive focus on SVM (shareholder value maximization).

To connect this point to the preceding section on the reason for the firm's existence, assemblages coded via corporate law are *useful* because they can be made to do, and thus want, things that other participants in the encompassing assemblage cannot (are not allowed to). They can engage in contracts, while other nonhuman actors cannot; they can command ordered distributed behaviour, including through platforms, while sole proprietors (human owners) cannot; they can protect assets via legal structures associated with limited liability, while other participants cannot; their products can be imprinted with brand identity while the firm itself can be decoupled from that identity, whereas individual humans cannot accomplish that separation.

Coding an assemblage as a firm also carries with it a model of claims to property via these Westernized corporate legal codes for corporations, LLCs, and B Corps. Returning to the Deleuzian conceptual apparatus, considerations of these types of coding are largely *arborescent* manoeuvres: they aim to produce clear lines of command and control and predictable manifestations of form, preserving the firm's ostensive purpose and the methods to be employed in accomplishing it for those managing occupying managerial positions. As the previous chapter argued, coding can always 'become other': arborescence may encounter the virtuality of the rhizome through the conduct of practice.

Logic(s) of practice

Corporate law is therefore an important participant in the assemblage that supports claims to property. Yet even law does not eliminate ambiguity about authority. When it comes to determining decidability, advancing claims to property is a 'storytelling battle' (Heller & Salzman, 2021, p 14) waged with logics like 'first come, first served,' 'physical control is legal control,' and 'you reap what you sow.' These logics are deployed to assert control over some asset and provide justifications for action, but what is particularly interesting is that each of these is frequently inverted (and often supported by the legal system in that inversion) to support capital accumulation of corporations and others whose interests are inscribed in the cultural/corporate code. An example of the inversion of one of these logics ('you reap what you sow') is in the claiming of internet users' data exhaust, a key to the surveillance capitalism articulated by Zuboff (2019) and mentioned in Chapter 1. These data – including physical locations, browsing activities, cursor locations, exercise habits, keystrokes, comments, ratings, and even sleep patterns – can be tremendously valuable to firms seeking to predict users' behaviour, shape their desires, and feed them content on these platforms. Data are also sold to other firms to develop user profiles for micro-targeted advertisements. This is no revelation to anyone at this point: the canard 'if it's free, you're the product' signals an understanding that users' interaction with these sites is a form of free labour not only appropriated by the firms, but which also may have pernicious effects on the users' experience. The logic, therefore, may well be 'the firm reaps what users sow,' supported by addictive technologies and government regulation. Yet this logic can never be *determinative*: data exhaust is the site of ongoing struggles over meaning, as data activists urge people to withhold data, demand reimbursement, or generate false data to push firms to alter their data mining (Milan, 2017), while governments increasingly move to restrict the data accessible to firms (for example, The EU's General Data Protection Regulation). From one perspective – the one likely adopted by most existing theories of the firm – data activism and government regulation are a threat to the resources the firm can call its own (its property) and which it can exploit to accumulate capital.

The example of data exhaust suggests two routes for advancing claims to property beyond the vocabulary provided by Heller and Salzman. First is that property is not reducible to the artifacts legally owned by the legal fiction called a firm (or by another participant in the assemblage), nor is it merely the VRIN/O resources that can be marshalled in production; property is a *claim* of the rights accorded to possession as those rights unfold over time. Bencherki and Bourgoin (2019) present what might seem like a hair-splitting distinction nicely:

> Property is an empirical matter; whether an organization has these or those members, buildings, brands, partners, missions, markets and so forth is an observable achievement, rather than an assured starting point for inquiry (see, e.g., Bencherki & Snack, 2016). Property concerns both what someone or something has and what he, she or it is, and we must resist defining people, organizations or other things before we study the possessive relations that constitute them. (pp 507–8)

What Bencherki and Bourgoin are arguing, then, is that possessive relations are *claims* to property: that understanding authority as shaping firm purpose (and trajectory) is less about the mere existence of assets and more about efforts to marshal them in one way versus another. Consequently, while there may be grounding in a legal code to assert that shareholding does not actually equal ownership and thus need not equate with influence over corporate decision-making (as mentioned in the preceding subsection), a logic of practice that justifies such a position can make that assertion moot. The interesting question for analysts of the firm then is another communicative one: how are such conflicts worked through in situated practice, and upon what resources do participants draw?

Importantly, my use of claims to property marks a distinction with competing theories of the firm. Conventional conceptions of property suggest that only the individuals who own its shares or with whom the firm (as legal entity) has direct employment contracts – as opposed to subcontracting relationships – can be considered inside its boundaries. Only the materials manufactured or purchased by the firm are to be considered its physical property. The CTF, in this respect, differs: it argues that the array of *practices* relevant to conceptions of the firm's existence, identity, and trajectory can be considered its property – and then only when those practices evince meanings that demonstrate attachment. The CTF interest centres, then, on how *claims to* (as well as denials of) property are negotiated, rather than on any determinative or comprehensive statement on how property 'counts.' What is 'proper' is a complex communicative accomplishment.

Claims to property, in short, participate in the constitution of authority – and, in turn, constitute what a firm *is* via the machinic attachments it makes. As these claims are taken up and embraced (or rejected) in decisional practices, the firm's logic of practice emerges.

The second upshot of the data exhaust example is, to underscore the point made earlier in this subsection, that claims to property are always *relational*. They depend upon legal codes and user expectations, yes, but not merely those. Possession of data – or claims to possess it – relies on the digitally mediated activity of persons, the (sometimes viral) passions that animate activity, a market for user data, the software/hardware infrastructure that delivers content to users and stores activity traces, measurement devices, nation-state regulations, and a faith in the economic value of attention. And if firms are authority machines that seek connections across an assemblage, it is the *attachments* that are both the source of claims to property and the potential for those claims' re-fashioning.

Any compelling claim to property is thus an accomplishment *of an assemblage*, not merely the discursive practice of a solitary actor. The question that should crop up, then, is about the key resource deployed in making claims to property – as well as promises of value. To address that issue, I turn to the notion of the authoritative text.

Authoritative texts

Authority is thus the product of promises of value and claims to property. But this tells us little about the organizing practices that make up a firm – in other words, how does authority exert influence over the becoming of a firm and the shaping of its trajectory?

Addressing these issues requires a concept that captures the mode(s) by which an assemblage (recall that organizations were framed as assemblages-within-assemblages in Chapter 3) acts as a *collective* in ordering, guiding, disciplining, and directing the dispersed practices associated with its existence. The concept would need to recognize that authority is distributed across many agents and emerges in interaction. Such a concept would also be required to provide analytical insight into the relationship between those local practices and the enveloping logic of practice, a narrative representation of the whole, that provides some representation of collective character and the agency behind it. Yet, keeping with the lessons of CCO and new materialisms, the concept should preserve the potentiality of the virtual and its immanent becomings, resisting the siren song of simple depictions of orderly internal integration. The concept must also allow analysts to trace how particular interests gain dominance over others in shaping portrayals of purpose. And it ought to be amenable to explaining how the deployment of a given logic of practice is associated with claims of collective performance.

That's a tall order. Fortunately, over the past two decades, several scholars have developed a concept for just this task: the *authoritative text*. The notion is grounded in the Montréal School's framing of the emergence of organization in the conversation-text dialectic, mentioned only in passing in the preceding chapter. CCO scholars see communicative practice as a coorientation system comprised of a text-conversation dialectic. *Conversations* are the interactions through which participants (not merely persons) generate, exchange, and build upon messages. Those messages are *texts*: the raw material upon which conversations form. Conversations are the 'lively' mode through which communication occurs because they're the site of sense-making, planning, coordination, and control (Ashcraft et al, 2009), but that isn't all there is to communication. Equally important are the texts that inform the conversations, make them possible, and serve as their outcomes are inseparably linked to broader communicative practices. And once we start looking, the presence of texts in communication becomes evident, as do the texts that become depictions of collective purpose and trajectory. Those texts are not exclusively inscriptions on paper (or in electronic form) like mission or values statements; they can also resemble the English constitution, which is an amalgam of unwritten principles, conventional practices, and codified laws more than a single foundational document (Barendt, 1997). Text, in this sense, is not merely a return to the textualism popular in academic circles decades ago but offers the sort of analytical apparatus to enable engagement with the epistemological slipperiness of assemblage.

Consider, for instance, Spee and Jarzabkowski's (2011) study of a British university's year-long development of a strategic plan. Observing a series of meetings, they noted how early wide-ranging conversations drew upon, and developed, several textual resources (including abstract rules for what a strategy should include, senses of the university's identity, and early statements of aims) that became the foci of subsequent conversations. As meetings proliferated and involved more participants, conversations' outcomes were inserted into drafts of the strategy texts, becoming both decontextualized from the moments of their emergence and recontextualized in succeeding conversations. The texts – specifically, the nascent strategic document – became *distanciated*: detached from any conversation's (or participant's) original articulation such that, in time, it gained the status of a *collective* creation. When the text accomplished this detachment, it 'provided the basis for legitimizing courses of action, without a reference to the talk which led to the manifestation of its content' (Spee & Jarzabkowski, 2011, p 1230). When it was drawn upon in other sites and times, it disciplined practices by establishing boundaries for both discussion and participation; in other words, it became authoritative in shaping decisional practices and charting the trajectory of the whole.

Another example is Koschmann's (2012) examination of a civil society collaboration, City Partners, to aid health, education, and economic sustainability in a large US city. Following an influential director's retirement, the remaining members encountered confusion with respect to the aims and scope of the organization. In one planning meeting, the new executive director offhandedly mentioned the role a dashboard plays in an automobile and likened it to City Partners' position with respect to other community organizations. Although the comment didn't seem transformative at the time, the dashboard metaphor was recorded in meeting minutes and recalled favourably in later meetings. It gradually became key to the organization's narrative, and Koschmann concluded that what became an authoritative text provided an identity that clarified the reasons for its existence, aided in the internal coordination of action, and guided its participation in the network of community organizations.

A more recent example is Smith's (2024) study of a loose collective of bicycle motocross enthusiasts in a large US city who design, build, and maintain dirt jump courses on public property without governmental permission. This case is particularly interesting because the collective lacked a coherent identity and site of governance that could exercise centralized control over the organizing practice; individual participants saw themselves as involved in a volunteer collaborative pursuit, but not as members of a formal organization. The collective expected users to contribute regularly to jumps' (re)construction and maintenance, emphasizing an ethos of obligation through repeating stories about conflicts with those who failed to contribute (including one fistfight) and making analogies to paid labour. The multifaceted text emerging from their practice often cropped up in conversation to emphasize a claim to property: those who identified with the collective either disparaged or disciplined those who refused, were ignorant of the expectation, or were too unskilled to work on the jumps. Thus the authoritative text, captured with the pithy phrase 'no dig, no ride,' ordered activity. But because it was open to interpretation and ironically led some members to believe that fully committed participation was required, it simultaneously *dis*ordered the loose collective.

These three illustrations demonstrate the inventiveness of those who have utilized the concept. Although I was the one to coin the term *authoritative text* (see Kuhn, 2008), in no way do I own the concept. That first articulation drew heavily on the pioneering work of James Taylor and colleagues of the Montréal School. And, like all useful concepts, it has been appropriated, extended, and modified in ways that have added more texture and utility than anything I could have written (see, for example, Holm & Fairhurst, 2018; Blaschke et al, 2014; Koschmann & Burk, 2016; Shanahan, 2023; Slager et al, in press).

At this point in its intellectual life, and based on these depictions, it is worth pausing to clarify just what is meant by the notion[7] of the authoritative text. First, in keeping with the CCO-new materialisms thinking from the preceding chapter, the authoritative text is *sociomaterial*. The three illustrations display that authoritative texts are not simply physical or digital documents and artifacts (*concrete* texts with relative stability); they are also, simultaneously, ideas, images, vocabularies, and narratives (*figurative* texts). Those figurative or metaphorical texts are 'abstract representations of practice sites ... inscribed with common or valued elements of the group and discourses of the surrounding environment' (Kuhn, 2008, p 1234).

Second, an authoritative text is a depiction of an organizational whole. A broad assemblage may be replete with forces, textual and otherwise, that influence organizational practice, but the authoritative text is designed to provide insight into an organization's (which of course is also an assemblage itself) mode of becoming via influencing the decision-making practices it claims to be its property. As such, the authoritative text is an organizationally generated narrative depiction of identity, obligation, and trajectory: *what the organization is* (and is not), *where it should be going*, and *how it's going to get there*. (Because these are often offered up by those professing to be 'inside' the organization, it makes sense to truncate these as assertions of the 'we': what *we* are, where *we're* going, and how *we're* going to get there.) The authoritative text encodes, and becomes the justification for, strategic choices about organizational aspirations (Christensen et al, 2013). Yet, as signalled, authoritative texts are agglomerations of those concrete and figurative texts, and thus cannot be reduced to 'official' mission or vision statements endorsed by executives. The authoritative text provides an encompassing logic of practice emergent from the firm's practices that, when invoked in decision-making, disciplines participants, shapes choice-making, and links practices to one another.

A related point here is that such narratives are not merely the site for *describing* that organizational whole; as philosophers argue, they are also crucial to assigning moral responsibility. Peter French (1979, 2017), for instance, asks whether the responsibility for a collective's *mis*deeds at one point in time might carry forward into its future (in other words, *diachronic* responsibility). Such a question is really one of agency: whether any agent – particularly a corporation – can be said to be the same across time and space, such that it can be held accountable for earlier actions associated with 'it.' French's response is to invoke the notion of *narrative coherence*, which suggests that an agent is morally responsible for a past action to the extent that the action coheres with the narrative the agent generates about itself (Matheson, 2014). When it comes to organizations like corporations, such narratives necessarily invoke decision-making:

> The corporate self-narrative is a developmental element of the policy aspects of a corporate internal decision structure. It is the story the corporation continues to tell itself (and others) about itself … for this story to function in the criteria of corporate diachronic responsibility it must be internally coherent and, crucially, it must be consistent with reality. So the 'bullshit' in advertising and rebranding (Frankfurt, 2005) and the delusional elements in corporate literature and communications are necessarily excluded. (French, 2017, p 62)

Though there is disagreement here – about how coherent we should expect narrative coherence to be (Hyvärinen et al, 2010), how narratives secure firms' temporal continuity (Plotnikof & Bencherki, 2023), and whether corporate agency should eclipse individual accountability (Maitland, 2017) – the point is that a narrative about decision-making as a model for grasping the organizational whole is simultaneously a device for ascertaining agency, trajectory, and collective moral responsibility. And decision/action communication is the practice by which that narrative unfolds.

Third, an authoritative text is the site of struggles over meaning. Though they rarely speak in these terms, participants know that depictions of the whole and its aims are political devices that privilege some parties over others. Whether the process is as overt and pronounced as in the Spee and Jarzabkowski case, authoring consequential (a better adjective than 'official') descriptions of the whole often involves participants seeking to inscribe interests on, or into, the authoritative text. Because an authoritative text will shape the organization's future, participants' efforts to shape its narrative contents will be deeply political. And in this sense, authoritative texts can be tools to trace not merely arborescent territorializing moves, but also the potential for rhizomatic deterritorialization.

Further, as mentioned earlier, strategic managers who believe that articulating a purpose for the firm confers control over its identity and trajectory are quite likely to be mistaken. The ontological multiplicity of both firms and purposes, along with the irreducible immanence of the virtual, imply that political manoeuvres to control firms via statements of purpose – which is a key route by which strategic managers employ authoritative texts to performatively squeeze singularity from the multiplicity (Law, 2002) – will be met with dis/organizational consequences that may, ironically, work at cross-purposes with those very moves.

An authoritative text, accordingly, encodes promises of value and claims to property, the two modes of authority discussed earlier. Its contents tender a vocabulary of the valuable, ruling some outcomes in and others out in the 'game' of participant attachment and capital attraction. Promises of value must thus appeal to the logics preferred by the authoritative text. And it also underwrites claims to property, since what is *proper* for the whole and which segments of the assemblage enjoy decisional control are inscribed in its content.[8] I attempt to capture this argument in Figure 4.1, which also includes a preview of the argument to come in its attention to dis/organization.

What authoritative texts accomplish: boundarying, branding, and binding

Just *how* does that narrative of the collective author the firm's present and future action? The authoritative text configures three key practices that 'write' its trajectory: boundarying, branding, and binding.

Boundarying

One of the four theory of the firm questions is about the location of the firm's boundaries; most contemporary thinking on organizations' boundaries sees them as fluid, shifting, permeable, and multiple. The residues of systems theory, as a dominant narrative of the social, are palpable here: to diagnose a system and grasp its systemic interdependencies, one needs to be able to draw its boundaries and explain how those boundaries are traversed. Yet any answer to the location of boundaries is contingent on the issue being considered (Heracleous, 2004; Oinas, 2006): managements of gig economy companies want drivers and taskers to be considered subcontractors rather than employees; the management of Shein wants #SheinGals to be kept at a controllable distance; marketers want to imitate other companies' guerrilla marketing or social media campaigns without paying for the privilege. Scholars of organization(s) know that boundaries are socially constructed, but the Deleuzian approach introduced in the preceding chapter goes further to show how boundarying is about territorialization, the *creation* of a domain of practice and the relations of authority that accompany it.

The key question for understanding firms is not, therefore, how one might draw unambiguous lines of demarcation. It's instead about understanding the resources that enable inclusion/exclusion to happen in and through communicative events (Bencherki & Snack, 2016). The CTF asks how an authoritative text's vision of property and value make particular attachments and relations in the assemblage (im)possible. Its answer is not that there is a single route toward boundary creation, but that claims to property and

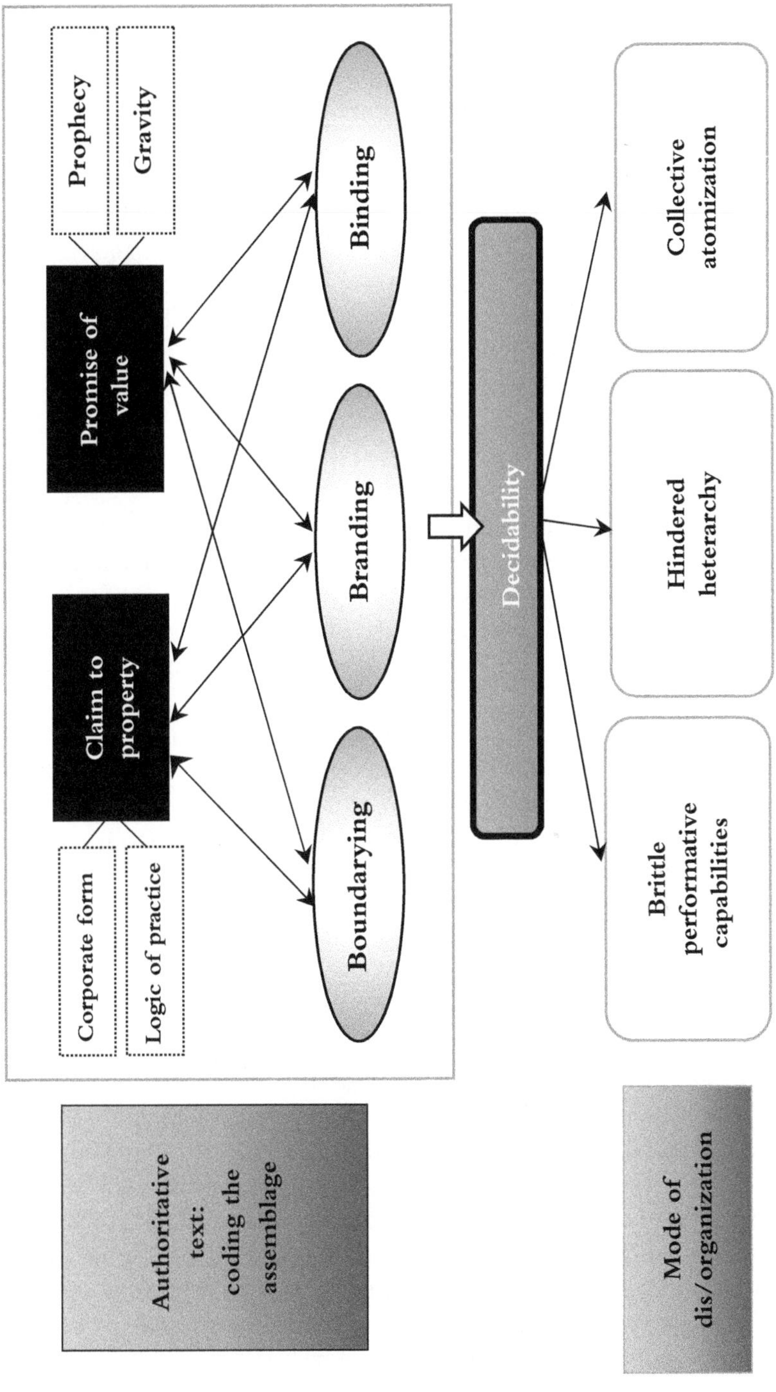

Figure 4.1: Contributors to, and consequences of, authoritative texts in the Communicative Theory of the Firm

promises of value are the resources for negotiation (see Dawson, 2017). Communication defines elements, which enables those dynamics of inclusion and exclusion; as Barad (2007, p 153) explains, the creation of entities and their borders 'is not a static relationality but a doing – the enactment of boundaries – that always entails constitutive exclusions and therefore requisite questions of accountability.'

As should be no surprise, the capacity to determine which practices and participants are inside and which are outside is also, simultaneously, a contribution to *ongoing* claims of property and value. It's about authority. Boundaries are thus not stable markers of organizational insides and outsides but are actions that 'continuously redefin[e] the actual out of a cloud of potentialities' (Spoelstra, 2005, p 114). The practice of boundarying is thus both the beneficiary of authoritative texts and their (co-)author.

Branding

The second practice authored by the authoritative text was discussed in some detail in Chapter 1. Even in entrepreneurs' early planning and fantasizing, conversations implicating 'the' organization make attributions about its identity or character (Cornelissen et al, 2021). Well beyond those early stages, practices implicating the firm simultaneously infuse it with associations that become elements of the assemblage. 'Haul' videos posted by #SheinGals, inspirational social media posts about a consumer product, and an activist's exposé of a firm's labour or environmental abuses, despite being outside the conventional boundaries of the firm, all participate in authoring the brand.

Of course, no single practice, including these illustrations, can claim sole authorship of the brand. Instead, brand*ing* is an ongoing communicative practice and, as such, is the site for the accumulation of a wide array of enactments of a given firm. The authoritative text is the mechanism employed *by* the firm to select and curate an image from the myriad dispersed practices, enabling a firm to claim *these* depictions as the firm's property and *those* as beyond its boundaries, thus marking some elements as 'our brand' and others as irrelevant to our preferred projection (and, thus as claims to property). Branding, thus, is often an attempt to establish a single purpose guiding the firm in the eyes of an audience.

Like so many other planks of the CTF, interestingness here lies in complexity: the competition among participants to articulate precisely what counts as 'the brand' might be cooperative or contentious, especially when those outside conventionally recognized boundaries – like those populating the aforementioned 'brand communities' – assert control over the meanings of a firm's public-facing identity (Iglesias & Bonet, 2012). When branding intersects with the contentiousness and ambiguity of boundaries, who and what represents 'the firm' is not only an empirical question, but a political one. The point is that the relations of value and property encoded into the authoritative text guide and direct branding, such that under communicative capitalism investigations of branding can never be divorced from resources for authority.

Binding

The final practice underwritten by the authoritative text is the cultivation of attachments that join practices and participants to the firm-as-enterprise. Recall, first, Callon's (2017) three modes of creating attachments discussed in Chapter 3: listening, co-production, and addiction. Those function well when thinking about persons' attachments to firms, but how do authoritative texts bind practices in the assemblage to the practices associated with the firm?

Although the typical response to questions like this in OS is positing interest dependence as the mechanism for extra-firm relationships, the CTF argues that the associations of value and property are more robust explanations for binding to the firm. Binding of this sort can occur with respect to the flow of raw materials into the firm, like employees with particular skills and characteristics, which bind, among other things, university educational practices to firms' claims to knowledge (and, consequently, value). It could be the sort of branding-induced connections mentioned in the discussion of gravity, which also underlie Callon's listening and co-production. It could also take the form of firms' affect capture, which aligns with Callon's notion of addiction. It might also look like efforts to affix responsibility for environmental damage to firms' value-generation practices, including environmentalists' drive to bind 'negative externalities' (historically rendered as societal costs) to consumption via product pricing, building a Pigouvian tax into the firm-consumer link.

Summary

These three communicative practices – boundarying, branding, and binding – describe the modes by which firms operate, the second question for a theory of the firm. And though only one is explicitly about the boundaries issue (an additional question theories of the firm must address), the three taken together show how the constitution of the firm revolves around authority and the authoritative text(s) that inform it. Another way of saying this is to note that these three practices emanate from the authoritative text, such that their specifics are the result of the narrative written into that text via its claims to property and promises of value. The authoritative text expresses the territorialized coding of the firm; in combination with the practices of boundarying, branding, and binding, analysts can find in the CTF a device to examine the operation – the organizing – of firms. The two remaining sections of this chapter build upon this to provide routes for engagement with what was introduced earlier as *the* key problem of the firm: purpose and its multiplicity.

Coding as a firm part II: the pursuit of profitability

What has not yet been explicitly addressed is the fourth theory of the firm question: *how do firms generate profitability (or competitive advantage)*? Indeed, many would consider a theory of the firm failing to convincingly address this question incomplete.

The conventional responses to this question are that firms reduce transaction costs, construct contractual relationships with asset suppliers, and configure resources to offer products or services that occupy a market niche. There is nothing particularly wrong with these responses; indeed, their depictions of firms have driven decades of valuable scholarship. But they tend to oversimplify practices that constitute firms – and, as I have argued, ignoring the communicative grounding of firms risks oversimplifying our understanding of the key issue of purpose.

Such oversimplifications tend to arrive in questionable assessments of performance as a metric of competitive advantage, both in terms of narrower conceptions of value than obtain in firm practice and in causal connections between practices and outcomes. Critics make clear that measures of performance or effectiveness are unstable and not linked to any so-called 'objective' features in the world (see, for example, Cameron, 1980, 1984, 1986; Quinn & Rohrbaugh, 1983; March & Sutton, 1997). The complexity of organizing, along with the logical fallacies suffered by individuals and institutions, makes determining which organizational factors lead to which outcomes nearly impossible (Denrell, 2005; Starbuck, 2005). The presence of multiple purposes and forms of capital, for instance, suggest that measuring performance is significantly more complicated than simple assessments of profit and loss can provide (and even those are frequently unreliable sites of creative accounting). Taken together, the logical conclusion is that performance, like the resources for authority, is a *persuasive claim* (one intimately tied to authoritative promises of value) – rather than a quantitatively assessable dependent variable – and should be studied as such.

Consequently, the CTF holds effectiveness/performance as a *point of inquiry*, one to be investigated with attention to claims made in, and about, practice. Unsatisfying though it may be, performance is a question rather than an answer, a source of insight into the continual becoming of a firm rather than an unambiguous outcome assessment. The question is more informative about the assemblage through which the firms operate than it is about a stable and secure advantage over competitors.

But that fourth theory of the firm question is not about effectiveness, exactly; it's about profitability and, usually, competitive advantage. And competitive advantage suggests relative effectiveness, a comparison with firms engaged in similar pursuits. The CTF answer is that, as authority machines, firms that outperform competitors are those that assemble a collection of practices (practices associated with claiming property and promising value) to foster attachments and attract capital from other points in the assemblage. (And recall that, following Bourdieu [1986], capital can be economic, cultural, social, and symbolic.) In line with the preceding paragraphs, it's thus too simple to suggest that firms attracting more economic capital have necessarily won the game, because there are *many* games being played: varied types of capital are valued differently across practice sites by firms that are many 'things' at the same time. Although coding as a corporation signifies to many assemblage participants that shareholder returns are to be granted primacy, a given firm may be playing the game of being a corporation for the accumulation of different forms of capital, like reputation or moral rectitude, and these can be done for their own sake (Weber, 1947; Etzioni, 1988) – as long as they're accompanied by economic sustainability. A firm may thus play the game of being a corporation to simply continue playing the game (see Kuhn, 2008); as the notion of purpose multiplicity emphasizes, the attraction of economic capital need not be the sole pursuit. Those advocating for *de*growth, for instance, argue for a very different logic of practice – one that re-imagines corporate purpose and displays that the conventional version of corporate wanting is not a necessary feature of contemporary capitalism (Chertkovskaya & Paulsson, 2021).

Obviously, *losing* economic capital is clearly not a viable long-term game strategy, but the degree to which growth in profits or shareholder wealth are essential features of the game is a refence to how other practices and practitioners in the assemblage exercise authority – how those participants shape the firm's decidability and trajectory. In other words, coding as a firm does not align with a single or simple embrace of competitive advantage; consequently, investigations should examine the wide variety of approaches to coding that become bound up in authoritative texts.

The analytical task is that competitive advantage is a *theme for inquiry* rather than a variable to be accurately and unambiguously measured. Inquiry about competitive advantage requires analysts to examine the collection of attachments associated with a firm with respect to a given practice to uncover why *this* firm's practices attract capital of a particular sort, or a particular mixture, from attachments at a rate greater than *those* firms. Foci for such an inquiry have been provided (modes of valuation and of claiming property), but any such examination would need to thematize the communicative constitution of flows of purpose and desire across an assemblage to understand the positioning of any given firm. Like all other elements in the CTF, performance is a complex communicative matter.

Coding as a firm part III: what do corporations want?

Bringing together the first section on the reason for the firm's existence with the second section on how firms operate, a logical question arises, the one animating this book as a whole: *what do corporations want?* Though it flirts with the problem of anthropomorphizing a communicative practice, it's a logical question: if firms (of all sorts, not merely corporations) are authority machines, they may not desire anything other than attachments. But if the authority guiding those authority machines is premised on promises of value and claims to property, there may well be some model of desire lurking in their attachment practice.

What does it mean to want?

It is unquestionably the height of naïveté to believe that such seemingly simple questions as *what do corporations want* have straightforward answers. Certainly, thoughtful critics have argued that self-interested individuals and the legal/ economic system that supports them *make* corporations pursue goals that are harmful for the planet and detrimental to the cause of social justice. Following a similar line of argument, those who follow the Chicago school tradition (the one associated with Milton Friedman) suggest that firms are devices that *should* be made to chase profits alone; the substitution of putatively 'social' goals distracts from the economic goods firms can bring. Others argue that corporations can be made to address pressing social and environmental problems if only their leaders and the practices they develop are sufficiently committed. Such stances resonate with debates on corporate personhood, a reference to how legal manoeuvres and public discourse have framed corporations as having rights and interests comparable to natural human beings. Answers like these portray firms as technologies that can be used, and abused, as their human creators desire. Firms then tend to be understood as fully human inventions, servants of human will that can take on the wants of those guiding them.

Do, then, firms *want*? Do they desire profit, do they yearn to generate shareholder value, do they crave a positive image, do they aspire to solve grand social challenges, do they long to enrich their legal owners? The answer pursued here is that starting with an identifiable entity called 'the firm' (or 'the corporation'), even one embedded in a socio-political milieu, limits our understandings of what it means to continually *become* a firm – which is a complex, unstable, and contingent undertaking.

It might be instructive to take a step back and consider a version of this question as encountered in the world of algorithms and machine learning.

When pondering the rather similar issue of 'what algorithms want,' Finn (2017) acknowledged that it is far too simple to conclude that humans writing computer code are algorithms' creators and controllers. Algorithms are the result of histories of mathematical logic, cybernetics, coding (and other symbolic) languages, public and private funding, and computing power. The agency we impute to them at present is a result of what he calls '"culture machines": complex assemblages of abstractions, processes, and people' (p 2). That complexity allows algorithms to embrace wanting of their own, independent of those creators and controllers. But algorithms' wanting is an accomplishment of that machine.

Correspondingly, starting with an identifiable entity called 'the firm' (or 'the corporation'), even one embedded in a socio-political milieu and shaped by human desires, limits our understandings of what it means to continually *become* a firm – which is a complex, unstable, and contingent practice. Like the algorithm, the firm is an ongoing product *of* its assemblage while simultaneously enjoying a semblance of independent agency *as* an assemblage. The complexity, instability, and contingency of wanting – whether by an algorithm or a firm – require a rejection of simple substantive entities and, instead, require an embrace of the assemblage thinking from Chapter 3.

Moving in this direction requires a return to the authoritative text that is in, and of, the assemblage. Firms exist because the logic of communicative capitalism requires nodes in the assemblage that, through their attachment-making, can coordinate and focus the assemblage's forces. Through those nodes flow the practices of production that attract and accumulate capital. Communicative capitalism assumes the existence of firms that monetize communication via affect capture, platformization, and branding.

Assemblages require authority to order and focus production. Firms are useful vehicles for concentrating authority in the assemblage; through claims to property and promises of value, they order production. And when these assemblages are coded as *corporations* (or LLCs or B Corps) – as noted, codings of the firm that imply a good deal of legal and social groundwork (Winkler, 2007, 2018; Baars & Spicer, 2017) – they can also be made to do things that other participants in the assemblage cannot. All capacities are well known (and were presented in the section of claims to property), but what is really interesting about placing firms in and as assemblages connects with where this book began: the problem of purpose.

Authoritative texts and the arts of attachment

If firms are authority machines that continually *become* through boundarying, branding, and binding, how do such attachments generate purpose? The most straightforward, and least interesting, answer has to do with simple accumulations of practices claimed to be the property of the firm: the acquisition or development of new productive capacities and the (non)human participants marking an assemblage, the extension of the brand into new domains, the presence of events that create new dependencies. Each of these could be understood as outgrowths of a firm's purpose, and simultaneously as inputs to future trajectories of purpose. More interesting answers emerge, however, when probing the value of communicative assemblage thinking.

The third premise of CCO introduced in the preceding chapter was about dis/organization, a notion highlighting the complicated relationship between order and disorder in organizing. As noted there, commentators often portray disorder as a temporary (yet potentially dangerous) deviation from a normal, and desirable, orderly state. *New York Times* opinion columnist David Brooks (2012) encapsulated conventional thinking on this theme: 'Most poverty and suffering – whether in a country, a family or a person – flows from disorganization. A stable social order is an artificial accomplishment, the result of an accumulation of habits, hectoring, moral stricture and physical coercion. Once order is dissolved, it takes hard measures to restore it' (Brooks, 2012).

Here, Brooks nods to the (communicative) work required to produce and reproduce organization, noting that it is the result of accumulated power-infused activity patterns. For him, as for most organization theorists, disorder is akin to weeds in a garden (Parker, 2022): a pernicious contamination that must be excised in the quest for the rational productivity of strategically managed action.

Yet disorganization and disorder are not the inverses of organization and order; disorder is not simply mess, chaos, or disarray, nor does it inevitably lead to poverty and suffering. Instead, dis/organization highlights Cooper's (1986) point – also a fundamental tenet of communication – that meaning simply cannot be closed, permanent, stable, or static. Meaning is forever marked by absences and surpluses, and the question of how actors encounter those absences and excesses is an expression of an assemblage's coding. Aligning with Brooks in the preceding paragraph, most organizing examined by OMT scholars understands absence and surplus as summoning systematization, classification, and control – for them, disorder *triggers* ordering. The potential for attending to the indeterminacy of meanings tends to be excluded from both managerial practice and scholarship, but Cooper argues that this is an ontological *choice* that neglects the necessary, and omnipresent, sites of communicative openings encountered in all organizing. As Vásquez and I (2019, p 5) interpret Cooper:

> The sign as meaning is always incomplete. Therefore, it can never be fully grasped: It is continually deferred by the multiple and potential meanings of the signifier. It follows that any attempt to fix meaning in the sign is a reduction, since the multiple other meanings are constantly

haunting it. In other words, disorganization is the excess, the surplus and abundance of meaning, the 'more than'; while organization, the 'less than,' is the attempt at reducing meaning, ordering it, controlling it.

Retaining the potential to imagine both order and disorder simultaneously (dis/organization) is the project of CCO scholarship, manifest in analyses of struggles over meanings across participants and practices, tracing the consequences of tensions and contradictions through assemblage relations, examining devices and instruments as vectors of dis/organization, and the potentials virtuality brings to organizational trajectories (Vásquez et al, 2022).

What dis/organization signals is the inevitable *excess* of communicative (and thus organizing) practice. Meanings can never be closed, permanent, stable, or static, regardless of any actor's efforts at fixity. Yet theories of the firm – indeed, theories of organization more generally – see the challenge of organizing as one of scarcity rather than excess. Although they recognize the potential for surplus capital generated from economic activity, the managerial challenge tends to be framed as claiming capital surpluses as the *property* of either the firm or the participants populating its practices (to repeat a point already made, such claims are processes of authority). Or they see the need to extract maximally efficient production from resources, since reducing costs and increasing output is the name of the game. In direct contrast, Andrew Abbott (2014, p 1) argues that:

[M]any great problems of our era are problems of excess: massive pollution, sprawling suburbs, a glut of information. Yet our social theories and normative arguments focus mostly on scarcity. Budget constraints, tradeoffs, impoverishment: These are concepts of scarcity. Confronted with excess, we nevertheless make scarcity the center of our attention.

Excess is marked by too many of one thing (what he calls *surfeit*) or too much of many things (*welter*). The rise of electronically mediated communication, for instance, creates both a surfeit of data and information, along with a welter of possibilities for (social) connection.

If the ontological multiplicity, part of the problem of purpose to which the CTF responds, can be operationalized by (a) a welter of attachments/ relations marking the assemblage, (b) surges in forms of capital attraction (another welter) by a given assemblage, or (c) an expansion of the boundaries of a given assemblage to incorporate additional practices (surfeit and/or welter), then it becomes clear that the problems are likely to be those of excess. But because theorists tend to translate experiences of excess into problems of scarcity, organization theory has a limited vocabulary for making sense of excess.

Abbott suggested several strategies for encountering and utilizing excess. These include developing bureaucratized procedures and delimited domain responsibilities (both of which delimit attention), pursuing ever-new fads and fashions, serial adaptation to novelty, and deciding to revel in the possibilities excess brings (see also Rehn & O'Doherty, 2007). What these approaches point up is that response(s) to excess are products of the authority marking an assemblage, coded into its authoritative text. A narrative of the 'we' and its guidance for boundarying, branding, and binding underwrite the strategy to any given excess. In short, if dis/organization is an immanent quality of assemblage, relations of authority between the firm and the elements of the assemblage become foci for problem-spotting.

Depicting firms as, and of, assemblages brings excess centre stage. Virtuality, the ever-present overflowing(s) in the relations marking an assemblage, shapes the assemblage's becoming and marks its potential for rhizomatic organizing. And, as noted in the preceding chapter, the character of that becoming is a matter of the problems and solutions the phenomenon/thing is made to face. That 'made to face' is important, for the *making* conjures up authority, and authoritative practices that restrict rhizomatic becoming provide an image of orderliness, of stability and security in the face of influences on firm practice scattered throughout the assemblage. Arborescence.

Take, for instance, the typical approach to stakeholders in OS: the injunction to strategic managers is generally to control the influence of stakeholder groups while simultaneously exploiting the resources such stakeholders supply. A more thorough engagement with virtuality and excess, however, would insist that the practices implicating a firm and stakeholder groups have the potential to become entangled with practices considered the property of either party. And, more to the point, the image of the assemblage suggests that there are lines and forces of entanglement always already existing; the *boundarying* that makes issues and interests the property of *either* firms *or* stakeholders is a communicative accomplishment of authority. Moreover, though the conventional approach to stakeholders may be oriented toward control and orderliness, surplus/excess meaning creates irreducible potential for the shared practice, as well as the organizations themselves, to become-other as a result of participation in it.

Another way of saying this is to note that if firms are ontologically multiple, excess is unavoidable. Most theories of the firm are, essentially, resources for strategic managers to assert control over the assemblage, providing them tools for performing unity from multiplicity (Law, 2002). But if dis/orderly phenomena can be leveraged by other participants in an assemblage – if they can use unintended consequences to reinforce multiplicity *in contrast to* managerial efforts to display unity – the immanence of assemblage might be maintained. Rhizomatic.

Taking stakeholder thinking as an illustration suggests that there are likely to be novel questions about organizing that emerge when one draws upon the CTF to examine the excess that accompanies firms' pursuit of purpose in entangled assemblages. There are several forms of dis/ordering analysts might expect from the three practices produced by authoritative texts (boundarying, binding, and branding), and a key value of the CTF is to aid in surfacing questions about (un)anticipated consequences of the complex practices of authority in the writing of firms' wanting.

Conclusion

This chapter has developed CTF responses to the four theory of the firm questions: why firms exist, how they operate 'internally,' where their boundaries are, and how they achieve profitability/competitive advantage. The typical coding of assemblages as firms, which is strongly shaped by existing theories of the firm, seeks to centralize control through restricting authorship of the authoritative text to strategic managers. Usually, those strategic managers are granted the capacity – the decidability – to define claims to property and promises of value. In constraining authorship, firms tend to also restrict the possibilities for (constrain the multiplicity of) purpose.

But this need not be the case. And, importantly, some unanticipated consequences arise when authority, as a force shaping decidability, is claimed in the service of a singular purpose. The challenge, then, is to find ways to allow purpose – as wanting – to be multiple in a corporate landscape that wants it to be singular.

One of the strengths of a CTF is that the framework it develops can help to make those unanticipated consequences evident. The three chapters to follow illustrate those consequences, and are already included in Figure 4.1: brittle performative capabilities, hindered heterarchy, and collective atomization. I now turn to those examinations.

Notes

[1] The company is reported to be eyeing a US Initial Public Offering, an attempt to make the company public, perhaps in the near future (at least at the time of this writing). Doing so would allow more transparency in the data and more confidence in the figures presented here.

[2] *Actant* refers to any participant who/that contributes to the development of a narrative, a move that meshes well with the stance on authoritative texts to be developed in this section.

[3] Such claims inevitably are based on the conceptions of property flowing through the encompassing assemblage; in most Westernized settings, the deeply entrenched influence of Roman law is palpable, where ownership over an asset, including a firm, provides the right to use it (*usus*), the right to enjoy its yields (*fructus*), and the right to destroy or harm it (*abusus*).

[4] See the Wikipedia page listing the many types of legal entities across the world for a more comprehensive view of the alternatives: https://en.wikipedia.org/wiki/List_of_legal_entity_types_by_country.

[5] The state of Delaware has, since 1899, attracted the lion's share of US corporations because it charges companies incorporated there no income tax. Estimates of its reach include half of the companies listed on the New York Stock Exchange, and two-thirds of the *Fortune* 500.

[6] There are corporations without the capacity to issue stock, known simply as non-stock corporations. More common as a form of incorporation of this sort is the LLC.

[7] The authoritative text is a *construct*: It is an analytical device useful in grasping organizational constitution and contestation. Constructs are tools, not truths (Kuhn, 2017b).

[8] Incidentally, these points suggest both a methodological logic for identifying the authoritative text (look for how claims of property and promises of value travel through decision-making) and a recognition of the recursion between participants' performances of authority and the writing of the collective narrative.

5

Boundarying: Inclusion and Exclusion in Dynamic Capability (Re)Development

Across the organization studies field, very few disagree with the assertion that firms, if they are to survive, must organize around sets of unique activities that allow them to adapt to external change. The managerial task is taken to be cultivating 'differentiated set[s] of skills, complementary assets, and organizational routines which together allow a firm to coordinate a particular set of activities in a way that provides the basis for competitive advantage in a particular market' (Dosi & Teece, 1998, p 284). The competency-based approach to the firm thinks of these characteristics as a firm's *dynamic capability*, its knack for adjusting its internal operations to the exigencies of its environment (Teece et al, 1997). Sustained competitive advantage is believed to be the result of exploiting resources that are Valuable, Rare, Inimitable, and Nonsubstitutable (VRIN; Barney and colleagues later substituted resource-exploiting Organizational capabilities for the N, producing the acronym VRIO) – that is, when they enable adaptation to environmental contingencies, when they are possessed by only a small number of firms, when they are costly for others to mimic, when alternative resources are understood to be inferior, and when an organization enjoys unique operational advantages (Barney, 1996; Sirmon, Hitt, & Ireland, 2007).

The resources desirable under communicative capitalism might not fit this formulation well. As I pointed out in Chapter 1, communicative capitalism urges firms to provide consumers with the emotional and aesthetic experiences they (have been conditioned to) desire. As authority machines, firms desire attachments with elements of the surrounding assemblage; when firms seek to engender consumers' emotional and aesthetic experiences, the connections that result are affectual relations. Reproducing (and perhaps altering or deepening) affectual responses over time is clearly a significant concern when, in a service encounter, the customer can simply choose a competitor for the next purchase. The authority machine desires desires, but also seeks recurrent desire.

Grasping how firms organize to foster, reiterate, and capitalize on customers' emotional responses requires a conceptual tool capable of encoding the claims about value production that become built into the service encounter. It is in the communicative performance of the service encounter that customer affect is generated and captured, but the authority that guides and directs those service encounters is distanced in space and time (usually situated in the strategic management function). The authoritative text is the conceptual device necessary to grasp both the influence of strategizers and the local re-imaginings of the service encounter, as this chapter will show.

Regardless of the contents of any given authoritative text, performances designed to elicit and capture customer affect are ambiguous and tenuous. As such, they threaten the stability of competency views' VRIO formulation. Experiential performances are *ambiguous* because they typically occur in ephemeral, rarely directly observable, potentially complex, imperfectly measurable, and poorly controllable episodes of communication. They not only depend on the unpredictable interactive moves and interpretations of customers (Llewellen & Hindmarsh, 2013), but they require employees to anticipate customer expectations and desires, routinely produce skilled performances, make sense of customers' responses, and respond in the moment. Assessing service performances is, as one could imagine, awfully tough (Vargo et al, 2008). Additionally, performative competencies are *tenuous* because they are not guaranteed by an external or structural force (such as regulations, spatial or technological advantages, or contractual agreements). They depend upon factors in the interactive context, and appear rather imitable through training, acquisition, or branding. Moreover, because performative competencies hinge on individual skill, making them 'scale up' to characterize an entire firm across space and time can be an enormous task.

Yet the drive for competitive advantage via dynamic capabilities is portrayed as an *existential* concern in competence approaches to the firm (Mazzarol & Reboud, 2020; Orishede, 2021). In terms of managing customer service performances, competence approaches argue that management's task is one of aligning resources that guide and direct individuals' efforts through relatively stable rules, task sequencing, routines, and decision making. (Re)producing the firm's dynamic capabilities thus requires *authority* which, in the competence frame, is situated directly in strategic managers. Yet when the competencies to be managed are ambiguous and tenuous – when they are, in other words, *communicative performances* – it is not at all clear how managers are to configure organizational practice to generate the competencies that produce the sort of outcomes they desire. Even less well understood are the unintended consequences of efforts to manage these ambiguous and tenuous competencies. This is where the CTF becomes useful.

Boundarying

Although most competence-inspired thinking on the management of capabilities references rules, routines, and decision-making, an oft-overlooked (and ontologically prior) practice of authority is boundarying. In a sense well-known to generations of systems theorizing, boundarying is an essential practice, because the very notion of assemblage suggests a multitude of participants whose complexity must be reduced for action (along with academics' analysis of that action) to proceed. If the notion of boundarying were reduced to the system theorist's simple act of system demarcation, it wouldn't provide much novel insight, nor would it be particularly interesting. Chapter 4's brief discussion of this concept noted that boundarying is not, however, merely about locating the lines that mark insides and outsides.

The communicative vision of new materialism presented in Chapter 3 elicits something more interesting. It's a vision aligned with Barad's (2007) notion of agential cuts, where organizing practices generate conceptions of the real that become eligible for inclusion and exclusion in practice. It is only *after* the production of elements *as* elements – as epistemologically distinct components of an assemblage – that inclusion/exclusion can proceed. Boundarying thus refers to *both* the *real*-ization of participants (the agential cuts making them manifest as real, distinct elements) and the moves that determine their degree of participation in organizing practice.

And, though it's perhaps obvious by now, boundarying is the product of the authoritative text that is medium and outcome of it. In the context of a firm, boundarying hinges on claims to property and promises of value: what is ours and what is not, what is 'proper' and what is not, what will bring benefit and what will not. These are tenets 'written' into an authoritative text. Though competence theories of the firm see authority as affixed to persons and positions in ways that appear stable, the CTF holds that authority requires ongoing communicative work for its (re)creation – a view that fits well with the ambiguous and tenuous character of distinctive competencies noted earlier.

The notion of the authoritative text is particularly useful here for its capacity to direct attention to both efforts to 'author' it – to write interests regarding property and value into its content – and to the consequences emanating from its incorporation into practice. The remainder of this chapter explores the utility of understanding a firm's approach to cultivating a dynamic capability as grounded in boundarying practices underwritten by an authoritative text. It uses such an understanding to display the limits of a competence-based approach and to display, in contrast, the value of the CTF.

(Re)claiming competencies at Metro Airways

To examine the boundarying of performative capabilities, one would want to span a firm's sites and functions over time by investigating both practice and reflections upon that practice. I was fortunate to have access to such a site. For over 2 years, I conducted a multi-pronged study of Metropolitan Airways ('Metro'[1]), a rapidly growing US airline. Founded less than a decade before this study began, Metro was immediately heralded as a unique entrant in the field; it modelled itself after the highly successful low-cost US carrier Southwest Airlines but, unlike other Southwest imitators around the globe, Metro provided services and amenities unknown on many low-cost airlines, such as reserved ticketing, all-leather seats, free high-quality snacks and soft drinks, and TVs in each seat back that included free satellite-based programming. Commentators noted several other advantages over more established carriers, including newer airplanes, a large reserve of cash, a complete lack of unionization, stylish branding, and friendly employees. During the time frame of this study, the company was adding a large number of routes and employees (a 20 per cent increase in employees over 2 years) and became one of the top ten carriers in the US for revenue and passengers.

A first visit to the headquarters (by former PhD advisee Renee Heath and myself) included a conversation with Metro's chief pilot and his team about an effort to enhance 'the Metro Experience' across the airline. I immediately asked what they meant by 'the Metro Experience' and, though the members of the team agreed that it was about the crewmembers' (the term used in place of 'employees' in Metro) actions that produced the superior customer[2] experiences that made Metro distinct from other airlines, the members voiced conflicting interpretations. Despite their multiple views, all acknowledged that it, whatever 'it' was, was strategically crucial. I was intrigued. Because of the notion's simultaneous multiplicity and organizational centrality, I decided to follow activities associated with it.

Notice here the boundarying already taking place. Not only is 'Metro' presented as an unproblematic agent, but 'the Metro Experience' was nominated as a key component of 'its' identity and competitive advantage. Even in that first conversation, the notion that the Metro Experience was a performance *by the crewmember* that generated an affective response in customers – and one that was strategically essential to the company's success – was evident.

Following that first meeting, I was invited to several venues to observe, and participate in, the development of the Metro Experience. Access to venues of this sort is relatively rare among studies of corporate strategizing. First were 'Customer Focus Conferences' (CFCs), quarterly gatherings of approximately 25 executive-and director-level crewmembers hosted by the President and CEO. These day-long meetings were designed to assess performance on, and to establish strategies for, a superior customer experience. CFCs were preceded by a working dinner the night before (a setting that promoted valuable informal conversations) and were held at a different US location each quarter. Second was 17 focus groups (ranging in size from six to 14 crewmembers), each consisting of crewmembers in similar roles (such as groups of pilots, flight attendants, ticket counter employees, airport supervision, baggage service, and reservations agents). These roughly 1-hour-long focus groups were conducted in the company's meeting rooms in Metro's primary airport, as well as in its local offices in a city in the Western US Third. I shadowed 13 Metro supervisors at that primary airport during their routine work for an average of 4 hours each, and followed each shadowing session with an hour-long interview in which I asked about events occurring during my observation along with more general questions about their work (see Vásquez et al, 2012). Fourth, I volunteered for a team crafting a survey for customers regarding every step of Metro's customer experience 'journey.' This team met via video conference call every 2 weeks for 3 months. Fifth, I had access to a large set of internal documents (such as reports on customer service from external vendors, internal emails, financial reports, yearly strategy documents, and training materials), along with a trove of depictions of the firm appearing in the popular press (newspapers, magazines, and books). These documents were sometimes the foci of meaning-making, and other times provided valuable supplements to frame the observations of practice, forming an important background of understanding of the firm and its strategic direction.

Authoring the authoritative text

The story of 'the Metro Experience' began in the firm's earliest days, when its founders gathered in a rented office in Metro City and concluded that the airline would compete not merely on price, but also on customer service. (Purpose was at the core of its earliest organizing.) The initiator of that team was James, the CEO, who years before had established a small regional airline that was purchased by a major US carrier. James went to work for the acquirer but was, not much later, fired for what he claimed was too aggressive questioning of his new employer's practices. The decision that Metro would compete on both price and service was in no small part a result of James's experience with the acquirer, suggesting a form of cross-assemblage influence from its earliest days.

While waiting out a 5-year noncompete clause, James gathered a group of airline industry insiders he had met over the years, including Jim, an executive at another major airline who would become Metro's president. Using the cash remaining from the sale of his airline and that raised from several investors, he founded Metro. In this narrative, James was central: his history positioned him as one who was a successful (and reasonably wealthy) entrepreneur, experienced in the industry, and able to attract both knowledgeable executives and ample funds. Taken together, these factors meant that employees were likely to consider James a valid representative of Metro's identity (a claim to property).

In this section, I first describe the contents that Metro members 'wrote' into the authoritative text, paying particular attention to the narrative that emerged regarding Metro's central features, competencies, and distinctiveness ('what we are' and 'what we are not'); the trajectory Metro saw itself following ('where we're going'), and its path to that end ('how we'll get there'). This section shows how the narrative of the 'we' encoded conceptions of value and property that became Metro's boundarying practice. In illustrating that narrative, I draw attention to points of contestation to show how the authoritative text is a site for the struggle over meanings, key to the notion of authority introduced in the preceding chapter. Following the presentation of the authoritative text, I discuss how the text was 'read' into Metro's managerial practices, drawing out an important dis/organizational consequence of this configuration.

Metro values 'soft' skills

The first plank of Metro's authoritative text, mentioned briefly earlier, was a key form of boundarying: defining the service encounter, and the production of a particular customer experience within it, as the central focus of the firm's routine practice. Accompanying this agential cut was a second: conceiving of crewmembers as the vehicles for eliciting that experiential response, which required so-called 'soft skills.'

Given its founders' desire to create a durable distinctive competency in relation to a well-established field, Metro's members portrayed the company as excelling in producing high-quality customer service. Knowledge of the competitive landscape is important, since Metro was a new entrant in a field of more established carriers with significantly more extensive flight offerings. And among low-cost carriers, one of Metro's primary rivals had recently purchased a sizable sum of fuel futures at a low price just before oil prices spiked, giving that airline a substantial cost advantage for the near term.

The organizational inculcation of a belief in the value of high-quality customer service began with a video shown to all new crewmembers as the first element of orientation:

> We'd like to be remembered as a company that transformed an industry. An industry that didn't care about its customers that much – that was more concerned about rules and regulations. And Metro has really changed the way that people have looked at air travel. (James, CEO)

Portraying Metro as the 'company that transformed an industry' through high-quality customer service articulated a promise of value. Because it is framed as a *choice* the company made, it also positions the senior managers (particularly James and Jim) as representatives of that vision. The function of customer service at Metro is well-defined: it not only produces differentiation, but generates repeat business and employee loyalty – and, one would surmise, survival. In other words, the high-touch customer service approach was designed to transcend the commodity character of air travel; it sought to enact this transcendence by attaching customers to the firm via an addiction to 'the Metro Experience' generated in the service encounter.

Further evidence of the value placed on customer service can be seen from my observations at the first CFC. Following introductory remarks by Jim, the president, Curt (Director of 'Customer Care') opened with a presentation providing data on 'customer compliments and complaints' from the preceding quarter, compiled and analysed by his team. Curt's depictions of customer service performance became the standard first presentation at each CFC, and always provided substantial fodder for discussion. In each, Curt also included data gathered by a third-party firm on general perceptions of Metro's service quality, which compared the company both against other airlines (Metro was always first or second on this measure), as well as against 'customer service leaders' from other industries, such as the hospitality and resort industries.

In this first presentation, Curt had separated the compliments into 'hard skills' (for example, features of the airplane, satellite TV service, ticket prices, or airport amenities) and 'soft skills' (those associated with employees' performances). Fieldnotes depict the discussion that ensued:

FIELDNOTES

Curt notes that most compliments were about 'soft skills' (87% to 13% soft to hard), while most complaints were about technical elements. Jim asks to quantify the comments/importance about TV service – and it's one of the most important negative responses. Jim suggests that the TV service 'is an important part of the Metro brand – [customers] don't fly only because of our people. What would happen to the data if we strip TV away?' Nathan (VP of Airport Services) then suggests that the Metro Experience is more about people – and that means it's about how employees on the flight, like flight attendants, handle technical elements like inoperative TV systems. The question, he argues, is how to handle 'hard' (material) problems – they always intersect with people, and that makes soft skills more important. He argues that 'the Metro Experience is all about people plus product plus things you can't teach that, together, produce an exceptional experience for customers.'

In this exchange, it becomes clear that customer service (delivered by employees and not TVs), while not only the source of customer praise, was prized by managers above the capabilities of 'material' contributors to experiences. Jim agreed, mentioning 'a recent University study' that showed 'the human side of the airline business is worth five times the product side.'[3] Here's a clear case of boundarying, in that it might have been possible for participants to frame the Metro Experience as the practice and product of an amalgam of human and nonhuman elements in customers' encounter with the company, but managers enacted a separation between 'hard' (material) and 'soft' (human) elements and chose to focus on the latter as their source of a distinctive competence. The promise of value creation, as a central element of authority, thus was connected to individual employees' performances; those who could provide evidence that their efforts produced reliably better performances could claim authority.

A focus on 'soft' skills entails that the delivery of high-quality customer service is likely to be ambiguous, since 'customer experience' can be rather opaque to those charged with providing it. This ambiguity suggested the instability of Metro's dynamic capability:

Crewmember 1:   I think the customer will let you know if you've delivered the Metro Experience or not.

TK: Let's say I'm a customer. What would I do to let you know?

Crewmember 2:   If you're trying to find out what a customer's going to do when they got the Metro Experience, my experience is that most customers are not going to say anything. Most people are not going to take the time and energy to go out of their way to come to somebody at Metro and say you guys did a good job. You know, they may say something to the flight attendant as they're getting off the plane or something, but they're not going to – most people aren't going to sit there and write a letter to the company, and I know I wouldn't. But what they will do is they'll go buy another ticket on Metro. And that's how I think, we may not get the immediate feedback, but I think the real bottom line is that if we deliver the Metro Experience, these people will go out and buy another ticket. And they'll buy them on Metro and they won't buy them on their old airline. (Focus Group #6)

Perhaps ironically, the criterion of repeat purchases was never tracked by Metro management (and those I asked had no knowledge of tracking it), limiting evidence of repeat purchases to the fill rate: the percentage of seats purchased on any given flight. Yet the reasoning enabled by the ambiguity of 'the Metro Experience' and a faith in members' ability to deliver it sustains the centrality of customer service in the authoritative text, because both success and failure could be attributed to employee performances, coupled to the unpredictability of customer response.

Additional evidence that authority at Metro operated with the aim of managing the provision of high-quality customer service was the development of a *customer journey map* (see Rosenbaum et al, 2017), a visual depiction of all the 'touchpoints' customers have with Metro employees. Created by a group of PhD students in logistics from a large US university in conjunction with one of Metro's vice presidents, the map provided an overview of Metro's customer-facing sub-processes, including advertising, reserving and booking tickets, contacting a customer service agent, checking in at the airport, waiting at the gate, flying to the destination, reclaiming baggage, and exiting the second airport. In a small internal videoconference, Tom, the VP of marketing, described the project:

FIELDNOTES

What we're in the process of doing is mapping out everything that falls onto that big picture. Breaking it down, ok, who takes care of that slice of the picture, where does the picture come together at one point and go apart … we're getting involved in pinpointing under each of those heads who does what. By identifying [customer concerns], we go back to the map and identify areas that we can put measurements in place where we can do kind of a proactive real time measurement to see what our own performance is.

The customer journey map was an artifact that represented the components of Metro's dynamic capability, inviting attributions of responsibility and understandings of relations between human and nonhuman participants. It debuted at the second CFC in the form of a large poster (approximately 1 metre high by 2 metres wide) taped to the wall of the conference room. Attendees were encouraged to inspect the map for touchpoints missing from the diagram and, perhaps more importantly, to identify both 'decision points' and 'trouble points' in a generic customer's Metro Experience. The artifact therefore invited managers to claim *property* in terms of both a function and connections between functions; such claims required both an assertion of representing a group (another claim to property) and a promise that value could be created by intervening at those points. In the notes circulated by email to team members following this CFC, one of the 'Key Takeaways' was that examining Curt's employee performance data and connecting it to the customer journey map 'must become a part of our culture. We should be mining our Customer and Crewmember data regularly.' Notably, there was no debate about the map's utility or the veracity of its depiction.

The customer journey map thus made materially present Metro's practices of authority: attendees at the CFCs used the map to provide a vocabulary for identifying problems in customer service and, in turn, to determine *managerial* responsibility for each step of customer contact, including which higher-level managers were responsible for smoothing connections between functions. Consider the following excerpt:

> '[The question is] who's the decision maker, how do we facilitate a healthy discussion when we (Metro senior executives) have such opposing philosophical views. It's different with [the Metro Experience] because people are so passionate and emotional about it. So I think it's tricky, but it's gotta start from the top and they'll have to do some talking. You can see it on the front lines. I fly out on Metro at night and I can see when things are inconsistent on the front line.' (Senior manager, on a customer survey team conference call)

This quote evinces important elements of the communicative constitution of the Metro Experience as authoritative text. It notes key 'philosophical' differences between Metro senior executives who participated in those CFCs, but it also reinforces boundarying in retaining decisional power for that senior management group ('it's gotta start from the top' and 'they'll have to do some talking') and the lack of performance 'on the front lines.' This excerpt also shows how decidability about the firm's trajectory, in terms of boundarying the Metro Experience, was a matter of contestation as different parties sought to inscribe their interests onto the map and, in turn, into Metro's authoritative text.

The customer journey map highlighted interdependencies between heads of functional areas, making lines of reporting evident; what became emphasized, however, was not the relations, the complexities of coordination, or the customer experience, but the *responsibilities of managers* one or more levels *above* the functions listed on the map. The map enabled the claiming of property, an assertion of decidability by higher levels of the managerial hierarchy when it came to specific customer-facing job functions. This enactment of authority, in other words, demonstrated Metro's boundarying of the service encounter as a property of crewmembers' performances and, in turn, as *proper* for strategic managers to guide. At the same time, the components of the assemblage considered material, those 'hard skills,' were *excluded*, rendered outside the customer service performance.

Metro fears dissipating distinctiveness

Palpable very early in my engagement was anxiety about, and allocation of blame for, a perceived slide in customer service performance from members. Although an outside market research firm contracted by Metro, along with an independent industry analysis, suggested that the company was regularly and continuously either first or second in industry-wide ratings of customer satisfaction, members at all organizational levels recurrently voiced a belief that customer service performance was suffering. This fear of decline was a subtext for a good deal of consternation and attempted reclamation.

Employees throughout the firm routinely located the source of what they perceived to be a decline in customer service (or a fear of an impending decline) as residing in newer employees, those hired during Metro's significant growth. This was often accompanied by a sense of nostalgia for Metro's early days, when employees were reputed to evince a passion for service alongside a selfless commitment to the company's success. For instance:

> 'Back when Metro was started everyone felt this entrepreneurial culture – that we're different, and we have to work extra hard to make this work. And now employees don't feel like they have to work extra hard to make this thing work. Those earlier people were especially motivated; these newer people are not especially motivated. Those older people could deliver the Metro Experience; those newer people, they could care less.' (Focus Group #3)

> 'If you ask any of those [older] employees, they would say the same: "I give the best experience, and I know what I'm doing." I think the difference is that they have seen it from the beginning and seen exactly what this company was when it started and where it is now. So, they have invested. And the newer employees, they're maybe not as invested.' (Focus Group #3)

Often, this anxiety was coupled with a concern about the development of an impersonal bureaucracy to accommodate Metro's larger size, which led to a reduced sense of community and loss of the 'entrepreneurial culture' mentioned in the first excerpt. Respondents routinely cast aspersions on newcomers while valorizing older employees, portraying the performance of the Metro Experience as the result of performance expertise possessed only by longer-tenured employees – those who truly cared about the company.

Usually, the problem was attributed to poor hiring and training practices, often described as inevitable given the increased need for more and more bodies to support Metro's rapid growth. The following excerpts from focus groups suggest that the 2 days of classroom training received by front-line workers (prior to starting regular shifts) was insufficient for the challenges of customer service work these new employees would encounter in airports:

> 'While American and Delta are losing 15, 20 aircraft, we're gaining four. So the mentality is hire quick, quick. What do we need? We need 100 [employees] here; we need 100 there. And I think the training process is they're trying to get them through the process so quick and no on-the-job training to get here [the airport]. Trainers are teaching the Metro values in the classroom, but when [new crewmembers] get here [at the airport] it's thrown out and they lose the whole thing.' (Focus Group #6)

Others, however, held that the problem was not too little classroom training time, but too *much* in comparison to on-the-job experience:

> 'They should be at the airport more instead of being in the classroom. … There is no interaction with a customer in the classroom. They get here and get nervous and they don't know how to react to certain situations. If they were at the airport a little bit longer, we would see how they work, so when they get here, we wouldn't have to watch them. In training, we know what kind of attitude they're gonna have, instead of waiting until they get to the airport and having to deal with it. That's what's been happening lately. They seem nice in class, but once they get to the airport, it's like Dr. Jekyll and Mr. Hyde. It's difficult trying to work with these people.' (Supervisor Interview #9)

Such human resource questions are outgrowths of the underlying claim that the older employees embodied the values of the firm, and the newer people simply did not. In other words, employees delineated the sacred and the profane (Douglas, 1966), associating the latter with the company's perceived slide into mediocrity. Scapegoating, the affixing of blame to particular bodies inside a system and expelling, eliminating, or cleansing the system of the offender (Gabriel, 1998), can be a powerful catharsis that ignores the underlying causes of organizational problems.

Evident here is thus a further sense of boundarying as a form of agential cut. To suggest that the cause of diminished competencies was incompetent or indifferent newcomers cemented the notion that performances were *individual* skills. Noting that inadequate training could be at fault for poor performances shifted a portion of responsibility back to Metro management, not-so-subtly challenging the relations of authority marking the firm (yet retaining the image of the newcomers as profane). As one ground operations crewmember stated during a focus group:

'[Resuscitating the Metro Experience] is always management's responsibility because I'm sure that I'm not the only person who knows these things. I'm sure Mr. James [CEO] knows it. I'm confident that Mr. Jim [President] knows it. And I'm confident that Mr. Nathan [VP of Airport Services] knows it. ... And it is their responsibility because first of all, you have to remember they're the ones who brought it to us. They're the ones who gave birth to it. They're the ones who created it. So you can't just drop it all of a sudden. And that's what Metro is founded on. The values, not the book with regulations and guidelines and policies and procedures. Like they said in orientation, it's the values. The values, that's the magic. And they could bring it back.' (Focus Group #2)

Arguments such as this reinforce the assertion, implied in the authoritative text, that top management decides how to manifest the Metro Experience, but it also inserts the firm's original organizing values as active participants in the competency reclamation project. It is a clear ascription of property to top managers ('they're the ones who brought it to us') alongside a promise of value ('that's the magic'), which together form an assertion of responsibility affixed to those individual executives ('they could bring it back').

The informal division of employees into the sacred and profane, the clean and the dirty, implied a hostile resignation to the company's enactment of authority, and a further sort of boundarying. It was not merely the case that respondents feared Metro's loss of camaraderie and distinctiveness as a host of new employees entered the fold; they additionally often waxed nostalgic for the early days of the airline when people purportedly worked together without regard for titles or functions, sacrificed for the good of the whole, and performed the service ethic that became known as 'the Metro Experience.' It was additionally the case that those registering such concerns resented their interdependence with employees they portrayed as unwilling to deliver high-quality customer service, holding that the distribution of capital to these workers (in the form of jobs and profit sharing) was a frustrating injustice.

Metro cares for its employees

The third component of the authoritative text was Metro's conception of itself as *caring for its employees*. 'Caring' was one of five values selected by founders at Metro's birth and inscribed throughout the firm, on concrete texts such as posters, business cards, annual reports, and the aforementioned orientation video. Many firms articulate sets of values that stand apart from practice, but caring was a term frequently drawn upon when members explained that the Metro Experience extended to employees as well as customers:

> 'There's people here that I consider as close as family. If they call and say, "I'm having a problem, can you cover a shift for me?" Whether it's convenient or not, yes, I will. It's just something you do for someone you care about. Check your values. Caring is one of them. It's important.' (Focus group #14)

> 'I always tell [subordinates], if they're dealing with a nasty customer, why don't you take a minute, get yourself a drink. The caring trickles down. It comes from the top. My manager cares about me. ... So we're all treating each other with that Metro Experience.' (Focus group #16)

Caring, and the feeling of interdependence associated with it, was widely expected to be part of all intra-Metro relationships. It thus was a key tenet of the firm's promise of value to its crewmembers. Yet not long after I began data collection, respondents began remarking on the *loss* of caring. They observed that within Metro there seemed to be a slippage in practices fulfilling this value:

> 'Caring was a value when I started. Over the last two and a half years, caring's gone out the window.' (Focus group #3)

> 'We were supposed to be a brand new culture, based on those values and stuff like that. And again, it's magic, why we were winning. And all of a sudden, it's like pulling away, we're becoming like the other guys, with no caring ... [no one asks] 'what's happening, how you feeling today?' You know, these [ground service employees] are freezing out on the ramp out there [on cold days]. ... All of a sudden there is no caring about what's affecting them when they're out there.' (Focus Group #6)

Statements such as these suggest contestation around the presence of caring as a characteristic of the authoritative text, a concern that the characteristic might no longer provide the security it once did. The concern these statements display about its absence emphasize caring's importance for Metro's sense of itself, as well as to its distinctiveness:

'You have to stay with the values. You have to stay with us working as a family, as a team, caring. Because that's the only thing that going to make you survive. ... We're the ones who came with the values. Business savvy and all this nonsense, everybody has that out there. What they don't have is the values. That's what made us what we are.' (Focus Group #5)

The expression of caring is an expectation about the activity that *should* characterize the firm's practice; they mark an endogenous distinctive competence that was not only a good on its own, but one which was understood to (re)produce individuals capable of delivering high-quality experiences to customers – Metro's competence distinguishing it from other airlines.

One interesting outgrowth of the authoritative text's emphasis on caring was a lenient orientation toward poor-performing employees. As mentioned in the previous subsection, anxiety about the company's decline was frequently connected conceptually with newcomers, employees hired as a result of Metro's substantial growth. The problem encountered in practice revolved around what was to be done with crewmembers not performing adequately; following the sacred/profane framing, one would expect that the profane employees would be eliminated, banished from the tribe as part of a cleansing ritual. During a coffee break at the second CFC, the VP of human resources pulled me aside and complained that Metro seemed unable to fire its poor performers, concluding that its human resource management was too 'soft' because the top executives were unwilling to, in his words, 'hold people accountable.' In focus groups, this frustration appeared as well:

Crewmember 1:	We could do a better job of getting wrong people either off the bus or in a different seat. ... But the people that aren't doing a great job are not getting reprimanded. They're not losing their jobs. These guys are ruining it for us.
Crewmember 2:	Amen.
Crewmember 3:	Every so often people slip through the cracks.
Crewmember 1:	Metro would rather wait for you to self-destruct than for them to do it to you. And it's a lot of paperwork to get rid of them, too.
Crewmember 4:	[Metro's Human resources is] exactly like that. They go one, two, three [points for infractions], you're out. [But in practice, we count] One, two, 30, 90, 100. I'm still giving you a chance. ... With any other airline, if you got a problem and you can't

do your job, you see those pink slips. But here, we keep giving people chances. (Focus Group #5)

The desire to give poor-performing employees multiple opportunities to rehabilitate or transform was, then, a source of considerable frustration because it sacrificed the Metro Experience while also threatening profitability (and employees' shares of those gains, as noted earlier). What the VP of human resources, in the conversation presented earlier, characterized as a 'soft' stance on dismissing workers can be conceptually connected not merely to Metro's need for labour power as it grew, but also to the value of caring written into Metro's authoritative text. Whether top management deemed those employees necessary for growth, keeping profaned crewmembers inside the boundaries rather than casting them out clearly created a tension between the value of caring and the pursuit of performance.

Another tension associated with caring emerged at the second CFC, where an event illustrated well the boundarying associated with Metro's narrative of caring for employees. James (the CEO) drew upon the customer journey map to make a proposal that displayed how Metro's version of customer service depended on individual employees, and framed top management as responsible for not merely training, but *monitoring* individuals' performances:

FIELDNOTES

During Curt's presentation of customer feedback data, James [CEO] consults the customer journey map and notes that compliments and complaints sent in through Metro's website could integrate with Metro's database of which employees were working a particular flight, so that a given customer's comments could be traced *directly* to specific flight crews, gate agents, and even ground crews. And, going a step further, senior management could even see which seat a customer occupied to figure out which individual flight attendant was likely to be serving the customer during the flight. This could extend to track each individual employee who 'touched' the customer at each point of the process – reservations, ticketing, and gate agents.

Nathan, VP of Airport Services, counters that 'that doesn't seem like *caring*; that seems very "Big-Brotherish." There are other ways to do that – maybe like an internal survey that enables us to get rid of rude people.'

Others seem to agree with Nathan, against James's proposal. James then reframes the proposal as *accountability*, saying 'no one can resist that.' He then suggests that using customer data in this way could be used to get rid of 'rogues' and also to identify 'star performers.' James notes that maybe senior management could have the stars train other employees.

The discussion then moves to how this could be used to also reward and praise, not merely to punish, employees since, as Nathan argues, 'that's accountability as well.' Later in the meeting, as Curt was presenting data comparing Metro's customer service scores with companies outside the airline industry recognized for high-quality customer service, James compares his initiative to 'secret shoppers' like those at Nordstrom and Disney. At the end of the meeting, Tom, the VP of Marketing, is tasked with responsibility for developing what members called the 'accountability initiative.'

This vignette illustrates contestation, a struggle over meaning about 'what we are (and are not),' as well as 'how we're going to get there.' It also involves competing meanings for *accountability*. When surveillance was challenged for its apparent violation of the previous element of the authoritative text – a lack of *care* for (and trust of) individual employees – James reformulated the idea with an appeal to a higher-order value, framing it as an employee's responsibility to customer service excellence, and that it was the responsibility of top management to construct a system of surveillance that could ensure accountability to *that* practice. In other words, James translated 'what we are' into a promise of value creation, one operating as an unemotional control over, and measurement of, activity in the name of efficiency, productivity, and personal accountability. The entire episode also operated on the implicit assertion that ensuring the routinized provision of the Metro Experience was the dominion of top management, such that it was proper for this group to gather data to control its provision via employee surveillance.

James's justification was resisted with an alternative, one drawing on the notion of *caring*: in Nathan's terms, caring meant that we, as senior managers, do not engage in 'Big Brother'-type surveillance of employees. If there was to be such a system, then it must be used to reward as well as to punish; James accepted this amendment. That James was able 'win' the disagreement and assign the project to a VP emphasized that a CEO's (and here, the CEO was also the founder) ability to marshal consent is a practice of authority – as deployment of property rights – rarely questioned in corporate life.

Yet authority relied not merely on property claims via positional rights, but additionally on an ability to promise value. James's appeal to personal responsibility and accountability functioned on a conception of value located in customer satisfaction achieved through an efficient system comprised of individual performances, whereas Nathan justified his argument with reference to the construction of a caring community. What prevailed in this case was the desire to recognize and respond to both 'rogues' and 'star performers' (to both punish and reward) and a concomitant belief that customer service was performed by controllable individual employees. Metro's executive-and director-level leaders were seen as properly qualified – *authorized* – to make those determinations with the aid of a surveillance system. Boundarying thus included both surveillance technologies and the practice of creating lines of demarcation to separate lower-level crewmembers from the CFC executives; it also included the firm's statement of values guiding its practice. What became known as the 'accountability initiative' operated on the data the executives could access, made available by digital ticketing, flight, and employment records, as well as the lack of a union presence in the firm to represent the concerns of the soon-to-be surveilled crewmembers. Yet it sat alongside the notion of caring for employees.

Summary

Metro's writing of its authoritative text, therefore, included three elements that articulate its sense of the 'we': Metro values 'soft' skills, Metro fears dissipating distinctiveness, and Metro cares for its employees. As suggested in Chapter 4, a firm's authoritative text characterizes its assemblage-as-practice; it is a narrative intimately bound up in its past organizing and future trajectory. For that reason, the inclusions and exclusions seen here would be likely to enjoy what Hernes (2003) calls *taxonomic authority*: the capacity a component of practice wields to sediment the distinctions marking that same practice.

One should be careful not to interpret this boundarying as *determinative* of the firm's practice, however. In addition to the valorizing of communicative performances and the division into sacred and profane, the boundarying discussed earlier displays a separation of the ideational and material, one relegating nonhuman elements to the periphery of the firm's authoritative text. Yet an important lesson of Chapter 3 was that the forces comprising an assemblage, perhaps especially those ignored in territorializing practices, remain immanent, virtual; they are the excesses poised to impose themselves on practice. This is not to suggest that nonhuman participants were *im*material (irrelevant) in Metro's reclamation of a dynamic capability, but to note that the firm's narrative of the 'we' privileged persons (those providing the performative competencies, as well as those managing them) and their symbolic action. In the next section, I delve into two dis/organizational outcomes of this enactment of authority.

Dis/organizational consequences of Metro's authoritative text

As noted in Chapter 4, identifying an authoritative text cannot be the *end* of analysis; the authoritative text is a device useful in gaining insight into the unfolding of the organizing practices that constitute firms. Given the promises of value and claims to property written into Metro's authoritative text – a model of authority likely to be widespread given communicative capitalism's emphasis on experiential affect capture and branding – it becomes logical to ask about the consequences of this form of boundarying.

Pressure on front-line supervisors

A first implication for practice was a high degree of pressure placed on the work of airport-level supervisors, the lowest level of management. The authoritative text, as mentioned, encoded senior management's claim to property with respect to monitoring and directing employees' service performances. The responsibility to monitor Metro's 'on the ground' practices was not senior managers' purview, however; that task fell to the supervisors of crewmembers in direct contact with customers (gate agents, ticketing agents, flight attendants, baggage handlers, ground crew, and reservations agents).

At many firms, low-level supervisors are responsible for only scheduling and monitoring functions but, in Metro, the supervisor was also the nexus for senior management's initiatives to enhance the Metro Experience. Supervisors were thus also responsible for motivating, developing, and coaching front-line employees. The customer journey map became a resource not merely for senior managers' territorial (property) claims, but for the expansion of supervisors' responsibilities as well: because the map displayed connections between functions, senior managers recognized that supervisors were the point of contact to bridge job functions. Because formal training was limited both in availability and on-the-job applicability, those supervisors became the axis upon which authority turned.

As a result, Metro's senior managers expanded the tasks to be performed in supervisory roles but did not provide attendant capacities (in terms of time and decidability) to guide customer service practice. Several supervisors, in interviews and shadowing sessions, remarked on their lack of influence over hiring and staffing processes and employees' lack of on-the-job training before beginning. An additional frustration was that supervisors were held accountable for ensuring that lower-level employees delivered the Metro Experience, but there existed no clear performance evaluations, and associated rewards, for those front-line crewmembers:

> '[Low-level employees'] morale is down because of not having been evaluated. They feel they need to be evaluated; they need to be recognized more. You have those employees who go beyond and they feel they are not being recognized, which brings the morale down and eventually the motivation down. That's why [two Supervisors] are

working on [employee recognition] projects outside our jobs. We want to bring the morale up. ... I want Metro to remain Metro, because that's what makes us unique.' (Supervisor Interview #10)

In addition to the insufficiency of training for front-line crewmembers, supervisors noted inadequate supervisory training, such that much of what they learned was the result of individual initiative and unstructured experiential learning:

'No one teaches you. I've never been coached. ... [When managing difficult subordinates] you don't know the right wording. You don't know what to do.' (Supervisor Interview #4)

'When I first became a supervisor, they didn't have training. It was go out there, learn, sink, or swim. ... Is it the right way? No, because you will make errors. You learn from your mistakes, but definitely it's something that you need to bring out of yourself.' (Supervisor Interview #7)

The boundarying mentioned in the preceding section noted that Metro's authoritative text accorded property rights to senior managers when it came to determining the emphasis on a customer service competency and the location for its conceptualization. Although supervisors did not contend with senior management's claim to property here – they agreed it was *proper* for top management to steer Metro in this way – they accused senior managers of failing to grasp the challenges of supervisory work. They argued that senior leaders remained physically and conceptually distant as supervisors were forced to muddle through their everyday activity. This led to a frustration with what supervisors saw as a lack of consistency both from senior management about expectations for supervisory work and across the team of supervisors in the airport regarding acceptable local practices:

'Consistency is our biggest problem. Following through on something that you (senior manager) say you're going to do, or you did, or it's in the works. I would say consistency-slash-communication. For example, the restructure of management and the leadership team. We're doing this, this, this, then the communication stops ... it's frustrating for every one of us supes. That leads people to believe there is favoritism. Leads me to believe there is favoritism.' (Supervisor Interview #3)

'There's no consistency. If I talk to this employee for punching out early, and another supervisor is not, then why am I doing it? It's difficult because you say, "why am I stressing myself and working hard if *you're* not going to do what you're supposed to do?" We do have a couple of [supervisors] like that. It means the person who is working gets burned out quick.' (Supervisor Interview #6)

Supervisors, in short, were made responsible for the performance of their subordinates, but were not given tools (including employee assessment devices) they saw as necessary to create the practices sought by senior management, nor were they given coherent messages from middle and upper management. This is ironic because, given the aforementioned fear of decline associated with lower-level newcomers' performance, a failure to measure performance meant that the attribution of 'profanity' to newcomers could never be meaningfully assessed. And if the fear of decline remained unexamined, it could not be challenged in a way that would either reduce the anxiety about customer service or alter the relations of authority.

Because Metro prized the production of high-quality customer experiences but operated in what might be understood as a commodity business – a highly competitive, low-margin business with high fixed costs and price-sensitive customers – the choice to compete on both service *and* cost meant that the 'service encounter' was a crucial site of competitive advantage. Employees thus had to be inexpensive, reliable, and able to engage in high-quality service work. This set of contrasting expectations fell to supervisors to manage. Consequently, supervisors' role was to both enforce the basics of the employment contract and aid in creating the possibilities for high-quality customer service. That Metro senior management failed to recognize the inadequacy of the tools provided to the supervisors suggests that many of the formal structuring and coordination devices associated with bureaucratized systems were rendered irrelevant, and informal communicative practices became central to the supervisory tasks of teaching and coaching (see Fortado, 1994). Because the task of monitoring and inspiring high-quality service fell to poorly supported supervisors, the ambiguity and tenuousness of performative distinctive competencies was likely to remain. The approach to boundarying, as a component of authority, ironically threatened the very durability of dynamic capabilities that Metro executives sought.

Disruption by IROPs

The second dis/organizational consequence of Metro's particular configuration of an authoritative text occurred when situations challenged the communicative performances intended to generate positive affect. Those situations were, in the argot of the industry, 'IROPs': IRregular OPerations.

An IROP was usually a reference to weather-related unexpected events (though others noted that it included cases of mechanical error, as when a luggage conveyor belt malfunctions or a computer system goes down), for which routine scripts for customer service performances did not exist. Events such as these, consequently, showed the intersections of material and discursive participants in assemblages while also exposing the dis/organization encountered by an authoritative text of the sort generated by Metro.

Consider this conversation at a CFC regarding a pilot's clumsy attempt at humour during a weather disruption to attendees also considered the problems unearthed by customer complaints:

FIELDNOTES

At the third CFC, members discussed a customer complaint that read: 'Our flight was delayed due to fog ... when we boarded the plane, the pilot told us we should cross all our fingers in order to guarantee us a safe landing in NYC.' After audible gasps and visible cringes from the attendees, Matt, the VP of Training and Development, gave voice to what I perceived to be the source of those gasps, saying that 'this could be seen as [the pilot] expressing a lack of concern over safety' that harmed passengers' trust. Another VP reframed it as the pilot using humor to 'make a human connection – he was bringing humanity back to the airline industry' (appropriating a line from Metro's branding efforts) and, thus, as an entirely appropriate response in the situation. Others called for this to be 'addressed in pilot training' to ensure that such unfortunate statements would never again be uttered from the cockpit. An alternative reading was presented by Molly, a pilot, who suggested that each of the customers on a flight might indeed have a different view: '156 customers have many different interpretations. They key is what we [the senior managers at the CFC] do with this information.'

This example encapsulates the challenge of performative capabilities as they encounter material challenge: when the model of authority urges unique customer service performances rooted in communication, but the material exigency provides a force of affect misaligned with the performance (such as passengers' anxiety about safety in foggy conditions), the response from those positioned as recipients of those performances may not support the performative aim. The conversation among CFC participants shows the excess of meanings pervading the assemblage, such that their interpretations protected the authoritative text from challenge: by suggesting that this was merely a misguided attempt at humour, the value of individuals' soft skills as the source of the Metro Experience was preserved – it merely required additional training. And the recognition that a multiplicity of interpretations required top management to shape future action retained decidability for the attendees at the CFC.

An IROP is, by definition, irregular. But they are rarely without significant precedent. Airlines have routinized their responses to such situations, standardizing their accommodations for customers whose travel gets disrupted. At Metro, however, these responses tend to flow through the supervisor. For instance, in one extended shadowing session at Metro's primary airport location, I observed an Airport Operations supervisor, AO#5, at the ticketing counter. Heavy fog had caused the multiple and frequently full flights to another city to be delayed, cancelled, and overbooked (overbooking was a practice Metro formally prohibited but sometimes practiced). At least once every other minute, lower-level crewmembers approached the supervisor and asked about how to get customers on flights; she responded with variations of 'here's what you can do' (further evidence of the increased pressure placed on supervisors). Later that day, AO#5 mentioned to me that the new batch of airplanes (from a different manufacturer than the existing fleet) created far more problems and that handling fog seemed to be a particular challenge for these planes.

The following day, I shadowed and interviewed AO#6, who expressed frustration because he had worked at the service counter in the gate area during the previous day's IROP. He mentioned that a flight departed after a long delay; 'it flew to [city], circled twice, and then they found out that it couldn't land, so it returned right back to [this airport]. Customers were *very* angry, because they saw that other airlines were landing.' When I asked him what he, at the Metro Customer Service desk, experienced, he said that he was able to obtain refunds for some of the customers, but that 'some gave me the finger.' When I asked other supervisors about how they're taught to handle irate customers, AO#7 mentioned that when his frustration with customers rises, he will seek to pass the problem off to another supervisor. The problem with such a response, however, is that during IROP situations, 'passing off' may be impossible since most supervisors are inundated with requests from both customers and crewmembers to address individual problems (as in the example of AO#5). These illustrations evince a tension: the Metro brand was built upon a friendly and caring image of travel but, in IROP situations, not only do problems flow to supervisors, but the supervisors handling customer problematic situations are expected to draw exclusively on impersonal routine while simultaneously providing satisfying customer service experiences. Friendly and caring come to seem impossible. There are precious few systematized resources in the assemblage enabling them to perform high-quality service in IROPs.

Summary

Taken together, these two dis/organizational consequences – pressure on airport supervisors and disruption by IROPs – can be seen as direct outgrowths of the boundarying of Metro's authoritative text. By situating the firm's dynamic capability in the customer service performance and then individualizing that performance by insisting that it's the result of employees' in-the-moment deployment of soft skills, Metro made the systemization necessary to accommodate growth the province of supervisors, but not of senior managers. Yet those supervisors existed in a contradiction where they were handed accountability but few resources.

This section displays the complex intersections between elements of the assemblage boundaried off from customer service performance in Metro's authoritative text. The excesses presented by sociomaterial incursions – here, weather, confusing incapacities of new airplanes, the lack of inter-airline operating agreements, Metro's inadequate training, comparisons with other airlines' accommodations, bureaucratic distances separating supervisors and upper management – dis/ordered the smooth individual customer service performances expected by the authoritative text. In the case of IROPs specifically, frontline employees and (particularly) supervisors were summoned to provide immediate responses because customers expecting high-quality experiences also demanded instantaneous remedies to their concerns and complaints. The boundarying enacted in the writing of the authoritative text excluded both the local control of supervisors and the unpredictability of IROPs, ironically threatening the very performances the authoritative text sought to generate.

Implications for a Communicative Theory of the Firm

It may not have been evident to this point, but this chapter's objective has been a novel answer to the theory of the firm question 'how do firms create profitability (or competitive advantage)?' Its answer started by complicating the dominant thinking of competence approaches to the firm and, instead of presenting *the* correct path to profitable performance, the CTF provides a set of conceptual tools to shift conceptualizations of the moment that capabilities become advantage.

Communicative capitalism urges firms to situate dynamic capabilities in performances designed to elicit and capture affective responses to customers' experiences. It is in the ephemeral experience of that moment that firms like Metro, which ride the wave of the experience economy, seek to turn into repeated consumption (Pine & Gilmore, 2011). As argued before, however, the ambiguity and tenuousness of those experiential responses threatens the VRIO formula. Performative capabilities' ephemerality requires reproducibility across time and space, yet the Metro case demonstrated the limits of such extensions. When the capabilities are the product of so-called 'soft skills' that depend deeply on individual employees' action, securing durable organization-wide performances is likely to run into the sort of challenges seen in this chapter.

Metro's response to the need to combat ephemerality was 'the Metro Experience.' It was the product of efforts to promise value and claim property, guided by an authoritative text, in an effort to constitute the firm. In constituting the firm, Metro's assertions of value and property generated boundarying, which *included* attachments between persons, skills, affective experiences, and customers, while simultaneously *excluding* (detaching) material forces, provisions for IROPs, and local supervisory control.

The notion of boundarying as a vehicle for both agential cuts and inclusion/exclusion practices is unique to the CTF, but the practices examined here are not restricted to either the theory or to Metro. A strict strategic/tactical divide is a well-worn model for corporate management, including in the management of human resources and the claim that management has dynamic capabilities of its own; indeed, it is a key plank of the RBV (Ambrosini & Altintas, 2019). The investigation of the dis/organizational consequences of Metro's enactment of authority demonstrated that its authoritative text may have worked at cross-purposes with the company's own aims. For instance, its inclusions and exclusions hampered both supervisors' action and the production of satisfying performances during IROPs.

The approach to boundarying inscribed into the authoritative text (and shaping organizational practice) therefore produced a *brittle performative capability*. The firm, as authority machine, desired not only attachments *but also detachments*, and the resulting performative capability was poorly transferable when meeting the demands of extension across time and space. Its brittleness was particularly on display under conditions of material peril, rapid growth, and overextended supervisors. But it was Metro's very valorizations that produced its fragility, as it prized individuals' soft skills, chose rehabilitation over removal, portrayed newcomers as incapable/profane, and excluded the obdurate material domain from its promise of value. Scalability was sacrificed; brittleness prevailed.

What, then, would constitute a CTF approach to performative capability (re)creation? It would start with questioning the location of authority. As noted earlier in this section, the common strategic/tactical divide centres decidability in upper management; doing so can deprive those on the proverbial 'front lines,' like Metro's supervisors, from a felt connection to the production of value. Collaboration in the production of an authoritative text, via broadened claims to property over experiential performances (extending the claim to the front-line sociomaterial practices, including their human practitioners), could foster the interdependence that might have tempered the development of the contradictions seen here.

From there, a CTF would direct greater attention to the content of the authoritative text. Doing so would turn to Jane Bennett's (2010) advocacy for asking what agency *fears*, which can be just as relevant as knowing what it desires. What an assemblage seeks to avoid is important as its productive aims. To think in the register of a practice 'fearing' and 'desiring' is not a simplistic anthropomorphism; it is, instead, a route for investigators to attend to the struggles involved in the trajectory of practice. The scapegoating was evidence of an affectual relation flowing through the Metro assemblage, and its influence made the performative competency more brittle than it might have otherwise been. Fear, manifest as scapegoating, enabled a displacement of anxiety onto the bodies (and soft skills) of newcomers while simultaneously precluding an interrogation of the reasons performative capabilities were poorly extended across time and space. In other words, the scapegoating built into 'the Metro Experience' obscured the representational practices that *produced the need* for a scapegoat in the first place. Charting the practices in which that fear materialized in practice would provide a capacity to intervene, to interrogate the assumptive ground upon which scapegoating unfolded.

Finally, the CTF encourages a rethinking of temporal shifts in the sources of profitability/competitive advantage. Much contemporary strategy research argues that firms require dynamism rather than stability in their capabilities: 'Companies may need to give up on seeking the once-coveted "sustainable competitive advantage" in favor of what some call "renewable competitive advantage," using one temporary position of strength to hopscotch into another' (Fiol, 2001, p 692). Most firms, however, would find it challenging at best to play hopscotch of this sort. Metro strategists could not have simply decided to hopscotch to advantages in costs, route maps, or technology, both because other firms occupied those niches and because switching capabilities is tremendously costly. Moreover, given its self-articulated values (and thus its inscription in its narrative of the 'we'), Metro's reliance on superior customer service was not a strategy from which it could easily depart.

The CTF instead suggests that the processes by which firms pursue competitive advantage are guided by multifaceted authoritative texts, producing consequences that are not only unintended, but which can work at cross-purposes with the firm's efforts to generate those very competitive advantages. The boundarying explored in this chapter might thus be augmented by a clearer focus on efforts to author the trajectory of the firm – to shape not only the current sense of the 'we,' but also '*what we should become*' (while acknowledging that this trajectory can be motivated by the fear Bennett mentions). Returning to the Deleuzian thinking upon which the CTF draws, augmented boundarying can enable the sort of rhizomatic *becoming-multiple* that allows for adaptation to potential futures. Imagining futures in which performative capabilities might be threatened by ambiguity and tenuousness yet where customer experiences could be collaborative communicative accomplishments could lead to a continual updating, an ongoing re-imagining, of the authoritative text.

Notes

[1] This is a pseudonym, as are all names in this chapter. There was a company called Metro Airlines that existed in the US from 1969 to 1993. Upon its 1993 bankruptcy, Metro was purchased and absorbed by American Airlines' holding company, so it no longer exists.

[2] 'Customer' was the company's term that replaced 'passenger' to both signal a relationship beyond the limited time flying on a plane and to frame employees' responsibility as one of service rather than conveyance.

[3] Despite repeated efforts, I have not been able to locate said study.

6

Branding: Hindering Heterarchy in a Startup Accelerator

With communicative capitalism's increased emphasis on branding as a manifestation of desire and mode of organizational/personal existence (as covered in Chapter 1), it seems logical to see corporations' need to present themselves and their products in a positive light as a justification for the profusion of branding. Those supposed needs appear to be found readily in firms' advertising and sponsorship, visual imagery, and public statements – but such symbolic and ostensibly intentional representations are only part of the story. In keeping with a theme of this book, branding is also about *excess*: any given corporation exerts only limited control over its ethos and 'feel' across the many and unpredictable events the brand encounters (Arvidsson & Peitersen, 2013). Not only does a CTF question the notion of intent built into the presumption of corporate agency, but it makes it clear that meanings outstrip firms' calculated self-representations.

Consequently, branding is more than what is found in a firm's marketing function, and brands are more than immaterial depictions of products or collective identities. As discussed in Chapter 4, branding, as one portrayal of a firm's promises of value and claims to property, is a site of excess because what counts as 'the brand' is unavoidably open to multiple influences distributed across an assemblage. Because every assemblage consists of participants vying to influence a firm's trajectory, branding is therefore also always a potentially contentious *political* endeavour (Lury, 2009; Ramaswamy & Ozcan, 2022).

Chapter 1 discussed the possibility that participants beyond those employed by a firm's marketing arm might assert control over a brand, and I connected this possibility to a relatively new development in the history of capitalism. This chapter advances that argument by situating branding not merely as the site of conflict over a product, but as the setting for clashes between contrasting domains of experience and valuation. The name given to these domains in one segment of sociological literature is *orders of worth*.

Orders of worth in entrepreneurship

Prior to the work mentioned in Chapter 1 on shifts in the 'spirit' of capitalism, French sociologist Luc Boltanski and economist Laurent Thévenot puzzled over why logics of practice differ so dramatically across situational and institutional divides. In *On Justification: Economies of Worth* (1991/2006), they traced six distinct *orders* (or economies) *of worth:* inspired, domestic, fame, civic, market, and industrial, each of which include contrasting criteria for evaluations of quality with respect to objects, practices, persons, conceptions of the common good, and forms of reason. (Thévenot et al [2000] later added a 'green' economic order that addressed the valuing of nature as a social good and mode of reasoning; these are depicted in Table 6.1.) Boltanski and Thévenot acknowledge that these 'worlds' do not mark distinct social spheres, but instead cut across social life, affecting all practices and persons (see Thévenot, 2001). For instance, a decision about a firm's potential promotional partner might assess the partner's notoriety (fame), passion (inspired), or reliability (domestic). It might also assess the cost of the partnership (market) or the specialized knowledge to be gained from the collaboration (industrial). Multiple evaluative principles shape practice, and those that become explicit *post hoc* justifications for action provide insight into the claims to legitimacy made on behalf of the firm (Patriotta et al, 2011).

The conceptual connections with the CTF's vision of firms as authority machines is perhaps obvious. Boltanski and Thévenot's work comprises a theory of value, and the promises of value written into the authoritative text necessarily reference some guiding logic(s) for such promises to have purchase; their work thus provides a vocabulary for understanding those logics. And the case is the same for claims to property, the other branch of the authoritative text: legal assertions of property rights might refer to a civic world, declarations of hierarchical role responsibility could draw upon an industrial order, and avowals of environmental responsibility would likely connect with both a market and a green world. Orders of worth, in other words, provide the ground from which promises of value and claims to property – the fundaments of authority – are built, asserting an ever-present ontological multiplicity into the conversation. Table 6.1 overviews the multiple elements of their scheme. It's important to recognize that, while the columns and rows make it appear that this is a scheme comprised of mutually exclusive categorizations, Boltanski and Thévenot make it clear that any single statement or action (or, I'd add, firm) is likely to be the product of *several* intersecting justificatory resources at once.

American sociologist David Stark has been the primary vehicle bringing this work into OS (see also Grattarola et al, 2024). Stark sees the orders of worth framework as useful for unpacking how firms deal with ever-present

Table 6.1: Boltanski and Thévenot's orders of worth, as articulated by Thévenot et al (2000)

	Orders of worth						
	Market	**Industrial**	**Civic**	**Domestic**	**Inspired**	**Fame**	**Green**
Mode of evaluation (worth)	Price, cost	Technical efficiency	Collective welfare	Esteem, reputation	Grace, singularity, creativeness	Renown, fame	Environmental friendliness
Test	Market competitiveness	Competence, reliability, planning	Equality and solidarity	Trustworthiness	Passion, enthusiasm	Popularity, audience, recognition	Sustainability, renewability
Form of relevant proof	Monetary	Measurable: criteria, statistics	Formal, official	Oral, exemplary, personally warranted	Emotional involvement and expression	Semiotic	Ecological ecosystem
Qualified objects	Freely circulating market good or service	Infrastructure, project, technical object, method, plan	Rules and regulations, fundamental rights, welfare policies	Patrimony, locale, heritage	Emotionally invested body or item, the sublime	Sign, media	Pristine wilderness, healthy environment, natural habitat
Qualified human beings	Customer, consumer, merchant, seller	Engineer, professional, expert	Equal citizens, solidarity unions	Authority	Creative beings	Celebrity	Environmentalists, ecologists
Time formation	Short-term, flexibility	Long-term planned future	Perennial	Customary part	Eschatological, revolutionary, visionary moment	Vogue, trend	Future generations
Space formation	Globalization	Cartesian space	Detachment	Local, proximal anchoring	Presence	Communication network	Planet ecosystem

uncertainty regarding evaluative criteria. Stark argues that entrepreneurial firms are the examples *par excellence* for examining the multiplicity of evaluative criteria because they work amidst *asset ambiguity*[1]: 'from ambiguity [entrepreneurship] makes an asset; and in creating assets that can operate in more than one game, it makes assets that are ambiguous' (Stark, 2009, p 15). That ambiguity, says Stark, enables entrepreneurs to play multiple games at the same time. When those entrepreneurs work across multiple orders of worth, advantage can be the result: 'Organizations that keep multiple evaluative principles in play ... foster a generative friction that disrupts received categories of business as usual and make possible an ongoing recombination of resources' (pp 16–17). Entrepreneurs, in other words, don't merely exploit the value of a novel idea, but exploit the tensions between contrasting models of value. Stark, then, offers an important connection between the problem of purpose (and its ontological multiplicity) with which this book began and the questions of performance animating theories of the firm.

In a series of studies, Stark and his collaborators examined this entrepreneurial capacity to utilize the dissonance across evaluative principles. Their settings included a new media startup in New York's Silicon Alley (Girard & Stark, 2003; Neff & Stark, 2004), a Hungarian factory operating under socialism in the late 1980s (Stark, 2009), and an arbitrage trading room (Beunza & Stark, 2004). One of the more interesting conclusions of these studies is that a particular organizational arrangement (a particular response to 'how do firms operate internally') appears necessary to enable the exploitation of the frictions between orders of worth. That arrangement is the *heterarchy*, a radically decentralized form where responsibility for innovation and firm trajectory is shared throughout a firm's many units rather than being centralized in a particular management function. Heterarchies are examples of distributed authority (Powell, 1990) that, because of their complexity and decentralization, require a high degree of collaborative communication across their multiple units.

Heterarchies deliberately avoid hierarchical rankings of valuation principles in their distribution of activity while also eschewing the possibility of a single logic for value selection (Crumley, 2015; Dekker & Kuchar, 2021). These are networks of action, and what becomes central is understanding the flowing of evaluative principles through the organization, which become assessments of value as actors 'interweave a multiplicity of performance principles' in accounting for choices (Stark, 2009, p 25).

Although authors have hailed the capacities of postbureaucratic, flattened, or networked organizational forms for decades, the heterarchy literature is unique in its attention to the *rivalry* between multiple registers of worth. As Stark summarizes, 'The manifest, or proximate, result of this rivalry is a noisy clash, as the proponents of different conceptions of value contend with each other. The latent consequence of this dissonance is that the diversity of value-frames generates new combinations of the firm's resources' (2009, p 27).

Such antagonisms have rarely been part of the literature on postbureaucratic organizations. But we should not delude ourselves into believing that such 'new combinations' offer an unalloyed good for organizations or the larger assemblages from which they spring. Indeed, if all organizing is about struggles over meaning (as the CTF claims), and if, as stated, branding is inevitably a political practice, analysts should be prepared to understand heterarchical organizing as a battle for control over organizational trajectories – one that could fetter the organization's performance capabilities. We should thus examine organizing practices that prompt a firm's authoritative text to enable or constrain the proliferation of multiple orders of worth. In entrepreneurship, a venue has emerged that practices prompting of this sort: the accelerator.

Accelerating entrepreneurship

The rise of entrepreneurship accelerators

Over the past couple of decades, entrepreneurship accelerators (also known as investment/seed accelerators or incubators) have sprung up across the globe to nurture startup businesses. Inspired, no doubt, by the astronomical monetary valuations attached to many startups (particularly in the technology sector) and the success of the well-known Silicon Valley accelerator Y Combinator, accelerators have become key parts of the entrepreneurial scene. They generally provide seed funding and a limited-duration experience to help entrepreneurs turn ideas into viable enterprises and, in exchange, the accelerators – which are firms themselves – take minority ownership stake in the nascent firm with the hope for a large payday provided by either a corporate acquisition or an initial public offering of stock (though increasingly startup firms eschew becoming public corporations in favour of private LLCs, as suggested in Chapter 4).

Most frequently, that 'limited-duration experience' involves a cohort of competitively selected startup teams gathering in a shared location for a duration that averages 3 months. In that location, the accelerator's leaders provide lessons on developing a business venture through (a) inducing experimentation with business models, (b) exposure to mentorship from accomplished entrepreneurs and subject matter experts, (c) conversations with potential customers, and (d) knowledge-sharing with other cohort members. Each cohort's conclusion includes a 'Demo Day' where the startup teams pitch their ventures to both potential investors and members of the local startup community. The jury is still out on accelerators' effectiveness in producing viable ventures (Hallen et al, 2020) and bringing technological innovations to market (Bernthal, 2016; Stayton & Mangematin, 2019), but their popularity appears strong.

As one might imagine, accelerators endeavour to mould the cohort's developing firms and shape their embryonic authoritative texts. Though it may not be on the formal agenda, startups experiencing an accelerator are likely to absorb what counts as value through both explicit and tacit lessons. Accelerators are, accordingly, excellent venues to observe the inscription of interests onto the authoritative texts that will guide these emerging firms' trajectories. One approach, therefore, might be to examine the developing authoritative texts of the budding ventures found in accelerators, as I did in a previous publication (see Kuhn, 2017b). Another could be to consider how the accelerator – again, as a firm itself – shapes meaning-making with respect to the multiple evaluative principles that, as Stark and colleagues note, confront entrepreneurs in their routine activity. This chapter takes that second route, examining how a particular authority machine, a startup accelerator in the high tech domain, developed practices that encouraged a model of branding that valorized a particular version of entrepreneurial wanting. The analysis to follow thus addresses the 'how do firms operate internally?' and 'how do firms generate profitability?' questions, which will add texture to the primary 'what do corporations want?' question.

The AmpVille case

AmpVille[2] is located in downtown Boulder, Colorado, a short bus ride from my office at the local university. Coded as an LLC under Colorado statutes, AmpVille focused on startups in the high technology sector, like its better-known forerunner (and Boulder neighbour) Techstars. The Denver-Boulder metropolitan area in which AmpVille operated fashioned itself as a hub for high-tech entrepreneurship and innovation, such that the links between universities, engineering-based employers, and entrepreneurial endeavours had been well established long before AmpVille was born (Feld, 2012). Boulder's status as fertile entrepreneurial ground of was one of the first lessons taught to each cohort by AmpVille, as captured in fieldnotes toward the end of the first week:

FIELDNOTES

Tony mentions Brad Feld's book *Startup Communities* and suggests how special Boulder is for startups. He says there's a distinct Boulder ethos: it practices a 'give first' mentality, which means that everyone in the community is expected to donate time and effort to the larger cause – which builds the startup 'ecosystem' – without expecting an immediate payoff. This works because, 'like karma, the benefit will eventually come to you. So always take a meeting, and always be kind in Boulder. Startups are everywhere. You never know who you're meeting with.'

He also says this is a hyper-competitive area for talent, that there's a .2% negative unemployment rate – and that there are more engineers in this region than anyplace else on the planet.

From the very beginning of their time in AmpVille, then, startup teams are told that Boulder is a special place, characterized by a magnanimous ethic that produces high levels of startup performance in a beneficial community.

For each of its 12-week cohorts, AmpVille's four directors (Tony, Steve, Juan, and, toward the end of the second year, Emma) select between 8 and 12 startup teams, typically consisting of between 2 and 4 entrepreneurs (usually the founders) who have little more than a rough, but intriguing, idea for a venture. The selection process is rigorous; as the directors claimed on the first day of each cohort, the acceptance rate at Ivy League universities was quite a bit higher than that at AmpVille. As is the case with most accelerators, AmpVille provided seed capital ($20,000 during this time period) in exchange for a 7 per cent ownership stake. And also as is the case with accelerators, AmpVille provided the startups with space to work, regular presentations on entrepreneurship (lionizing it while describing its significant personal demands), routine sessions for preparing and polishing Demo Day pitches, and volunteer mentors from the local startup community.

At the beginning of each session, the directors assigned each team to a two-table row in one large room (of AmpVille's five rooms) in the basement of a medium-sized office building (see Figures 6.1 and 6.2).

It was in this room, which measured approximately 15 metres long by 6 metres wide, that most presentations from directors and subject matter experts occurred, but a more open space behind this photo's vantage point

Figure 6.1: The left side of AmpVille's main meeting room, from the back

Figure 6.2: The right side of AmpVille's meeting room

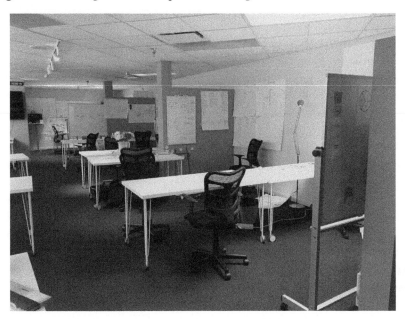

was used for informal gatherings and happy hour meetings. Although most of the everyday work in which teams engaged occurred at these tables (witness the writing and posting on the whiteboard walls), there were, additionally, two enclosed meeting rooms for more private conversations.

I was provided access to this site and its startup teams for approximately 2 years. I sat in the back of the room observing presentations and routine work, attended informal gatherings, interviewed team members, engaged in small talk, and offered feedback on products and investment pitches. My aim was to understand how the practice of AmpVille's branding promoted particular evaluative principles as (un)desirable among the startups.

Branding AmpVille, branding startups

As AmpVille taught the startups experiencing its program how to become viable enterprises, it made two simultaneous branding moves: it evinced a model of value-producing activity geared toward the accelerator itself, while also advancing a conception of branding as valuable for the startups it coached. Valorization was thus key to AmpVille's practices. In terms of this book's title, AmpVille's activity demonstrated its own wanting while also shaping the wanting of the startups it honed. Honing those startups consisted of three interconnected valorization practices, associated with (a) the technologically cool, (b) mentorship, and (c) funding.

Valorizing the technologically cool

In an accelerator devoted to high-tech entrepreneurship, it should come as no surprise that technological sophistication was an expected attribute of the startups AmpVille attracted. It's also unremarkable that AmpVille's practices urged startups to brand themselves as technologically creative, since businesses able to demonstrate a capacity to capitalize on technology's cutting edge would be more likely to attract investment – which, in turn, would grow toward financial returns for AmpVille.

For instance, early in one cohort experience I had an informal conversation with a founder whose company sought to digitize automobile parking in cities using electronic sensors on paid street parking areas linked to an app. The founder described an instance early on the 12-week program where AmpVille co-director Tony, after receiving a description of the team's idea, challenged them to think about the possibility of capitalizing on the data generated from the parking transactions. The working revenue model had been that the company would take a small percentage of each parking fee paid through the app. Tony wondered aloud whether they 'might be able to do something with the data those transactions make.' A few weeks later, I observed the two co-founders meeting with one of the mentors assigned to them. They presented the potential to capitalize on users' data exhaust as a major novelty, one fitting with what the most innovative companies working directly with consumers (as presented in AmpVille sessions) were doing. They also presented the sale of data to third parties as not only an additional source of income but as a bulwark against the vagaries of city parking demand and city governments' unpredictability, such that their technological sophistication made their business a strong bet for success. They did not credit Tony for the idea, but in further conversations with the co-founder it seemed clear to me that they believed the expropriation of data exhaust was such a common approach to value creation in AmpVille that they would have eventually stumbled toward its allure. As this example suggests, AmpVille didn't merely expect startups to have 'cool' technology, but to develop a technologically-informed practice – often one capitalizing on data – that startups could narrate as they depicted their brand.

At an evening event linking startups with the local mentor community in the first week of a cohort, three of the AmpVille co-directors stood in front of an audience of about 40 mentors, alongside the roughly 20 members of the cohort's startup teams. The co-directors mentioned that 'in the first week, the aim is to create an open, growth mindset. The teams must be willing to 'thrash' [to experience the frustration and confusion of not knowing their startup's direction]. In the past, we failed to give them a system to feel safe thrashing. There's a pain point, and they need to get there.' Juan then projected the following 'Thinking Tools' on the monitor at the front of the room:

1. Customer personas
2. Business Model Canvas
3. Value proposition
4. Get out of the building
5. Update canvas
6. Journey mapping (and then validate assumptions)

These are largely taken from Ries's (2011) materials and curriculum for 'lean startups' (compare AmpVille's assemblage with those described in Bruton et al, in press). The element that brought together many of the lessons of that curriculum was item #2, the Business Model Canvas from Strategyzer AG, as depicted in Figure 6.3. This artifact forced entrepreneurs to articulate what were taken to be the central features of any fledgling business: key partners, key activities, key resources, value propositions, customer relationships, channels (to access customers), customer segments, cost structure, and revenue streams.

These 'thinking tools' are assignments that entrepreneurs are to complete, and the continually revisable physical artifacts hang on the walls (see Figures 6.1 and 6.2) to display those entrepreneurs' past imaginative connections between interesting technologies and potential value. 'Entrepreneurs,' said Tony at the event mentioned in the preceding paragraph, 'should be bringing these artifacts to their meetings with you, their mentors.' He added, 'mentors: use these artifacts as a tool set to overcome resistance, to challenge the entrepreneurs.' Because this message is also directed toward entrepreneurs (and not merely mentors), it's clear that Tony's urging engages in a form of *prophecy*, wherein the co-directors promise that startups will create future value if AmpVille's techniques are accorded decidability in entrepreneurs' practice.

One meeting between a mentor and a startup team midway through the 12-week program showed the importance of bringing these artifacts together with the technology through which the startups worked. After presenting their Business Model Canvas, a three-person team working on an advertising technology business presented what members considered to be technologically cool:

Entrepreneur: I wanted to introduce you to [name of algorithm], dude, this was a big part of what we did last week. ... I realized that I had really been obsessing over building the predictive analytic model, but what we really had the opportunity to do was build a fairly simple descriptive model that no one's done before, that adds direct value to the platform. So, one of the questions that we've been getting is, 'well, what if the small business owner doesn't know who to target or who his clients are, or something like that?' What it is, is, we tie into the client's social feeds – Facebook, Twitter, LinkedIn, what have you – bring that information up, expand it, or augment it against the data warehouses that do nothing but augment data, then will crunch it through our algorithm and come out with descriptive assets. So also we'll come in and tie their Facebook and Twitter into it, bring that data up, married again some third-party data, crunch it out, and then be able to come back to [local small coffee shop] and say, 'hey, 40 per cent of your engaged audience online are women in this zip code between these ages. We think we should target that automatically, and that will inform the [advertising] campaign, straight out.'

Mentor:	That's neat.
Entrepreneur:	It's fucking awesome, is what that is.
Mentor:	Sorry, that's what I meant to say. Neato. Peachy keen. So that's what you would patent?
Entrepreneur:	[emphatically] Yes.
Mentor:	It's a good thing to patent, anyway.
Entrepreneur:	Yep. And it adds some very specific value into exactly what we're doing. ... So, I don't know how that's going to work yet, but this is the way we are moving, in that direction.
Mentor:	Yeah. Once you, once you run it, once you make it, and you are seeing what comes out of it, you'll have a better sense of the value.

This excerpt provides a useful illustration of the branding exercise induced by AmpVille. Branding was the practice of linking a narrative of the (developing) firm to a claim of distinctiveness, propelled by a firm's property, which enabled a compelling promise of value. As such, branding was clearly about generating an authoritative text. A brief conversation like this displays

Figure 6.3: A Generic Business Model Canvas, from Strategyzer

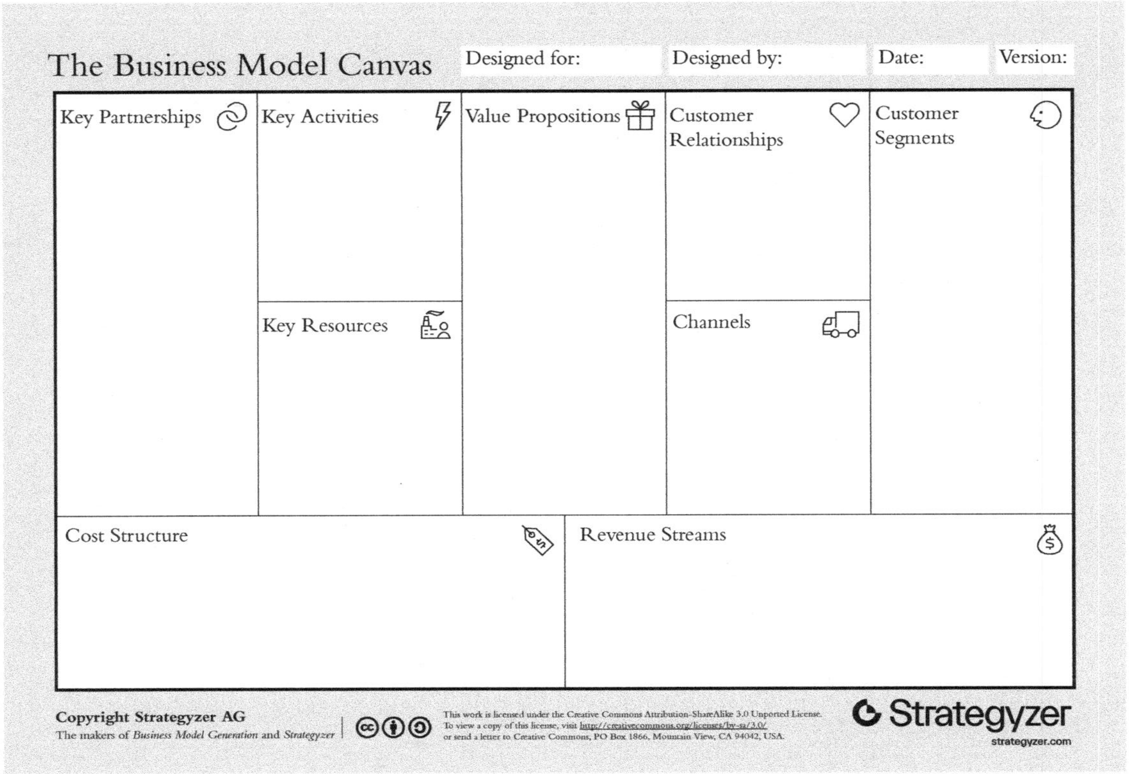

Source: Strategyzer

the constitution of the budding firm while simultaneously exhibiting an AmpVille operating logic (see also Kuhn et al, 2017).

Although AmpVille's co-directors didn't *force* startups to embrace technologies capable of mining data exhaust, being a technologically sophisticated startup was an expected characteristic, a component of the accelerator's branding. And when AmpVille's co-directors prompted entrepreneurs and mentors to deploy artifacts like the Business Model Canvas as a sociomaterial device to scrutinize claims to the technologically cool, they were prying open the black box of branding.

Interestingly conspicuous by their absence were references to the material 'stuff' making the technologically cool possible: the digital and satellite infrastructure, the heavy elements comprising computer and smartphone componentry (and the mining that uncovers those elements), the physical spaces of city streets and US automobile dependence, or the computing power required for an algorithm to sift through voluminous data and place advertising bids on content websites. Factors like these receded to the background as assemblage participants that could be *assumed* in the development of business plans – they weren't made to matter in startup practice but were an unarticulated background for the conversations AmpVille engineered between entrepreneurs and mentors. And, as the next subsection shows, attachments (bindings) between AmpVille, entrepreneurs, and mentors further shaped the practices of wanting in ways that made branding central.

Valorizing mentorship

The second practice characterizing AmpVille was its emphasis on mentorship, which was instrumental not merely to nurture its budding firms, but as a component of its own branding endeavour. When I asked co-director Juan about the most important elements of the scene for startup success, he replied:

'I think mentorship, definitely. A lot of these entrepreneurs are in their early to mid-twenties, they weren't around when the (dot-com) bubble popped. Other people have been making mistakes for decades – why duplicate that? They were smart people too, and they made the mistake they did, why do you think you are better than them – try to avoid their mistakes by taking advice.'

I then inserted a question: 'Why do *mentors* do this? It seems like a significant investment of time; what's in it for them?' Juan's response:

'First thing is that you're learning a lot, you are helping these startups deal with challenges that you may or may not have dealt within the past, that they are then getting to learn, say, okay, this is how I would approach it, and then getting to see, did that work? ... as you (the mentor) build a relationship, then the startups will say, "I want to continue past the 12 weeks with building a relationship with you and have a more formal relationship." You know, mentors still help past the 12 weeks – it's not like they stop, but they say, let's have a more formal relationship, join my board of advisors, and usually there is some kind of equity exchange that happens there. And the mentor *can't* initiate that discussion during the program. The startup can if they want to. So, there is some reward, long-term, if they put in – if they give first. But the best ones don't come in with that expectation.'

In another interview, co-director Steve portrayed mentors in a similar light, suggesting that mentors felt excitement about guiding startups' early steps:

'There is so much buzz and excitement around startups in Boulder, that I think for some [mentors], it allows them to tap back into that early stage. ... So they like being around, the excitement, and it's amazing that it works out that way. And we're really explicit with the mentors about the fact that this is all volunteer, but for relationships that do work out, typically after the program's over – not typically, it's on a case-by-case basis – if it's a really valuable relationship, that mentor will often be taken on the board of advisors, and then it's not atypical to offer them some equity. But we really try to screen for mentors where that's really not their goal.'

Evident in Juan's and Steve's similar responses are the multiple functions mentors serve for AmpVille. Commissioned by AmpVille, mentors drive a good deal of the learning and refining in which the entrepreneurs engage. Not only do mentors provide valuable perspectives and business advice for getting a company off the ground, but they may also continue to shape the firm's trajectory after the time in AmpVille concludes.

Also evident in the co-directors' comments is mentors' multiple motivations for participation. Another example of this comes from a conversation with Emma, a mentor from the local community – and someone who (as indicated earlier) later became one of AmpVille's co-directors. During the second cohort I observed, Emma entered the space, greeted me, and the following conversation ensued:

Emma: Today's my 'gauntlet' day – I'm working with each of the teams for half an hour each.

TK: That's a lot of work you're donating to these teams. What's in this for you?

Emma: I enjoy working with them. But, to be honest, I'm hoping to get some consulting work, working with these startups in their business plans and value propositions down the road. It's always a bit challenging with these guys, the accelerator model, because they (the entrepreneurs) don't see the need to hire someone to do the sort of work I do on their business models. They feel like they don't have the luxury of thinking through that unless they really need to; they don't appreciate the value of someone forcing them to think critically about their model and their future. When they only have 10 thousand dollars left from their funding, paying for anything outside of immediate needs is tough.

TK: So maybe not in their best long-term interest?

Emma: Right. It's short-sighted. But, you know, the forms I use (these included the business model canvas in Figure 6.3) are publicly available, and they think they can do it themselves – well, they're often mistaken. They don't see how much value I can add through challenging them and getting them to think differently.

TK: How do you help them see that?

Emma: Well, the larger hope is that it'll drum up some business in the future that'll help me make the case. A lot of my work is with larger clients, around 50 (employees) – they're in a different place, they have the ability to think that. What I get for a week with a client like that is almost as much as the teams get all together from AmpVille, so it feels unwise to them. But I'm working with a team from the last [cohort] now, so there may be opportunities for working with these teams down the road. So maybe some contracts in the future.

Emma voices the sort of complex mentor motivation written into an accelerator like AmpVille. She connects her mentorship directly with the important work of developing a business model, acknowledging that the value of her work often goes unrecognized. But the emphasis AmpVille's co-directors place on this form of mentorship is clear, prizing a mentor like Emma's influence over this crucial part of the narrative the startups develop. AmpVille thus is a site of *gravity*, because the attachments on offer from AmpVille – and, in the narrative, only through AmpVille – promise to spark startup performance. Branding AmpVille as a site for startup development via the web of mentorship attachments thus implied branding startups in a similar mode.

All three respondents in this subsection discussed the 'give first' ethos, where participants were expected to contribute to the larger community before they received any remuneration. Mentors, with their particular sets of skills and connections to the Boulder startup scene, were those from whom AmpVille wanted to prompt giving. As one mentor noted in speaking to an audience of AmpVille mentors at another evening event, 'We're all entrepreneurs, so we know where they're (the startup teams) coming from. I believe this is the value that separates successful accelerators from the rest. Safety and comfort is sitting down with someone who has the wisdom – and that's you (mentors), in this room.'

AmpVille's valorization practice thus provided the likelihood of encoding mentors as crucial elements of startups' wanting while also urging startups to want mentors' guidance; the valorization of mentorship simultaneously encoded AmpVille as a site where mentors' multiple interests could be met.

Valorizing funding

An attention to funding was a result not merely of startups' need to financially support their growth, but also of AmpVille's needs as an enterprise (since the accelerator's profits depended on its startups' subsequent financial success). Given the focus of this chapter, however, the more relevant question is how practices associated with attracting funding privilege a particular order of worth.

Juan (again, one of AmpVille's co-directors) depicted the importance of funding as a need felt by the accelerator – again, as a firm itself. Given that need, many accelerators cater to the desires of investors. Investors participate in the program as mentors, consult with AmpVille's directors on which startups are most promising (which are likely 'winners'), and attend Demo Days:

> 'A lot of accelerators have started focusing on the investor, and have begun to raise bigger and bigger funds, follow-on funds, try to get people to invest in their winners and everything. They're re-asserting the investor, and even if they claim that they're not, they're going to have to make decisions based on how to optimize for those funds that they're building, right? In our case, we definitely serve the investors *and* serve mentors. And even when our primary customer is the entrepreneur, and we make decisions based on, "is this going to be best for the entrepreneur?," sometimes it does mean let's focus on the investor. We have them as a primary customer.'

Here, Juan articulates the tensions across the key participants in AmpVille's assemblage, situating investors and mentors as central nodes shaping decidability in AmpVille. He maintains that for AmpVille's co-directors, the startup teams (the entrepreneurs) are still the primary focus, but his attention to the funds the investors provide – the funds without which AmpVille could not operate – suggest that the model of authority recognized that its purpose was tied closely to the interests of the investor class.

AmpVille's emphasis on locating funding was evident in everyday decision-making as well. These practices were often associated with branding – branding not only the accelerator, but also the startups found in it. A representative example came from an interview with a startup founder, Simon, conducted 2 months after his 12-week AmpVille experience concluded.[3] During the program, Simon's company, a peer-to-peer financial technology firm, attracted a $25,000 'angel' investment from a high-profile founder of a much larger and more established firm in (roughly) the same industry. That other firm had just gone public and netted its founder a large windfall and international recognition. An investment from such a figure was a branding victory for Simon's startup, a moment to claim both legitimacy and worth in that field – and, as he noted to me, also the potential for 'lots of contacts with players in that space' otherwise unavailable. This branding-via-attachment would not have occurred without the exposure and attachments provided by AmpVille.

A central AmpVille lesson was that branding-via-attachment is a key element of any firm's narrative of value. This was the case both for AmpVille (as a venture) and for the startups in its cohorts. AmpVille's co-directors repeatedly made the case that, in venues such as Demo Day, startup founders needed to make the case for 'traction' (momentum and progress) to investors via a vocabulary of users, revenue, and external investment. Simon made that case in his Demo Day talk and, despite his company having no revenue at that point, the attractiveness of the idea and the endorsement of the high-profile investor appeared persuasive, supporting AmpVille's argument about branding.

In another interview 4 months after the conclusion of his AmpVille experience, Simon recounted the events that transpired following Demo Day, which further demonstrate AmpVille's practice of valorizing investment. He mentioned that, at a reception immediately following the Demo Day presentation, he was approached by a representative of a venture capital (VC) firm interested in his company. A meeting was scheduled for the following week, and at the meeting the VC firm offered a $500,000 investment in exchange for a 30 per cent ownership stake in the company. Simon consulted with the AmpVille co-directors, whose advice was to accept the offer. Simon reflected on the exchange:

> 'Tony, from AmpVille, has been pressuring me like hell to take the money. They're our shareholders, so we told them about this offer – and they're also our advisors still, so we keep them close and informed. ... It became very clear when the money was on the table, that the advice they were giving was advice *for AmpVille*, and not advice for [my company]. I understand. Tony's got his own [business], he's got to run it, he's raising more funds for the next two classes, he's got to have some success stories. I get it. But it's also

short-sighted. Tony needs results today because he's going to go talk to his own investors tomorrow. I need results 2 to 3 years from now.'

Simon explained his thinking, balancing claims to property with the development of his startup's value. In his estimation, the offer exceeded the startup's needs at that moment and would have sacrificed substantial control (property rights) for the future:

> 'They wanted too much of my company – they wanted 30 per cent for half a million. And it's like we don't need that much money right now – where we are, we can do a lot of growth, we can get really far on much less money than that. [The VC firm] also wanted board control – they wanted the sun and the moon, so we just said no. ... I think that if we demonstrate any kind of traction – if we got that offer when we were essentially pre-revenue, what's it going to be when we have 10,000 users? ... and if we had accepted that deal, they would have owned more of the company than [my co-founder].'

The tension between AmpVille's branding for its primary audience ('Tony needs results today because he's going to talk to his investors tomorrow') and the desired trajectory of a startup is laid bare in this example. Although AmpVille sought to exert influence over decidability, Simon expressed elements of an authoritative text's conceptions of property and value as extending across time; relying on these resources led him to decline the VC firm's offer despite Tony's advice.

As the preceding example makes plain, co-directors' urging of startups to accept funding is closely coupled to the metrics of success to which AmpVille must respond. Steve mentioned in a presentation to the cohort teams that AmpVille:

FIELDNOTES

'[P]repares you for how to talk to investors, to make sure that they have all the paperwork and term sheets, everything really professionally done, so that we make sure that every single startup has all their paperwork in place, and is working with CFOs, financial advisors, ahead of time. Honestly, there's a lot of stuff, and it's constantly changing.'

A few weeks later, Steve dropped by where I was sitting in the AmpVille space, mentioning that he was checking on a company that hadn't been showing up recently. It was in the latter weeks of the session when teams don't need to be physically present in the AmpVille space each day, but he noted that this startup 'didn't turn in some homework we had assigned the teams.'

Connecting with the preceding practice, Steve mentioned that this absence was a potential concern for AmpVille's relationships with its set of mentors, but noted that this is even more a problem for attachments to *investors*:

'Our funders, investors, want to know who's a good bet. They come to [the co-directors] to get advice on which teams to pay attention to. And sure, we have our favorites, but that changes based on what goals they meet, what milestones they hit, whether they get a UI (User Interface) operational, and whether they leapfrog other groups. Look, we (the co-directors) and AmpVille are judged on how many teams get funding after coming through – so a dropout is a problem. That's a problem as we think about how we're going to grow and evolve AmpVille.'

Echoing the example from Simon, Steve here notes how the practice of valorizing investor funding is an instrumental goal for AmpVille, one that becomes part of the tacit curriculum of the accelerator. Like many practices, there is no bright line between valorizing investment and valorizing mentorship, but Steve signals how an allegiance to investors drives the accelerator's practice.

Summary

On the face of it, none of the three practices presented here – valorizing the technologically cool, valorizing mentorship, and valorizing funding – would seem to occur in the conventional register of branding. Each appears to be about the resources for a budding business to prosper, and thus not merely about the image the startup conveys to the external world. From the perspective of the CTF, the interestingness of branding is not the symbolic depiction of a firm or its products (though those can certainly be fascinating); instead, branding reveals struggles over meaning carried out in the everyday practice of a firm's continual becoming. Branding is about developing and deploying firms' authoritative texts in ways designed to bind audiences to the firm. In this way, branding allows analysts to trace the sources of (the influence over) what becomes their wanting; the economies of worth literature aids in making sense of the logics applied to firms' appeals.

From this perspective, AmpVille's business model was clearly based on conveying the value of branding to its startup teams. By centring the three practices discussed, AmpVille engaged in its own branding endeavour, developing an authoritative text to appeal to those in the Boulder startup assemblage to whom its work was obligated: investors and mentors. Those investors and mentors brought AmpVille into existence, nurtured its startups along their developmental path, and invested in those same startups to create a significant financial payout for the accelerator.[4] AmpVille, in other words, engaged in prophecy: predicting the future returns of these forms of valorization to promise value to startups, mentors, and investors simultaneously.

Moreover, these practices display that branding exceeds the symbolic domain.[5] Valorizing funding, for instance, would appear to emphasize the material, in that funding would appear to be about the attraction of financial capital – what is typically taken to be matter. But the communicative stance on new materialism pursued throughout this book argues instead for practices of matter*ing* as the site to discern the forces that flow through assemblages. When it comes to funding, consequently, the important question is not about the existence of dollars as material entities, nor is it about those dollars' signaling capacities (indeed, money has never *not* been sociomaterial, as Simmel [1907/ 1978] argued over a century ago). The question, like most questions in this book, is what firms want funding to *do* for them – and, in turn, about where such wanting might originate and where that wanting would take the firm.

The same goes for valorizing the technologically cool: the important question is about how 'cool' can be marshalled as a marker of distinctiveness that connects with other forces characterizing the Boulder startup assemblage. The focus on coolness with respect to the business model, as noted, also directed attention away from the material infrastructure enabling such plans (in other words, those elements weren't *made to matter*). When attention turns to mattering, the examination of the multiplicity of forces shaping branding – a multiplicity that is demonstrably the case among AmpVille's nascent firms – displays the intersections of a myriad of forces. The CTF's conception of assemblage highlights the points of connection, the nodal points, through which those forces flowed.

AmpVille's wanting shaped startups' wantings. The model of property and value inhabited by AmpVille – its brand – was simultaneously the reason startups congregated in that Boulder office building basement *and* the vehicle for the valorizations seen here. The final section returns to the notion of orders of worth to explore the implications of this particular configuration of wanting.

Conclusion

This chapter addresses the theory of the firm questions regarding the mode of ('internal') organizing and the generation of profit. AmpVille's funding depended on the financial success of the startups it nurtured (and in which AmpVille had a financial stake), and startups' futures depended on the access to mentorship and funding in the surrounding assemblage made possible by their participation in the accelerator. The coupling between AmpVille and any given startup was loose, in that sources of funding and mentorship are available without the assistance of an accelerator, and AmpVille was not dependent on financial returns from *each one* of its startups to fund its ongoing operations. Yet AmpVille and its startups were tightly connected at several nodal points, as illustrated through the three practices seen in this chapter (again, valorizing the technologically cool, mentorship, and funding).

The preceding section argued that AmpVille's wanting was a response to its business model and position in the startup assemblage. Specifically, what AmpVille wanted was to draw upon the Boulder startup community (along with established models of startup creation) to configure startups that, in turn, created value for that community. In creating value for the community, startups would themselves attract value via funding that would, in turn (and in time), produce financial returns for AmpVille via its ownership stakes in the startups.

The notion of 'creating value,' used twice in the previous paragraph, is a common trope in the startup world. Perhaps because of that ordinariness, it is rare to see an interrogation of 'value' when it is deployed. Boltanski and Thévenot, with whom this chapter started, would not countenance such an oversight. The practices characterizing the Boulder startup assemblage would, from the data presented in this chapter, appear to draw primarily from a market order of worth, where the startups that are AmpVille's product are to be judged on their ability to successfully compete for funding by investors. At the same time, however, there are elements of the industrial order of worth that shape AmpVille practice, where business plans that build on the technologically cool serve as technical objects that demonstrate the competence and expertise of the startup team members. The same logics appear to apply to AmpVille's co-directors, who recognize that the viability of their firm hinges on the ability of their brand to attract the attention of mentors and investors in a competitive startup market (recall that the much-better-known Techstars operated just a few blocks from AmpVille) and to also demonstrate technical efficiency in cultivating startups that will, over time, pay financial dividends.

AmpVille's practice, in other words, drew largely on the *market* and *industrial* orders of worth, the first two columns in Table 6.1. AmpVille's desire to create itself as a viable enterprise relied on its own market competitiveness and technical competence, demonstrated primarily through the startups it nurtured (and promoted to both mentors and investors). Given these domains, the tests of worth (Boltanski & Thévenot, 1991/2006) involved AmpVille's startups receiving investment funding or being approached as acquisition targets by larger firms. And because AmpVille could display several successes on these fronts to the Boulder startup community, it could claim to have passed its tests.

The contradiction is that the entrepreneurs running through the accelerator program drew on a broader range of justificatory logics. Startup founders were well aware of the centrality of market and industrial orders of worth in the entrepreneurial game, but they voiced several additional modes of evaluation. For instance, one founder of an advertising technology firm described the need to speak to an additional form of value as he hired software developers in the 2 years after his time at AmpVille:

'[Developers] are very mission-oriented; they're really in search of a *why*. I'll give you an example. So I need to hire developers, right? What [other entrepreneurs] see is that there's four jobs for every developer, and every developer is making $200,000, and I just can't compete with that. And I recognized that pretty early on. So when I sit down with a Millennial, who can choose to go anywhere, and I can't compete on salary, but I do have a sense of purpose. So for me it was, how do I construct a narrative for a very drab ad tech application, like who the fuck wants to do work in advertising? How is that exciting? Frankly, just *as* advertising, it isn't. But the motivator is that, generally, engineers like to solve big problems.'

This entrepreneur described his conversations with potential hires, telling them about the scale of the projects on which they could work, likely appealing to an industrial order of worth, where value is to be found in engineering competence. He made an interesting move as he continued:

'And the problem we're addressing expresses itself into a larger societal equity conversation, even if it doesn't look like that from the outside … I go into the larger problem. The problem is, [this large-scale ad tech problem] is overseen by fucking powerful interests. And what kind of society do we live in where only those powerful guys can access it, because they're the ones who can hire the ad agencies? How about seeing something relevant to me and actually getting traction from local businesses and the little guy? And that's going to require us to do the following kind of work. By the end of it, I have these kids jumping at the chance to work for me. And then you have to back it up – that's got to be the central mission and purpose of your company, and that's going to be what we do to make an impact.'

This entrepreneur displays how at least one additional order of worth displayed in Table 6.1 – the *civic* (and perhaps also the *inspired*) – is central to the multiple purposes flowing through his firm. The desire to be on the side of 'the little guy' and to engage in a noble battle with powerful and established corporate interests appealed, in his telling, to interviewees' sense of equality and solidarity. Such a David and Goliath narrative was present for another co-founder who, when asked about the value of startup entrepreneurship, replied:

'It's about disruption, the disruption of corporate power – at least that's what *we're* trying to do. You know, most businesses in the US are small businesses, but large corporate entities set the tone and have the most influence. Startups have the potential to challenge that dominance.'

As amorphous as 'corporate power' may be, challenging corporate domination was an additional justificatory logic legitimizing startup entrepreneurship. Many startup entrepreneurs gathering in AmpVille saw themselves as engaged in a righteous battle against corporate power. Such assertions invoked an anti-corporate solidarity, one that appealed to conceptions of justice beyond the bounds of the market and industrial orders. This is clearly a model of branding active among startups, but largely ignored in the program AmpVille presented to entrepreneurs.

Any scepticism about whether such models of activist branding map directly onto practice would miss the point of heterarchy, as discussed. If heterarchy is built upon the entrepreneurial drive to keep multiple evaluative principles in play and profit from their tensions, any narrowing of orders of worth would present a threat to that entrepreneurial endeavour. In its restriction of value to market and industrial registers, AmpVille constrained startup founders' ability to exploit those frictions. In other words, they *hindered heterarchy*, narrowing the evaluative criteria applied to startups to those associated with the market and industrial domains. If Stark and collaborators are right that exploiting the interplay of multiple evaluative criteria is key to organizational profit, AmpVille's branding would appear to impede its own interests with respect to shaping the startups coming through its program.

It is the CTF's assertion that branding is a communicative practice *constitutive of* the firm; it is not merely the superficial presentation of a desirable image for consumption by an audience. Unique to the CTF is an understanding of branding as the communicative production of territorialization, which is both situated in and expressed through a firm's authoritative text. It is precisely this vantage point that creates a capacity to see the dis/organizational consequence in the AmpVille case. As an authority machine operating in, and as, an assemblage, the accelerator's promise of value to its customers (mentors and investors) revolved around shaping its products (the startups coming through its program) as technically competent commodities valuable in a marketplace. The forms of valuation encoded into AmpVille's authoritative text thus influenced the narratives of the startups becoming enterprises in its (physical and conceptual) space, and did so in ways that potentially confined the evaluative principles that could be met in those startups' own branding – their own narrativizing of the 'we.'

Branding, as a practice of organizational becoming and an expression of organizational wanting, is always a product of the possibilities established by the coding of the assemblage. In a startup community like Boulder, the expectations for a firm like AmpVille – a firm that produced startups for both its key constituencies and for its own profitability – developing a brand like the one depicted in this chapter may well be a logical positioning. What the CTF allows, however, is an analysis of the complex ways the enactment of the brand-as-business model generates unanticipated tensions that may be inimical to a firm's longer-term interest. And if branding is also always about an excess of meanings, it is unlikely that AmpVille's influence could ever fully contain the impulses associated with other orders of worth. A recognition of hindered heterarchy could, therefore, lead to a rhizomatic challenge to AmpVille's mode of startup creation.

These issues can serve a heuristic function in driving future research. But there exist also *ethical* questions: to what extent can branding practices that constrain the becoming of other participants in an assemblage – even when those participants are a firm's *products*, as startups were for AmpVille – be defensible? And how are assessments of such practices' (in)defensibility transformed by recognitions of the boundarying practices (for example, excluding the material elements required to produce data exhaust) that make a given mode of branding possible? Also, how might the recognition of multiple modes of evaluation constrain critique? Few ethical questions have simple answers, but one of the hallmarks of the CTF is that it both makes visible and forces a consideration of precisely these issues.

Notes

[1] This is in contrast to the notion of asset *specificity* developed by Riordan and Williamson (1985) as a key contribution to the transaction cost theory of the firm.

[2] All names of AmpVille participants, as well as 'AmpVille,' are pseudonyms.

[3] An expanded version of this case can be found in Kuhn (2017b).

[4] As of this writing, AmpVille claims that of the over 200 startups that have come through its programs, 94 per cent are generating revenue. It also asserts that the accelerator's portfolio of investment stakes in startups is valued at roughly $1.5 billion.

[5] It's also important to note that the interview responses, as well as the conversations occurring with actors in the scene, are not to be considered the *doings* of practice themselves. They are reports and recollections of practices; as such, they may generate performative effects in the scene (Mazzei, 2013), but the aim here is to provide insight into the conduct of the accelerator, where such utterances are taken to provide access to those practices that would escape my ethnographic observational activity.

7

Binding: Collective Atomization
and B Corps

With respect to corporate purpose, the corporate social responsibility (CSR) debate noted in the Introduction is, in one respect, over. Those who, like the representatives of the Chicago School of Economics, argue that the sole purpose of a corporation is to deliver profits to shareholders seem to have lost the argument to those who contend that corporations must be responsive to a much broader set of stakeholders, at least in the public square. Some corners of legal scholarship, however, continue to hold that a commitment to shareholder value maximization (SVM) is gospel truth: 'it is black letter law, according to most scholars, that corporations exist to maximize shareholder wealth' (Mocsary, 2016, p 1320).[1] Assertions of this sort tend to rely on the notion that shareholders own the property of the firm and thus deserve (have property rights over) its profits, though some hold that the question is less about ownership than an agreement between those who have provided capital to the firm in exchange for residual claims on its assets (recall Grandori's [2022] argument here, presented in Chapter 4). Others advocating SVM declare that it is explicitly *not* law, but rather an efficient and sensible ideology superior to any dogma that accords the authority of governance to an array of *stake*holders (Macey, 2013).

Staunch proponents of SVM have all but disappeared in public discourse, replaced by those who acknowledge a need to attend to a wider array of concerns in corporations' action. Sometimes these aims manifest in 'ESG' (Environment, Social, and Governance) programs, sometimes it's the 'triple bottom line,' sometimes it's about the need to embrace circular economics, sometimes it's the summoning of business leaders to address 'grand challenges,' and sometimes it's about development aimed at the 'bottom of the pyramid.' Regardless of the route to using business to produce social benefit, when powerful corporate forces like the US Business Roundtable or the elites at Davos agree that businesspeople must deploy their economic clout to solve vexing social problems and to take a stand on international conflicts, there's no denying that the tide has turned against Friedman and his ilk (see Rhodes, 2022; Kelley, 2023; Wright, 2023).

Irrespective of the earnestness with which such pronouncements and injunctions are made, there are *many* reasons to be skeptical that corporate practices are as enlightened as the discourse appears (Kuhn & Deetz, 2008; Hanlon & Fleming, 2009). Skeptics acknowledge that 'good business' can be just as much about drawing attention to a firm's branding endeavour as it is about creating substantive change in the world inhabited by the firm. Rather than assessing CSR initiatives as greenwashing or purpose-washing – two interpretations that draw heavily on questionable distinctions between talk and action (Marshak, 1998) – the CTF stance instead directs attention to the *character of attachments* that arise when authoritative texts highlight a firm's putatively ethical commitments.[2] Instead of asserting that an analyst can know the 'true' intentions behind action (which would violate the ontological multiplicity of purpose guiding the CTF while inserting a dodgy anthropomorphism), the move here is to interrogate the bindings that unfold when the firm *wants* to be implicated in positive social change.

A question like that is not about the firm's founders or strategic managers; it is about the assemblage through (and because of) which the firm and its wanting emerges. And rather than starting with the firm as a focal entity and then tracing its connections with other participants, it makes sense to turn the issue around. If, as the CTF argues, firms are the *result* of assemblages – if they are necessary devices for encompassing assemblages to (re)produce communicative capitalism – one might instead ask how desires flowing through the assemblage guide and direct the creation of particular renditions of corporate purpose. In other words, we might ask *how the assemblage's participants and practices play a role in writing purpose(s) into a firm's authoritative text* – along with *what consequences that writing creates*. Fortunately, one relatively recent effort to shape firms, benefit corporations, provides fertile ground for engagement with this question.

Benefit Corporations as platforms

Benefit Corporations, or B Corps[TM], mentioned briefly in Chapter 4, are relatively new entrants on the corporate scene. In conventional corporate legal guidelines, a firm's governance commits to the 'best interest of the corporation,' a line that has traditionally been interpreted as producing SVM and the arborescent assemblage accompanying it. In contrast, B Corps work into their charters explicit *stake*holder commitments; that they pledge to benefit the environment, workers, and local communities through their everyday activity. The ambition is grand:

We envision a global economy that uses business as a force for good. This economy is comprised of a new type of corporation – the B Corporation – which is purpose-driven and creates benefit for all stakeholders, not just shareholders.

As Certified B Corporations and leaders of this emerging economy, we believe:

- That we must be the change we seek in the world.
- That all business ought to be conducted as if people and place mattered.
- That, through their products, practices, and profits, businesses should aspire to do no harm and benefit all.
- To do so requires that we act with the understanding that we are each dependent upon another and thus responsible for each other and future generations. (B Lab, 2023a)

Because these commitments are centrally codified and standardized, B Corps, despite their efforts to create new social realities, generally exhibit an arborescent coding of the firm similar to more conventional corporate forms (see Dobusch & Kapeller, 2018).

Key to thinking about that centralized codification and standardization – that arborescence – of the B Corp 'movement'[3] is to see it as a *platform*. In the US, it all started in 2006, when Jay Coen Gilbert, Bart Houlahan, and Andrew Kassoy – three friends who met as undergraduates at Stanford – sought to provide an alternative to businesses' traditional focus on SVM. Believing that the challenge to enable that alternative resided in legal codes and accounting systems, they launched B Lab™ (https://www.bcorp oration.net), a nonprofit that provides resources to companies seeking to (re)define themselves as public benefit corporations (Marquis, 2020). Since its founding, B Lab has successfully lobbied governments worldwide to accept B Corps as legitimate corporate forms; as of this writing, there are over 8,200 Benefit Corporations operating in 96 countries; in the US, 35 US states and the District of Columbia allow companies to operate under this banner. Legislation is thus a crucial participant in the becoming of individual B Corps, not to mention as an enabler of the larger B Corp community (Lucas et al, 2022). The reliance on legal codes underscores the arboreal character of the platform, but I'll argue that there's a rhizomatic side to be found here that is in tension with the narrative power of aborescence.

Becoming and remaining a B Corp requires significant effort, and certification is tightly controlled by B Lab. Being a B Corp isn't a mere matter of declaration; representatives of a given firm – from a startup[4] to a large multinational – must participate in a rigorous certification and re-certification process. A host of resources is available to certified and potential B Corps, including narratives of successful B Corps on the B Lab website (as well as on social media) and regular webinars describing the B Corporation mission and processes of certification. Moreover, there are 'B Local' chapters across the world that run events celebrating existing and aspiring B Corp businesses, provide networking opportunities, and coordinate volunteering endeavours.

Some of the event and celebration activity could be considered proselytizing – preaching a gospel of ethical business to the converted (and not-yet-converted) – but it also provides a set of lessons for becoming a member of the community. Attendees at webinars and in-person events need not be members of existing or aspiring B Corps companies (incidentally, there exists a separate 'B Academics' arm), but the presence of interested parties who unfailingly express strong support for both the B Corp movement and companies pursuing certification generates a sense that this is a noble vision with the power of community support and moral rectitude on its side.

As one might imagine, there are several critical examinations of the B Corp movement in both OS literature and the public eye. Observers express concern for its ambitious aims, its impacts on firms' growth, and the potential for 'purpose-washing' of conventional corporate practice (Gehman et al, 2019; Parker et al, 2019). Others allege that B Corps can divert attention from the need for large-scale governmental change (Wilken, 2015; Woods, 2016; Gilbert, 2018). The aim of this chapter is not to settle such irresolvable questions, but to probe the implications of deliberate efforts to make corporations *want* to both be 'responsible' and change the very capitalist assemblage they inhabit.

Although its tools aren't app-based or AI-enabled as in much of communicative capitalism, firms become B Corps both through the certification regimen *and* the valorizing of B Corps' practices. In this sense, B Corps, and the B Lab organization that grounds them, is not simply a social movement pressing for purpose-driven and ethical business; it is thus also a *platform* providing resources that simultaneously enable and constrain the actions of the firms that secure legitimacy from the association. This is a key sense in which B Corps serve as a platform, in line with the discussion in Chapter 1: the platform operator (here, the global enterprise B Lab) provides a set of tools and expectations that allow users to establish a presence on the platform, with rules established by the owner (a claim to property is thus present from the very beginning). Successful completion of certification carries with it both full membership in the community and the capacity to use the B Corp logo on products, storefronts, and publications.

Restating the reason for firms' existence from Chapter 4, B Lab and the B Corp community *need* individual firms to become and remain B Corps to advance this atypical corporate form and to usher in the re-configuration they desire in the larger capitalist assemblage. The question for this chapter, accordingly, is how the B Corp platform participates in authoring its firms' authoritative texts. Because there is an obvious attachment between the platform and member B Corps, this chapter will explore how binding unfolds through the platform–firm relationship. As such, the focus turns not to the communicative constitution of any particular B Corp, but to the relations of authority and associated logics of practice that shape the *becomings* of these firms.

B Corps and making firms want: forms of binding

Authority, as articulated in Chapter 4, is a matter of both promises of value and claims to property. Authoritative texts are the products of, but also resources for, the firm-implicating communication practices that I called boundarying, branding, and binding. Those communication practices unfold in and through an assemblage, making the practices of binding, or attaching, a key question for understanding both the constitution of authority and the trajectory of the firm (as authority machine). The assemblage provides the potential for becoming – and also for rhizomatic dis/organization via the virtual domain. In the case of B Corps, there are two forms of binding associated with the platformed development of purpose.

Participating in purpose

The first binding practice involves cultivating attachments between the firm and elements of the surrounding assemblage. Many of the practices associated with B Lab and B Local chapters is, as mentioned, evangelical in orientation, where one aim appears to be cultivating converts: persuading individuals associated with not-yet-B Corps to pursue certification while also appealing to others to support the movement through philanthropic donations to the B Lab nonprofit organization (B Lab, 2023b). There is also substantial preaching to the choir: convincing leaders of current B Corp firms that they are on a righteous path as part of a social movement for social and environmental justice. Coming from a central location, this would again seem to be an instance of arboreal organizing: a platform operator aligning the wanting of its many constituents. However, I'll show how the picture is more complicated.

One way this binding appears is in B Lab's Theory of Change (B Lab, 2023c) which makes the movement's need for individual firms evident. At a webinar[5] directed to a Canadian and US audience (B Lab, 2021), a B Lab officer presented the movement's model for how the ambitious change agenda could be accomplished. Two slides from her presentation exhibit the logic:

The argument advocates a widespread socio-economic change, one that involves the intersections between business laws, norms, and behaviours. She argued that because only *behaviours* are immediately controllable,

Figure 7.1: The B Lab™ model of large-scale systems change

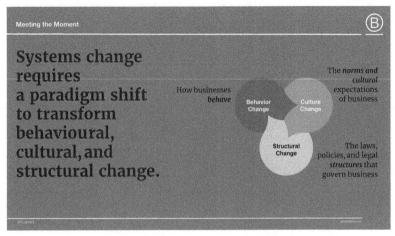

Source: B Lab

urging businesses to shift their practices to full engagement with stakeholder thinking – 'becom[ing] a force for good' – is the spur needed to change the capitalist system. The means by which that 'inclusive, equitable, and regenerative economic system' will materialize is not spelled out, however:

> 'At B Lab, we know that in order to change the system, we must take a holistic approach. We must change not only how businesses behave but also the cultural expectations of businesses. The laws and policies and legal structures that govern businesses and the markets that we operate within. So we have to take this holistic approach. Doing so will allow us to move toward our global vision re of redefining the role of business, so that it is truly a force for good, and eventually changing the economic system so that it that it contributes to equity regeneration and wellbeing and redistributes power instead of consolidating it. ... So we understand now the levers of change, those are the culture, the behaviours and the structure that surround business and also the vision and the objectives that we want to achieve.'

The predicted transformation, in this officer's eyes, will be the result of a critical mass of similarly guided B Corps that inspire more widespread change among *non*-B Corporations, and the passion of the movement will instigate normative and legislative change (as depicted in Figure 7.1).

In a separate presentation, a B Lab Senior Insight Analyst discussed the devices designed to induce that change (Glasgow Caledonian New York College, 2022). Those include (a) a community of thousands of 'credible leaders,' (b) B Lab's 'impact assessment' and the injunction that B Lab must

Figure 7.2: The B Lab™ call to alter the role of business in society

Meeting the Moment

The change we seek can only be accomplished by shifting the role of business

so that it becomes a force for good – changing the nature of the system itself and moving towards a more inclusive, equitable, and regenerative future.

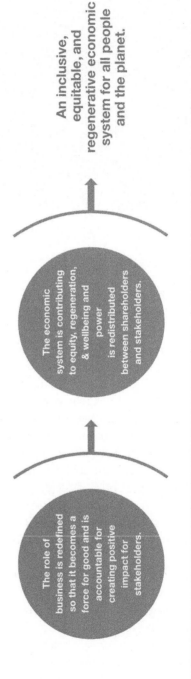

The role of business is redefined so that it becomes a force for good and is accountable for creating positive impact for stakeholders.

The economic system is contributing to equity, regeneration, & wellbeing and power is redistributed between shareholders and stakeholders.

An inclusive, equitable, and regenerative economic system for all people and the planet.

© B Lab 2021

bcorporation.net

Source: B Lab

'create tools to make it easy for millions of other businesses to follow,' (c) a 'communications [*sic*] infrastructure to inspire millions of consumers, workers, investors, and others to support businesses who are a force for good,' and (d) the Benefit Corporation as a legal framework for changing policy. In this second talk, what is evident is not merely the grandness of scale, but a call to the audience, urging them to participate in 'shifting the role of business' (as also seen in Figure 7.2).

This articulation of the transformational ambition alongside the need to join the community was articulated in that previous B Labs officer's words in 2021 as well:

'I want to stop and talk about why we believe that this community of B Corporations are credible change agents – why we believe that you can really help us to create this change that we seek. It's really because you've gone through an incredibly rigorous journey. It's because of what makes you a B Corp that measuring and improving your holistic impact, embedding benefit governance that changes your operating system, committing to the ongoing transparency and third party validation that's required for certification and joining this community, and ultimately coming together to mobilize is this holistic and rigorous journey that makes us credible.'

Later in the talk she described the significance of that community:

'so that looks like continuing to recruit companies that demonstrate their commitment to using business as a force for good and encouraging them to join our B community. We'll do that not only on our own, but we will continue to and increasingly work with partner organizations who are supporting these companies to bring them into our community ... our strategies are really in a cycle, we know that we must first start by, by recruiting the right companies and supporting them in really deriving value. And then from there we'll continue to foster opportunities to connect and learn from each other, join the network space and identity impact area and more.'

One important move in the practice of 'Participating in Purpose' is thus to enrol B Corp firms into a 'community' where all members are deeply committed to transforming the economic system. The architects of the platform recognize that constituting an assemblage in which individual firms spark behavioural change is necessary in the transformation of the encompassing capitalist assemblage. Binding thus involves creating attachments between firms and the constituents of community. The B Corp movement prizes this interdependency as key to its aim of re-imagining capitalism. Inviting participation is, then, a form of Callon's (2017) *co-production*, discussed as a mechanism of attachment in Chapter 3.

The practice of enrolling participants in the B Corp purpose is also evident among those member firms. Suppliers and customers are frequently presented as networked participants to be configured as contributors to a shared pursuit. In a B Local event (for community members in a particular geographical region), in response to a question about how B Corp leaders extend their influence outside the boundaries of the firm ('how do I spread this knowledge, this way of thinking, outside my own corporation?'), one panellist responded that her business devotes 20 per cent of sales to charities and nonprofits. Another B Corp panellist chimed in with a note of evangelization:

> 'we focus on spreading the message of B Corp to all our clients. Basically, anytime we either talk to a client or have a new client, we ask them if they know what a B Corp is, that's kind of our first step. And a lot of the time they don't, and that's when we give them a very tiny, non-intrusive elevator spiel about what a B Corp does. And then a lot of times, what these companies end up coming to us for, not only what they've asked, but then talking about a CSR program – so, corporate social responsibility in some of these companies that are not a B Corp, they end up wanting to start small. ... So a lot of it is having that conversation, not forcing it to become a B Corp, just having that conversation in a very non-intrusive way, and seeing what they're already doing in their company and how they can talk to their audiences and their clients ... just having that conversation is really important.'

At the same B Local session, a second panellist weighed in similarly:

> 'For us, it's not necessarily clients, but contractors. We're trying to help people use their spending money to help make the world better; we try to do the same thing as a company. So we have a stated policy that when choosing contractors we always give preference to certified B Corps, and when we're choosing between two different agencies and we told one of the contractors, "you know, it's close, we kinda like you both. But they're a certified B Corp, and you're not. Will you become a certified B Corp if you want our business?" And they said that they would. And another, the partner businesses we work with are already at a pretty high level in terms of social impact, but for businesses that don't quite make the cut, we won't just say no, we'll say, "why don't you go take the B Lab impact assessment. Become a Certified B Corp, and then come back to us."'

Significantly, the commitments of a firm's contractors and suppliers are a component of B Lab's certification process, such that becoming and remaining a B Corp *requires* firms to configure their networks as seen here: with an eye toward those sharing the value stance that being a B Corp requires.

A final example was offered at another B Local event, where a panel was assembled to discuss the relevance of B Corp status on company operations. One panellist, the CEO of a small company, described a difficult financial struggle in the early days of her business. She invoked the uniqueness of B Corps on three fronts: for intra-organizational decision-making, for the clients they attract, and for the extra-organizational sources of support they enjoy. She began by describing the transparency with employees implied in operating as a B Corp, and attributed a successful response to that financial struggle as an outgrowth of the values implied in being a B Corp:

'It was because of being a B Corp that actually helped us through that situation. And when I say that, it's not because of the B Corp certification score. ... When we actually answer those questions on that (certification) assessment, it's a representation of the character of our company. A representation of how we operate, and how we function – and because of our dedication to social impact, the types of clients we attract are generous and kind. And because we deliver great service, they were actually going to prepay for the work. And they helped us. And they knew that we were in a bind and wanted to help us. And it's not just the relationship with our clients – it's also the relationship with each other, with our team. Because the transparency and the trust with each other, because we had the ability to have a conversation about "we know we don't want to go bankrupt, so let's figure this out together." It meant that everybody's job mattered; it meant that everything that they wanted to bring to the table made a difference to our company and the trajectory of where we were going to go. We did make the next payroll, and the next. And then I bought the company. [Cheering from audience]

The truth of it is, being a B Corp, the values that we hold actually created this culture that allowed us to get out of that situation. So it's so much more than just the assessment and the certification. It's how you operate as a company and how you function as a team. It created hope for us when probably, there really shouldn't be much hope. But it was built into our DNA, to have trust, to collaborate, and to work together. To trust our community and to bring them into that conversation.

I actually called several B Corp CEOs and asked for advice: "Have you ever been in this situation? Because I need help." And because of this community, I got the help I needed. And that's how we got out of it.' [followed by raucous applause]

In short, then, the logic of being a B Corp, on display in sessions instructing new potential B Corp members about the value of community (such as proffering the platform, locating assistance in the local community of suppliers, employees, and other B Corp leaders), summons the binding of participants to the firm. Prophesying the benefit of sympathetic connections creates a promise of value.

In the language of the CTF, this section shows both the shaping of firms' authoritative texts and the consequences of those texts' deployment in routine practice. The platform urges individual B Corps to portray themselves in terms of their membership in a community committed to using for-profit business to make local and global transformations in capitalist practice. In displaying the authoring of authoritative texts, the section also provides insight into the sources of corporations' *wanting*: the coding of their authoritative texts proceeds through the binding of firm to platform, as well as in the binding of contractors and clients/customers to the firm. These bindings occur in the certification process, in public presentations, and in everyday events involving (more or less) routine firm activity. What becomes evident, however, is that the wanting is not merely an outgrowth of the B Lab directives or the B Corp platform as interpreted by these firms' strategic managers; the cases also imply the involvement of other participants in the assemblage (contractors, logos, customers, employees, other B Corp executives, certification scores, alongside flows of trust, morality, and ownership) in the production of wanting. The following section addresses a somewhat different form of binding that nonetheless writes authoritative texts, illustrating how wanting travels through assemblages.

Narrativizing materiality

A second form of binding is the building of attachments between the platform, firm, and nonhuman elements of the assemblage. Here, I focus particularly on what is rendered as the domain of the material world encountered by current and potential B Corp members. The focus here is on the narratives that come to characterize the firm and its logic of practice; because such narratives are components of firms' authoritative texts, they are useful vehicles for analysing platform influence over the conception of the material in firms' wanting.

One manifestation of this platform-level influence was B Lab's announcement of its agenda for the B Corp community. The 'three pillars' of the B Corps movement were (and, as of this writing, still are) climate equity, racial justice, and stakeholder governance, but at that June 2021 webinar – roughly 1 year after the murder of George Floyd that sparked protests for racial justice around the globe – the first B Lab officer announced that B Lab was advancing that second pillar as the most crucial for its overall aims:

'As a community, we know that it's incredibly important that that now, at present, we focus in on racial equity and this is because, well, research and history have shown us that, in order to address equity for all – for us in the US and Canada again this is based on over 400 years of systemic oppression, and so this means focusing *first* on racial equity in the pursuit of equity and justice for all. As just an example to paint a picture of what this might look like, we're going to work together with you, with the B community and our partners to develop our specific calls to action. You can imagine that this focus might mean something like calling on business leaders to pay a living wage to all employees. This supports equity for all, but it will especially help those low-wage and front-line workers that are disproportionately black and brown. As we are addressing racial *in*equity, we're recognizing that racial *equity* is inextricably linked to all forms of oppression. And as we focus on both climate justice and racial equity we'll take an intersectional lens, really centring the experience and the impacts on the most historically marginalized groups such as black and indigenous women.'

The question, then, is how racialized bodies, along with climate justice, are imagined by the platform to be instilled in firms' wanting (in the language of the CTF, how these become part of their promises of value built into their authoritative texts). The punctuating moment of global protests for racial justice offered the sort of disruptive event that created the potential for rhizomatic dis/organization. That potential, however, went unrealized, as I discuss in the remainder of this section.

Conventionally, racial justice practices invoke bodies – bodies coded as Black, indigenous, and people of colour (BIPOC). And though my analysis doesn't have direct access to the engagement with the materiality of the nonwhite body in firms' everyday practices, it can examine the rendering of racialized bodies in the platform's charge to member firms. By way of example, during a 2022 US and Canada webinar entitled *A Blueprint for Racial Equity in Business: Building a Just Future Together* (B Corporation, 2022a), most of the five presenters described demographic shifts, the state of economic insecurity, and the limited actions regarding racial equity in North America's largest corporations. Reporting on racial equity in non-B corporations in the US, one presenter from a financial services nonprofit noted:

'[L]arge companies, as measured by US employment size, are highly likely to disclose commitments but they are far less likely to report out on corporate actions that in part illuminate the state of their actual performance ... [her nonprofit agency's report] highlights actions companies can take across three different domains. These are the company itself, its surrounding community, and the wider society. These domains recognize the systemic wide-ranging reality of racial inequity while also reinforcing the notion that B corporations must center equity throughout their business.'

By drawing attention to the gap between talk and action among large corporations, this presenter enjoined the B Corp audience to attend to her organization's 'blueprint' for eliminating the talk/action chasm. She then urged B Corp leaders to:

'[R]ecognize the structural nature of racial inequity and that companies must be willing to wield their political influence to impact the policies that promote equity within their surrounding community. And finally, the community actions of the blueprint reinforce the importance of bringing that broader racial equity lens across the company's community impacts by elevating the reality that, for example, communities of colour are disproportionately impacted by environmental harms. [This recognition] elevates the reality again that companies are resourced and highly influential and that they must be willing to use it across communications, through their industry influence, within their policy engagement and political donations, and through direct investment in historically under-resourced and marginalized communities.'

As another presenter (an associate director of a social impact consulting company) argued after this statement, 'what is needed now is a shared language and approach for building equitable corporations and advancing racial equity in the private sector.'

Current and potential B Corp leaders thus learn that racial equity is a moral responsibility not merely for individuals, but for businesses as well. It's a commitment framed as inherent to being or becoming a B Corp, a non-negotiable duty a firm and its leaders must exhibit. It must become, in this presenter's thinking, part of every B Corp's *purpose*. Importantly, it is also presented as a point of differentiation from conventional corporations – an important narrative distinction of the 'we' to be woven into a firm's authoritative text.

The lesson provided by the platform is that B Corps' engagement with materiality is found in the narrative a firm tells about itself. Those stories, as witnessed in leaders' accounts of firms and their actions, are understood as bringing about *operational* benefits to the firm (in an update to the well-worn 'business case for diversity'). The important question, then, is how B Corps make commitments to equity (in terms of bodies' materiality) *tangible* in everyday practice.

At one point in the online B Corp presentation 'A Blueprint for Racial Equity in Business,' the CEO of a building materials B Corp, a self-identified white cisgendered man, spoke. He recounted the company's first failed effort at B Corp certification, where the B Lab assessment 'showed me all the different things that I could be doing a better job with to create a more just, equitable, and better business.' He then turned his storytelling to the B Corp expectation of shared ownership:

> 'For us, and this is so much of the B Corp community, [sharing company ownership] has very much been based on this belief that we have an obligation to do better, leveraging frameworks like the B Impact Assessment or the Blueprint for Racial Equity as guides and benchmarks for what we can do to be better, taking steps all along the way to find little improvements, whether in benefits, pay, ownership, so that we could do a better job and push ourselves to be a better company. And the result of this is we have a really happy team, we have a great culture, our employee Net Promoter Score is north of 40, which is a phenomenal score. We have great retention, we're able to recruit and attract incredible teammates and for myself. I feel like I've been able to do a part in trying to get to a more equitable place for [company name] and be a leader in setting an example for others.' (B Corporation, 2022a)

The story is one of valuing racial (and gender) equity, placed in the context of this CEO's narrative of the firm. With respect to the notion of the authoritative text, the claim to property here differs from that which has been seen to this point in the book: it is not that decidability is being claimed for one participant over another based on a claim to ownership, but that sharing the firm-as-property with employees moved toward both racial equity and employee satisfaction. In the terms of Callon's forms of attachment, this CEO signalled the value of *co-production* for its capacity to induce employee attachment; it's apparent that this plank became part of the firm's authoritative text, its conception of *what we are* and *where we're going*. The company's espoused commitment to (the material act of) distributing ownership across employees is described as not merely a move for social justice, but a contributor to a smoothly functioning firm. The implication is that firms of all sorts, but particularly B Corps, should *want* to use their corporations to advance the agenda of racial justice. There is a form of prophecy here as well, a prediction that pursuing co-production will generate several positive outcomes.

As a further example, consider an excerpt from a webinar held by the US and Canadian arm of B Lab. In a session titled 'Behind the B,' executives spoke about their experiences and reasons for pursuing B Corp status. One featured presenter identified as a Black woman who owned a small organic farm. Acknowledging that she doesn't embody the conventional image of a farmer, she noted:

> 'I strongly believe in organic growing, and we are also advocates for equity in agriculture. We started levelling the playing field, an initiative focused on equity in agriculture, in 2018. We believe in regenerative and reparative agriculture, unapologetically Black woman led. ... [We became a B Corp because] we wanted to formalize our existing commitments to social and environmental responsibility. Social and environmental responsibility weren't things that we had to be proven, that they were valuable due to business outcomes. But we wanted to have some formal acknowledgement of that commitment.'

She went on to describe the benefits to her firm of being a B Corp:

> 'We have people that contacted us and said 'hey, I only buy from B Corp organizations.' So there's that external validation and it also provides validation within industry, within the various marketplaces that we are in. It provides access to best practices and resources. We know that there is space that needs to be taken up by indigenous farmers, heritage farmers, other BIPOC communities, and other businesses outside of agriculture as well. But it does provide you with access to [resources] like networking with other B Corps; it allows you to get to know other B Corp leaders, whether they're on the executive side or sustainability experts. It's been tremendous and really connecting with some companies that we now have partnerships with. ... And for me the overall value of the B Corp certification is it allows an opportunity to better communicate the social and environmental impact of BIPOC farmers, of women farmers, of black women farmers to the B Corp conversation.' (B Corporation, 2022b)

In discussing environmental responsibility and racial equity in agriculture, it's interesting that the farmer did not address the material challenges facing organic farming, nor did she attend to the ways B Corp certification aligns with her firm's commitment to bodies infrequently seen in agriculture (at least as farmers in the US; agricultural *labourers* are often nonwhite). She mentioned, instead, the utility of the B Corp brand for attracting attachments and for evangelizing for a movement for social justice.

In the B Corporation public fora, statements such as these were common; the genre appeared to be one where speakers depicted how B Corp certification could serve as a branding move that provided (competitive) advantage while also addressing social/environmental exigencies. What becomes evident in statements like the farmer's is that the material domain – land, organic produce, marked bodies – was portrayed as the medium for binding the firm to other assemblage participants. But that binding could happen *only because* the material domain was captured in compelling narratives.

A similar move can be seen as a high-ranking executive of a teamaking firm described the materials used in production at a B Local event:

'[W]e source our teas, you know, 100 per cent organic, we use compostable materials. It's more expensive and it's a pain in the ass, but we do it because why wouldn't you make better choices every step of the way? You know, why wouldn't you use products – and I'm a big fan of consumer products and tactile, you know, *things*, tools for education. You know, much more than just selling products. We're, you know, we're trying to change the world in our little way. And I think also when you're operating in any commodity sort of category, having those different points of difference you know, that you're organic, you sustainably grow your own peppers – it's a really great way to set yourself apart. You know, from commodities – and it's, it's a way to tell a story, you know I think that's a lot of value. A lot of work, but it definitely does result in stickier, loyal customers and consumers, and you have more impact ultimately.'

As in the previous example, the claim about narrativizing the material becomes clear: a company would choose the 'pain in the ass' route because it allows a better 'way to tell a story': a distinctive brand that binds customers to the firm. Moreover, those 'stickier, loyal customers' are important to expanding the movement the platform desires. Those customers attach because the firm makes a promise of value, one with a gravitational pull toward the firm.

Across these examples, what becomes evident is that materiality gets bound to the firm chiefly through the firm's self-narrative – its authoritative text. The B Lab platform's focus on racial and environmental justice insists that B Corps demonstrate a *wanting* with respect to these forms of materiality; indeed, a firm cannot become a B Corp without making such commitments explicit. The forms of binding induced by such commitments are many, attaching firms to participants in the assemblage such as production partners, employees, consultants, and the community of B Corp leaders.

But it's the binding between the firm and the material domain that is particularly interesting. The capacity of those bodies, sites, and objects to offer (immanent) new becomings appears to be eclipsed, or perhaps merely disregarded, by executives' narrative reductions. In other words, the possibilities for reconceptualizing firms, such as urging them to become warriors against racialized injustice, were translated into relatively conventional and instrumental business-oriented aims by B Corp leaders. The potential for rhizomatic disruption met the platformed force of arborescence. Perhaps this is less than surprising in firms legally devoted to profit just as much as they are to people and the planet; these *are* still corporations, after all. And centralized certification of a relatively new organizational form could also be expected to be a force of relative standardization. But the B Lab officers' lofty rhetoric regarding firms' wanting, connected as they are to B Lab's Theory of Change, may not work its way into the lived practice – and thus the living authoritative texts – of member firms as those articulating the platform might imagine.

The product of B Corp practices: collective atomization

As should be clear by this point, the CTF is centrally focused on questions of authority. In this chapter, the relations of authority are illustrated by the B Corp platform, as expressed by B Lab (specifically here its US and Canada arm), which proffers claims to property and promises of value to individual B Corps. Were that top-down form of influence the only contribution of this chapter, however, the CTF would offer very little beyond existing perspectives on corporate practice.

The evidence presented here suggests that – in the language of the CTF – firms are authority machines that territorialize through binding (attachment-making). The authority they generate, their capacity to guide and direct practice, is a product of the claims to property and promises of value encoded into their authoritative texts. B Corporations, like all authority machines, *want* attachments, and the lines of their desire are inscribed in their authoritative texts.

Recall that, in Figure 4.1, the arrows of influence between the authoritative text and the practices it authors were double-headed. The implication is that authoritative texts do not merely induce binding (and boundarying and branding); they are simultaneously *the ongoing product of* binding practices. How, then, do the participants attached through a firm's binding encode interests into its authoritative text?

The first source of authoritative text inscription occurs via the platform. If the B Corp 'movement' functions as a platform, as suggested, we might assume that, like other platforms operating in communicative capitalism, it *atomizes* participants. The platform atomization thesis suggests that platforms detach providers – usually firms and persons as independent operators – from platform owners such that those independent operators become disposable and interchangeable. Atomization also implies that separation of this sort makes it difficult, if not impossible, for independent operators to join together, to create solidarity and realize their shared interests. As seen in Chapter 1, the typical telling of platform capitalism depicts atomization as a tactic enabled by advanced computing, such that algorithmic management steers the process of management toward control without accountability and responsibility (Heiland & Schaupp, 2021; Pignot, 2023). Of course, the B Corp platform is not like Uber, Amazon, or Shein. The B Corp platform, as articulated by B Lab and endorsed by numerous B Local chapters, consisted primarily of centralized certification processes and efforts to evangelize; the algorithmic element typically associated with platforms was absent. And the frequent opportunities to connect with other B Corp adherents offered not merely opportunities to make claims for the moral worth of their efforts, but also served as a vehicle to trade insights on the practices of becoming and being a B Corp.

As discussed in Chapter 3, however, efforts at (arborescent) territorialization are likely to meet (rhizomatic) *de*territorialization as they encounter excess. In other words, the basic storyline – that a B Corp's trajectory is a matter of its leaders' interests as conditioned by the top-down shaping of the platform – is too simple a tale. The focus of this chapter, the practice of *binding* as a key component of authoritative texts, provides evidence for how deterritorialization might unfold. A bit of prudence is wise as we consider those lessons, though, since the CTF's argument for fluidity and shapeshifting would require more longitudinal evidence than is available here and would also demand fewer data emanating from the mouths of B Corp leaders. Consequently, this section engages, speculatively, with potentialities. Yet if the inflection point for firm trajectories is decision-making, if decidability is a matter of authority, and if authority is guided by authoritative texts, then considering how inscribing those authoritative texts provides (or constrains) possibilities for authority machines' wanting-via-purpose can be instructive.

Forms of binding and firms' wanting

First, the B Corp platform operated with a legal structure that obliged a tripartite purpose, enforcing via certification that social and environmental aims were to be weighed in a manner equivalent to profit. There is a key contingency implied in this obligation: although corporations operating under mainstream corporate law make those firms want SVM (or at least that's the story commonly told), an alternate legal structure can make them want differently. The upshot is that firms *per se* have no desires; it is the wanting inculcated in them by the corporate forms their leaders espouse that produce their trajectory. B Corps' practices, consequently, are bound to both the legal structure and their leaders' values. In the B Corp world, there are accompanying assumptions that these leaders *hold* or *possess* those values (and that the holding or possessing doesn't run in the other direction), and that their values are recognizable *as* values in the register of an unequivocally progressive movement. In short, then, one form of binding occurred as the legal apparatus attached (leaders') values to the firm and its purposes.

Three other forms of binding were also evident. The second type occurred as the platform instructed individual B Corp leaders to bind with the larger B Corp community/movement, suggesting that the community offers resources of advice and support for the challenging task of making a non-traditional business operate. Although 'community' can be an ambiguous notion, the referent here appeared to be leaders of other B Corps, the members of B Lab, and affiliated interested parties (such as consulting groups and B Academics).

Third, the platform required in its certification processes that B Corp leaders bind suppliers and customers to their purpose, since enrolling others in a noble crusade was intended to both provide the security of shared principles in the supply/value chain and build the groundswell of activism necessary for the platform's theory of change. Fourth, the platform presented racial and environmental justice as the key planks of the movement's desired social change, pressing B Corp leaders to bind with BIPOC bodies, traditionally exploited sites, and objects associated with sustainability in their routinized practices.

One form of binding curiously *absent* across the myriad pronouncements from the platform was the matrix of desires that shape conventional corporations' focus on SVM, often using share price as a proxy. Most B Corps were, and continue to be, small and privately held companies; though they are corporations with Boards of Directors, stock ownership tends to not be widely dispersed. B Corps have thus been relatively overlooked by the analysts, shareholder activists, and professional investors that comprise markets for corporate control (Thompson & Davis, 1997; Gourevitch & Shinn, 2005). Few B Corps have 'gone public' as do more conventional corporations; several of those have issued Initial Public Offerings of stock, and in most instances either investors have pushed the firms away from the B Corp legal structure or the now-public B Corp has been acquired by another firm (see Davis, 2021a, b).[6] One of the world's largest B Corps, Paris-based Danone,[7] pushed out its CEO, Emmanuel Faber, in 2021 after two shareholder activist groups convinced the Board that Faber 'did not manage to strike the right balance between shareholder value creation and sustainability' (Abboud, 2021). As Faber noted in an interview following his removal, 'The global financial markets are increasingly reluctant to fund [B Corps]. So far, ESG has been sort of an easy path for CEOs and boards that wanted to look good, but weren't ready to really walk the talk. That's the whole question of greenwashing' (Walt, 2021). Clearly, the legal structure of the corporate form is a relevant template for binding, but the limits and risks of the B Corp form are infrequently mentioned in the B Corp platform's shaping of its member firms.

Disrupting arborescence

Calling attention to these forms of binding highlights a binary around which 'purpose-oriented' firms like B Corps operate. The forces of authority are generally understood as *either* internal or external, or some tensional admixture of the two. Decidability on any given firm's practices and trajectory is, conventionally, reduced to either the choices of a firm's leaders or the forces of the social surround, such as the bindings noted here. (And it's important to recognize here that saying 'a tension exists between opposed forces' runs the risk of simply re-inscribing the ontological status of those forces as distinct entities.)

As demonstrated in this chapter, the CTF's conceptual tools of claims to property and promises of value are useful in making sense of binding-induced tensions for firms. In the B Corp case, they can also point toward possibilities for transcending the binary. Across the forms of binding observed here, regardless of the level of acknowledgement in B Lab's discourse, is an expectation that firms' authoritative texts set decision-making in the person of a leader (or leadership team) in a way reminiscent of most other arborescent organizational forms, including LLCs (see Chapter 4). Decidability with respect to both values and routine business choices is consequently framed as the *property* of those 'certified leaders': it is *proper* that they are the site of decision-making.

Yet the stakeholder model upon which B Corps operates insists that decision-making is a collaborative endeavour; the evidence shows that many other parties (boards, suppliers, the B Corp community, governments, the environment, employees, BIPOC bodies) are to be considered property rights holders, depending on the decision in question.[8] There could, undoubtedly, be a threat to existing firm governance were decidability truly distributed across stakeholders; scholars who investigate co-creation and co-production know well the erosion of control, displacement of responsibility, and increase in transaction costs accompanying mutistakeholder decision-making (see, for example, Brandsen et al, 2018). Nevertheless, the B Corp 'theory of change' seen in Figures 7.1 and 7.2 relied on the advent of a movement of 'millions of consumers, workers, investors, and others'; just *how* those masses would materialize and support firms' decision-makers in justifying their pursuit of capital beyond the mere economic was a question never answered (and, even more importantly, never asked).

At the same time, there exist multiple models of *value* running into one another in the platformization of B Corps. To return to a tension introduced in Chapter 6, the explicit aim of the B Corp form – to produce viable businesses that join in a social movement devoted to overhauling a damaging capitalist system – requires firms that inhabit different 'economies of worth' to simultaneously pursue social justice, environmental sustainability, and profitability. B Corps must make nuanced promises of value that resonate with the multiple participants that/who, according to the doctrine of the movement, are holders of property rights – even though those property rights are not what conventional theories of the firm would recognize. In short, there exist many potentially competing claims to property and renderings of value, and adjudicating among them is framed as *a decision* made by individual B Corp leaders. In making such decisions, those leaders must display a compelling purpose to several audiences simultaneously.

There is, thus, a *collective atomization* at work. In borrowing this term,[9] I intend to signify the tension, even contradiction, of situating a firm as a *collective* in terms of its participation in a movement and the stakeholder influences running through it while, at the same time, understanding its atomization with respect to the individualized site(s) for decision-making and value propagation. The B Corp 'purpose platform' is thus a source of tensions that are left to individual leaders of these firms to resolve.

Those who study the constitution and consequences of tensions, paradoxes, and contradictions in organizational life (for example, see Poole & Van de Ven, 1989; Fairhurst & Putnam, 2024) suggest that these potentially paralyzing forces can be *generative* of action when actors find ways to use them without denying their existence. Accordingly, it may not be surprising that, when considering how to engender racial equity and climate justice, the leaders of firms seen in the preceding section turned not to practices directly involving materiality (bodies, objects, and sites) but to narratives of their firms' value as expressed in branding. Authoritative texts can be vehicles for encoding the tension between forces illustrated here that – especially when inserted into the domain of branding – can operate with enough ambiguity to enable freedom of movement, potentially even transcending longstanding conflicts between claims to property and promises of value.

Yet, as mentioned previously, simply noting tensions between opposing forces does nothing to disrupt binary or arborescent thinking. The CTF, in conceiving of collective atomization as not merely another version of the individual-social tension but a recognition of the distribution of authority across the array of participants and practices animating an assemblage, transcends that binary logic. We begin to see that value and property are *constitutively entangled*. The continually unfolding practices of participating in purpose and narrativizing materiality, along with the (more-than-human) bindings found in them, show that authority is fluid, shifting with the multiplicity of values and property claims at play. Rhizomatic thinking (re-) enters the frame.

When a firm faces a decisional challenge, as in the aforementioned case of the B Corp managing a financial struggle with the help of multiple stakeholders, value and property are distinct only analytically: assistance from clients, employees, and other B Corp leaders works because the pursuit of future value required the distribution (and perhaps renunciation) of control over decisions, and claims to ownership of the firm's trajectory only work because they're intimately bound up with the multiple forms of capital implied in the case. What counts as value and where proper decision-making is to be located are the *outcomes* of an assemblage activated in communicative practice – a practice we only see in the rearview mirror of the speaker's recollection. It is in this shifting of authority that *de*territorialization – the dis/organization that engages with the virtual to create new becomings – becomes evident. It is not that decidability is necessarily located in the person of a leader who is responsive to a set of stakeholders from the social surround (that's the limited conception of collective atomization); it's that the surfeit of forces suffusing firm practice require attuning to the possibility that firms can be made to move in several directions simultaneously. In such a setting, focusing on strategic managers' decision-making is likely to miss the ways complex organizations' purposes and trajectories can become both manifest and manifold as a result of struggles over the meanings of value and property.

A claim like that summons scholars to examine the longitudinal unfolding of firms-in-and-as-assemblages, an analysis exceeding the scope of this chapter. Yet even episodes like those recounted in this chapter show that participation in decision-making is multiplicitous, a practice involving the more-than-human participants only rarely considered in the decision-making literature. The notion of collective atomization thus signals the ontological multiplicity of purpose in domains that valorize either individuals or institutions as possessors of values and property rights (and that domain includes B Corps). The story told in this chapter suggests that only when we attend to the array of relational forces found in, and running through, the assemblage will we grasp the complexity and multiplicity of authority over firms' trajectories. And only when we see the assembling of those forces in the communicative practices of binding will we be capable of tracing *how* corporations become sites of wanting – where wanting is inscribed onto the firm. The authoritative text, which is written by the communicative practices of binding, can provide a handy tool for that tracing.

Conclusion

To state the case clearly: collective atomization articulates a novel understanding of *what corporations want* in its rejection of the binary between firms' leaders (such as strategic managers) and extra-organizational actors (such as the B Corp platform) when it comes to authority. Because firms are authority machines, they desire bindings across an assemblage; the resulting surfeit of bindings disrupts any simple determination of decidability. That excess of bindings produces a fluid multiplicity in authority, and fluid multiplicity implies that firms' agency moves in multiple directions concurrently. But platformization simultaneously constrains the potential for multiplicity by framing individual leaders as the sources of inspiration and action.

What, then, do (benefit) corporations want? Conditioned by the platform, they want bindings, the sort that align with the branding and emotional capture presented as pivotal to communicative capitalism in Chapter 1. Through those bindings they want to accomplish the multiple purposes inscribed into their authoritative texts. And with the fluctuating forces authoring that authoritative text, grasping what corporations want is not a matter of reading mission statements or executives' pronouncements (those are never adequate operationalizations of an authoritative text), but is about understanding how those forces enable or extinguish the various streams of activity associated with complex organizations. *What corporations want* is not merely what they are made to want, but is the ongoingly contingent product of contests over value and property in the multi-participant constitution of the firm.

As might be evident from this chapter's preceding pages, the question of multiplicity suggests that the boundaries drawn around firms matter substantially for understandings of claims to property and promises of value. The metaphor of an assemblage makes just that point, suggesting that the bindings associated with B Corps forces both actors and analysts to attend to fluid multiplicity in authority, despite pervading logics that point toward simple conceptions of control.

Notes

[1] Among those advocating SVM, very few ever really advocated the ambiguous notion of value *maximization* as such, but were more interested in keeping share prices high to benefit the firm's reputation and because stock is often used as a form of currency by the firm (Lazonick & O'Sullivan, 2000).

[2] Of course, a Friedman-esque commitment to SVM *also* embodies an ethical stance. It may be the sort of ethic activists disdain, but there can be no position on corporate purpose outside ethics. And, as mentioned in the Introduction, corporate managers may not be equipped to meet the needs of multiple and conflicting stakeholders.

[3] See https://www.bcorporation.net/en-us/movement/about-b-lab

[4] Because B Lab requires both a history of performance and clear lines of responsibility for practices, it's unlikely that a startup firm could emerge as a B Corp.

[5] Much of the broad availability of the platform's messaging was enabled by the broadcast technologies of videoconferencing and always-available video recordings associated with information and communication technology tools, which saw burgeoning growth during the COVID pandemic's shutdowns. Though the data collection for this chapter began prior to the pandemic, the participation of electronic tools (like all participants in the assemblage) in the process of platformization is inseparable from the becoming of these corporations.

6   Marquis (2020) argues that there is an ideological transformation afoot, and that such illustrations will fade away as the financial class becomes more accustomed to, and accepting of, this relatively new corporate form.

7   Danone's North American arm operates as a B Corp and 70 per cent of its sales are through B Corp entities the corporation owns, but its Paris headquarters operates under France's *enterprise à mission* legal structure.

8   Those property rights are likely not legally grounded; they may influence leaders' decision-making, but would be dubious grounds for making claims on assets in legal proceedings in locations where B Corps operate.

9   In writing this book, I learned that this term is quite close to Husted et al's (2023) notion of atomization in 'prepper' collectives. The conceptualization here differs from their use, especially since they tie it more directly to the experience of organizationality.

8

A New Future for the
Theory of the Firm

The Coinbase case

In June 2020, during what the world would eventually recognize as the early days of the COVID pandemic, employees working for the cryptocurrency trading firm Coinbase gathered virtually. It was a week after George Floyd had been murdered under the knee of a Minneapolis police officer, and protests around the globe seemed to signal a readiness to reckon with histories of anti-Black racism and institutionalized violence. This meeting, called by an internal group of Coinbase employees calling themselves 'Colorblock' for their largely nonwhite membership and their commitment to fighting racism, sought to make public the conversations many employees were having in channels of the company's online collaboration tool. They were hoping for Coinbase to join the ranks of many other Silicon Valley companies and issue an official denunciation of pervasive racism, one that would lend the company's endorsement to causes like the Black Lives Matter (BLM) movement.

Coinbase's CEO, 38-year-old Brian Armstrong (a white man who co-founded the firm in 2012), had been noncommittal on the issue to that point. He had emailed employees noting his personal sorrow around Floyd's death but mentioned that his attendance at this meeting was to listen and observe. Attendees described the meeting as 'raw' and emotionally taxing, and Black employees complained that the company had failed to understand the pain and trauma they experienced both within and beyond Coinbase.

The following day, Armstrong held an all-hands meeting. According to several sources, Armstrong acknowledged the pain expressed in the previous day's conversation but held that a statement on anti-Black racism was beyond Coinbase's scope. He argued that Coinbase was committed to economic freedom and that the company was apolitical; he refused to pledge to use the words 'Black Lives Matter' in any corporate pronouncements, saying more understanding of consequences was required and that he thought such a statement would be divisive (though he did say that he personally believed in the BLM movement).

Employee reaction was strong. And overwhelmingly negative. Employees across the company staged a virtual walkout, shutting down the firm's operations. Armstrong responded on his public Twitter account, with a now-deleted thread mentioning his personal support for BLM and committing to stronger internal diversity efforts at the company. Employees believed they had made progress, but over the ensuing weeks new controls were instituted, including restrictions on discussing the impending US presidential election during working hours.

Not long after, things got really interesting. On 27 September, Armstrong wrote a blog post (and an accompanying email to all employees) that made his stance clear. Holding that Coinbase was 'a mission-focused company,' he declared that discussions of 'social issues' would be *forbidden* in the (physical and electronic) workplace, because his observations of other tech companies suggested that 'political' disagreements created challenging internal strife (Barber, 2020). He wrote the following:

[A]lmost every year there will be some sort of event which tests the culture. My goal is to create clarity for all employees going forward about how we're going to operate. I suspect the vast majority of people will be excited to proceed in this direction – after all, the mission is what we all signed up for and is what Coinbase is uniquely positioned to achieve as a company. But for some employees, working at an activism focused company may be core to what they want, and we want to prompt that conversation with their manager to help them get to a better place.

Armstrong's post went on to note the behaviours (un)acceptable at Coinbase:

We won't:

- Debate causes or political candidates internally that are unrelated to work
- Expect the company to represent our personal beliefs externally
- Assume negative intent, or not have each others [*sic*] back
- Take on activism outside of our core mission at work

We will:

- Fight to get on the same page when we have differences
- Support each other, and create team cohesion

- Assume positive intent
- Put the company goals ahead of our teams or individual goals

Paradoxically, by being laser focused on our mission, we will likely have an even greater impact on the world, through our products and growing customer base. (Armstrong, 2020)

Armstrong acknowledged that some employees would be likely to resign due to this stance, and even offered severance packages to those who were simply unwilling to divorce their experiences, values, and traumas from their work at the firm (Chaparro, 2020). Although around 60 left (about 6 per cent of the workforce), those who remained asserted that Coinbase's mission was intricately tied up with institutionalized racism, as were the lives of employees. Among other points, the Colorblock members noted that women and persons of colour were both underrepresented and paid less than their white and Asian counterparts at Coinbase (Popper, 2020a, b).

Employees also held that no company is an island able to separate itself from the waves crashing upon its shores. They argued that there is no position outside the politics that Armstrong sought to place beyond the firm's boundary. One former employee noted that 'Crypto is political, so the sense is that doing this stems from leadership not agreeing with certain political stances. It's easier to just prohibit any discussion at all' (Ongweso, 2020). Then-Twitter CEO Jack Dorsey also weighed in with a tweet on 30 September 2020, referencing Armstrong: '#Bitcoin (aka 'crypto') is direct activism against an unverifiable and exclusionary financial system which negatively affects so much of our society. Important to at *least* acknowledge and connect the related societal issues your customers face daily.' Former Twitter CEO Dick Costolo, in a tweet from that same day, echoed the sentiment but went further in his castigation: 'Me-first capitalists who think you can separate society from business are going to be the first people lined up against the wall and shot in the revolution.'

One more piece of background is germane: during this period, Coinbase's executives were working with investment bankers to take the company public. On 14 April 2021, that plan was actualized, as Coinbase's Initial Public Offering hit the NASDAQ exchange. At the end of its first day of trading, the firm was valued at almost $62 billion, above where initial estimates thought it might be. Despite the rough waters for cryptocurrency since that IPO, the point is that managing the company's brand in the eyes of some important stakeholders (potential investors) seemed to influence Armstrong's stance on so-called 'political' conversations in the workplace. The fear of both a negative brand image and workplace disruption, alongside the desire to maximize the IPO valuation, likely shaped Armstrong's engagement with the voices in the firm urging a stronger stance on a dominant social issue of the time.

Connecting Coinbase and the CTF

This case lays bare many of the issues brought up in the preceding chapters; it also illustrates why a Communicative Theory of the Firm is conceptually crucial for the OS field. The case revolves around the firm's purpose (Armstrong used the term 'mission') and returns to the point made in the Introduction that purpose is contested terrain. It's doubtful that any members of Colorblock would have argued that Coinbase's reason for existence was to engage in the sort of discussions Armstrong sought to extinguish, but they held that, in the widespread social awakening to the horrors of anti-Black racism, becoming an advocate for positive social change through becoming actively antiracist was a necessary part of the firm's purpose. To return to a theme introduced in Chapter 4, they were urging the attraction of social and symbolic capital in addition to economic; they urged participating in a different game than the one Armstrong sought to play. The contest over whether the firm's purpose would be narrow or somewhat more expansive was thus at issue, with the codicil that Armstrong's claim to purpose was quite likely tied up with the aim of attracting a good deal of economic capital via the planned IPO. Armstrong's statements framed these two trajectories as mutually exclusive, whereas employees associated with the movement for internal change saw them as necessarily bound together. Both sides, however, wanted Coinbase to *become-other*, with very different desires animating the trajectories they sought.

The parties therefore had irreconcilable differences regarding what 'Coinbase' signified – what it was taken to be and the ends it should serve. Clearly, the case demonstrates a contest over authority, with each side making claims to the contents of an authoritative text associated with the identity and trajectory of the collective called Coinbase. Both asserted claims to property and value. Armstrong invoked his position in the governance structure, his control over resources (employment contracts and severance packages), his connections with other Silicon Valley CEOs, and his observation-based prophecy that so-called political conversations would impede productivity. Concerned employees sought to inscribe into the firm's authoritative text a refusal to divorce what they saw as an essential sociopolitical issue from the content of their work, insisting that the materiality of race and financial inequity were constitutive features of Coinbase's business. They asserted claims of property in citing their embodied experiences of racism and, in temporarily withdrawing their labour in the virtual walkout, clarified how value generation occurred in the firm.

Moreover, both sides placed the practices of boundarying, branding, and binding front and centre in the conflict. Armstrong's effort to exclude political conversations from work was obviously boundarying, but employees' efforts to expand the limits of conversational practices pertinent to 'Coinbase' were likewise designed to shape boundaries by including practices that had been excluded. Both Armstrong and the employee group were involved in branding the firm, with Armstrong seeking to project an image attractive to investors while the group of employees sought to create a workplace that exemplified the values they held dear. Both also endeavoured to bind participants to the firm, whether those were investors, financial capital, and 'mission-focused' employees in Armstrong's case; or BLM-associated interests, social media critics, putatively enlightened Silicon Valley companies, and future hires for the employee group. The three core CTF practices were clearly sites of struggle. 'Purpose' is a summoning to dis/organize.

Illustrating the CTF's worth

The degree of insight available here is understandably constrained by the data (having access only to popular press reports), but one could reasonably ask what a CTF could provide in a case like this beyond the deployment of a novel vocabulary. One vector of novelty offered by the CTF is a basic recognition of the centrality of this illustration: one could argue, as Armstrong did, that political conversations were a step removed from Coinbase's 'real' business, but the effort to restrict or expand internal communication practices and to control the company's brand made it clear that these participants recognized, even if only implicitly, that their communication practices *constituted* their organization. Such a recognition is an ontological shift, one that implies that what 'Coinbase' is taken to be, how it operates, how it establishes boundaries, and how it generates profitability are the result of decisions produced in communication, and nowhere else. Further, those decisions are shaped by resources of authority that are *also* established in communication. The sociomaterial practice of communication, outlined in Chapter 3, is the genesis of, and scene for, all organization.

In conventional theories of the firm, 'the firm' is too often black-boxed. This book is an attempt to pry open that box and to re-imagine this body of theorizing in a very different register than is typical. The CTF, with its foundations in CCO theory and Deleuzian new materialism(s), is the tool for that prying. When the box is undone, firms' complexity, indeterminacy, ambiguity, and dis/organizing come into the open. Yet participants, in Coinbase and beyond, frequently seek to impose order on these untidy practices, making the authoritative text a particularly useful analytical device. The authoritative text allows researchers to trace efforts to insert interests in the abstract conception of the 'we,' knowing that a myriad of participants attempt to influence that text's contents to alter the firm's trajectory. Purpose is multiple, which means, once again, that it is contested terrain.

A second is the CTF's acknowledgment that diagnosing a situation like this requires attention to the multiplicity of participants populating an assemblage and, simultaneously, to the forces animating that collection. Rather than painting a picture of a CEO squaring off against employees, the CTF shows that a wide array of human and nonhuman actors are implicated in action, and not all of them are 'inside' what we'd conventionally consider to be Coinbase. It is the *excess* of desires and fears flowing through the relations between persons, positions, affect, capital, and assertions of property and value (among others) that created the Coinbase controversy described previously. And it is that excess, that potential for rhizomatic virtuality, that an analyst would trace to grasp the dis/organizational consequences in the CTF. One potential rhizomatic dis/organizational outcome generated by the Coinbase assemblage could be a continued (yet novel) claim on property among employees: 2 years after the events recounted earlier, lower-level employees circulated a petition (on both Coinbase's internal platform and on public websites) calling for the removal of three of the company's executives for inept management that produced low morale. Armstrong, not mentioned in the petition, unsurprisingly criticized the petition, especially concerned that it was carried out in the public eye (Roach, 2022).

Coinbase provides a vivid case, one that highlights the challenges communicative capitalism (particularly its affect capture and branding themes) presents to firms. Moreover, it illustrates the ontological multiplicity running throughout this book: what is Coinbase, and what is its purpose – or, rather, what are its purpose*s*? As analysts, do we simply defer to the articulation of purpose offered by the CEO, or do we acknowledge that promises of value and claims to property, as the components of authoritative texts, are fluid sites of contestation, such that no privileged position to determine a single purpose exists *a priori*? If we pursue the latter, the analyst's task becomes examining how resources for authority both make possible particular conceptions of purpose and, at the same time, engineer unanticipated dis/organizational consequences. This is the framing of the CTF, and the rest of this final chapter explores the theory's claims, its status as a theory of the firm, and its heuristic utility as a tool for imagination.

Encapsulating the argument

Theories like the CTF are, at base, *explanations* for important phenomena. Though the explanatory devices and criteria differ markedly from the theories described in Chapter 2, the argument here has been that a theory of the firm that generates fresh insights into (and asks new questions of) an element of our social scene we thought we knew well, needs to start with the shifting logics of capital accumulation under contemporary capitalism. Those logics revolve around communication practices associated with affect capture, platformization, and branding, suggesting that value production has become thoroughgoingly communicative.

The central argument of this book is simple: communicative capitalism makes corporations want – makes them pursue purpose – in ways that create ironic dis/organizational consequences that interfere with generative new becomings. That message depends on the following planks:

- The world is made up of assemblages: sociomaterial gatherings of more-than-human participants animated by the forces that attach them to one another in the conduct of practice. Assemblages are thus practices where agency resides.
- Firms – which are also assemblages – exist because encompassing assemblages *require* them for capital accumulation. They are nodal points in the assemblage that organize disparate participants and practices.
- The communicative emphasis of contemporary capitalism summons from those firms particular models of wanting. It fashions them as authority machines that desire attachments that attract (multiple forms of) capital.
- Wanting is expressed by the purpose(s) a firm pursues.
- Although no firm's purpose has ever been unitary, communicative capitalism reveals purpose to be ontologically *multiple*.
- If purpose is ontologically multiple, it is contested terrain, and organizing (and managing) is a matter of vying to author a firm's trajectory by influencing decidabilty.
- The primary device for authoring the firm's trajectory and managing its pursuit of purpose(s) is the authoritative text.
- Authoritative texts are the ongoing product of practices in which assemblage participants advance claims to property and promises of value.
- Firms, as authority machines, seek attachments across the assemblage, and the authoritative texts they generate foster practices of boundarying, branding, and binding.
- Authoritative texts seek to order the firm, but because assemblages are characterized by excess and rhizomatic virtuality, they are inevitably sites of dis/organization, and always carry the virtual possibility of the firm becoming *other*.
- The dis/organizational consequences of typical approaches to coding (territorializing) via a firm's boundarying, branding, and binding can work against the ostensive purpose(s) of the firm. These consequences include the generation of brittle performative capabilities, hindered heterarchy, and collective atomization.

This set of claims recaps the novelty of the descriptive framework of the CTF. Its value, I've argued, lies in its radical re-imagining of firms' purpose as ontologically multiple. *What corporations want* is thus a matter of authority, but authority is a far more communicatively complex force than conventionally understood.

These claims also provide the foundation for the CTF's responses to the four theory of the firm questions. As noted in the Introduction, a pragmatist impulse argues that all questions are premised on prospection: what we want the answers to *do* for us. Because the CTF insists that theories of the firm should be tools for imagining new becomings rather than implements of managerial influence, answers to those four questions look quite different than the governance and competence approaches discussed in Chapter 2. I condense them here:

- *The reason for the firm's existence*: firms are necessary devices for capital accumulation in/through the (communicative) capitalist assemblage; they are the nodal points that organize participants and practices. The assemblage summons forth the firm.
- *Mode of (internal) operation*: after problematizing the internal/external distinction, the CTF argues that firms are authority machines guided by authoritative texts – which are the result of claims to property (made up of corporate form and logic[s] of practice) and promises of value (comprised of prophecy and gravity). Authoritative texts inspire (and are the result of) boundarying, branding, and binding, which produce dis/organizational consequences.
- *Location of boundaries*: an invention of the inclusion/exclusion dynamics underwritten by the authoritative text that creates a territory of activity, boundarying practices allocate the firm's property and responsibility to participants in the assemblage.
- *Production of profitability/competitive advantage*: a *point of inquiry* rather than an axiom or definite object, pursuit of profitability (or performance) must attend to the fundamentally ambiguous assessment devices and the criteria of the capital attraction 'game' a firm's purpose(s) prompts it to play.

Across all these, one theme is clear: the CTF, at least in its current embryonic stage, is in the business of providing novel points of departure for inquiry into firms' practices. It aims to disrupt, and provide an alternative to, governance and competence thinking while also providing a route for OS scholars to (re)claim the theory of the firm as vital conceptual territory. Further, as suggested in the Introduction, the CTF aspires to be a critical rather than administrative theory of the firm, one that inspires imaginative possibilities for firms' becoming – including possibilities we haven't yet envisioned – that align with the ever-mutating desires of assemblages. And it shows how the drive for control over corporate purpose – over corporate *wanting* – provides only illusory control over firm identity and trajectory, because forces throughout the assemblage dis/organize even the best laid plans for constitution.

As made evident in Chapter 2, most theories of the firm are deeply normative in orientation. As suggested in the response to the fourth theory of the firm issue, they assume a particular dependent variable and then describe the configuration of structured inputs and processes they see as necessary to make that outcome happen. It's a version of contingency theorizing, one that follows 'if-then' reasoning. Such a logic, however, makes no sense from a stance that frames firms and the purposes they serve as ontologically multiple, since to suggest that a firm must align its boundaries and organizing architecture behind only one set of desired outcomes is to oust possibilities for alternative becomings. And those becomings are core to what the CTF seeks to understand.

Accordingly, normative claims about how to bring about profit-generating forms of growth haven't been the objective of this book. But given the desire to bring about new becomings (new facets of organizational multiplicities; forms changed into new bodies), what does the CTF have to say about how to organize (or, rather, *dis*/organize) differently? The next section pursues a few possibilities.

Inducing rhizomatic imagination: the CTF's claims for firms becoming other

To address the imperative but elusive 'so what' question, this section postulates three practices that have the potential to deterritorialize firms and usher in new becomings. Each is speculative in its normativity and, in conjunction with the case studies in Chapters 5–7, take up the question of whether anyone should *care* about a Communicative Theory of the Firm and work toward its future refinement.

One the key contributions of Deleuze's approach to new materialist thinking was, as mentioned in Chapter 3, the distinction between arborescent and rhizomatic models for assemblages. Rhizomatic thinking, as articulated by Deleuze and Guattari (1987), is simultaneously an analytical device that fosters radical imaginings of organizational possibility and a profoundly distinct mode of organizing an assemblage. Deploying rhizomatic reasoning can foster the sort of experimentation that stimulates virtuality in the deterritorialization of arborescence. This is the version of critical theorizing mentioned in the Introduction: a commitment to interrogate and challenge theory and practice's status quo to move from a hermeneutics of suspicion to a hermeneutics of imagination and affirmation (Dey & Steyart, 2015).

Yet this reasoning does not necessarily offer a new and better approach to organizing that corrects existing shortcomings. Not only are arboreal and rhizomatic forms intertwined throughout social practice, but an all-encompassing attitude is not the style of the rhizome: 'the rhizome does not seek to create any universal order or ethical code for the sake of control, but rather to inspire multiplicities and legitimate marginalized voices and practices' (Hsu, 2022, p 10). The question, then, is whether there are elements of the communicative capitalism assemblage that could be practiced differently to stimulate the virtual domain to fashion new firm becomings. It's a matter of probing assemblage to re-imagine the desires constituting firms (that which makes them *want*). Desires/wants, as suggested throughout this book, are manifest in practice.

Returning to the Introduction, where I invoked the opposition between contrasting purposes – *desires* – for the firm, the challenge becomes clear. The contrast between SVM and pro-social purposes are typically presented as if they were positions on a continuum, with some suggesting the potential to circumvent the opposition by either finding a middle ground or by folding one desire into the other. On the one hand, this opposition is evidence of a crucial change, one led by decades (generations, really) of writing critical of the SVM thesis and the social problems it has wrought. On the other, however, it re-instantiates a binary choice, one that limits organizational purpose to what *human* actors summon from 'the' firm and, in so doing, ignores additional possibilities for conceptualizing purpose. The issue is not which human motivations could be marshalled to lead firms to move toward one or the other of these purposes, but what *practices* beyond this binary are likely to lead authority machines to new becomings (to forms changed into new bodies). Another way of saying this is to ask: *how might the CTF provide conceptual resources to understand how today's practices alter the authority relations undergirding what corporations want tomorrow?* A few possibilities illustrate how research can probe practices to locate the possibilities for deterritorialization.

The digital undertow

First is the practice of digitalization. The increased reliance across assemblages of all sorts of digital mediation is well known, as are digitalization's disruptive effects on both 'spirits' of capitalism and sedimented sectors of the economy. But when firms organize their practices around digitalization, what deterritorialization can occur? How might inhabiting digital architectures as a key component of organizational practice carry the potential for disruption of an arboreal model of the firm?

An answer can be found in Scott and Orlikowski's (2022; Orlikowski & Scott, 2023) thinking on the 'digital undertow.' Although they don't use the image of assemblage, they employ the related notion of an *apparatus*, drawn from Karen Barad's (2003) notions of agential cuts and constitutive exclusions, to highlight the stabilization of practices that reference relationships between firms and institutions. They are interested in how waves of digitalization flowing through firms materialize in industries and economic sectors, along with the consequences those waves bring. Using examples from book publishing and the hospitality industry, Scott and Orlikowski describe how digitalization disrupted elements of practice that wouldn't seem, at first blush, to be the focus of digital transformation, including forms of cross-industry standardization and accreditation. The digital undertow, 'the unwitting yet consequential effect of digitalization efforts that are aimed at core business activities' (Scott & Orlikowski, 2022, p 315), is for them a deeply sociomaterial force that escapes human efforts to corral it. An undertow works beneath and against the waves on the surface, and the unforeseeable effects of digitalization also summon changes in the larger assemblage (for example, attempting to create new standards to adapt to those displaced as irrelevant). In short, then, the unintended consequences of digitalization – a set of forces seen across many industries, which also characterize a good deal of communicative capitalism – cannot be understood by examining only individual firms' practices. Understanding these deterritorializing, dis/organizing impacts of digitalization requires an attention to the recalcitrant desires of sociomaterial participants in practice, a stance foreign to conventional conceptions of the firm. Thinking with Finn's (2017) question regarding what algorithms want, tracking how digitalization can *want* deterritorialization as the disruption of the assemblage (and thus also of firms' practices) summons from our theory and research a thoroughgoing examination of the sort of constitutive boundarying practices discussed in the CTF. If the norms and rules of digitalization thus present logics of practice to firms, they also present possibilities for those firms' new becomings, and those new becomings would be evident in the narrative that is the firm's authoritative text.

Dwelling in the natural realm

A second practice that can unsettle arborescent organizing is firms' dwelling in nonhuman nature. Of course, I'm referring to *what gets coded as* nonhuman nature, or the natural domain – not what the natural domain *is* (since the 'is' is always the result of agential cuts). A refusal to perform agential cuts *a priori* on assemblages in favour of conceptions that seek to transcend dualisms, even when they involve unwieldly terms like 'sociomaterial,' '(non)human,' or 'natureculture' (Haraway, 2003), was a central point of the framework set out in Chapter 3. To some extent, of course, all firms inhabit the natural world, since even those with an exclusively virtual presence still rely on bodies, flows of attention, the 'series of tubes' that is the internet (Kliff, 2011), and the server farms that make electronic access and storage ever-possible. Nevertheless, some firms' practices are attached to natural resources in ways that mimic the addiction form of attachment mentioned in Chapter 3, where the interdependence is deeply inscribed in their authoritative texts' conceptions of the 'we' such that substitutes are impractical. For firms fitting this description, like Anglo American from the Introduction, the question is whether rhizomatic disruption might result from practices occurring in assemblages experiencing threats associated with climate change (such as ecosystem transformations, species extinctions, threats to food supplies, extreme weather events, and geopolitical migration and associated armed conflicts). In firms whose practices are intimately linked to the hazards of climate change, might they encounter deterritorializing disruptions from factors such as these?

Fortunately, Wright and Nyberg's (2015) *Climate Change, Capitalism, and Corporations* documents common corporate responses to such destabilizations, including practices like enhancing energy efficiency, reducing waste and emissions, developing a 'green' corporate culture, branding products as environmentally conscious, lobbying for change, and building alliances. The problem with this set of practices is that each involves merely a new activity or a refocusing of effort on a slightly different target, both of which keep a firm's existing purpose and trajectory largely intact. Each practice, in other words, is a minor tweak that is likely to avoid challenging the fundaments of a firm's authoritative text.

Yet one of those practices holds promise for deterritorialization. What Wright and Nyberg refer to as *alliance-building* can provide moments where substantive change – even if only temporary and partial – is possible. It's not clear whether Wright and Nyberg had this sort of potentiality in mind – they describe it as 'Building links with other businesses, industry groups, think tanks, and NGOs as a way of promoting a company's environmental and climate policies and objectives' (p 24) – but communication scholars have long recognized the possibility for identity and narrative renovation when engaged in authentic dialogue (Deetz & Simpson, 2004; Gergen et al, 2005). If it's true that no dilemma is more vital than climate change, and if an alliance were the sort of cross-sector collaboration from which a unique conception of organization could communicatively emerge (Koschmann et al, 2012), and if that collaboration were marked by an openness to (and willingness to be led by) the demand of the Other (Dutta & Elers, 2020), the potential transformation in the conceptions of property and the model of value characterizing a given firm, as represented by its authoritative text, could lead toward more rhizomatic forms of corporate being and becoming. Alliance-building could, of course, be merely about making connections to preserve a pre-existing identity, as Wright and Nyberg observe, but it could alternatively be the practice through which a firm's relations of authority explore new potentials for purpose through the re-configurations of an assemblage occasioned by climate change.

The key to the difference in tenor is the character of communication making alliance-building happen.

Becoming advocate

A third opportunity to deterritorialize the coding of the authority machine is made possible by pulling on the thread of corporate advocacy. Typically, advocacy is understood as a form of activism, what groups identified as outside the firm's boundary do *to* a firm as they attempt to influence it in a direction associated with a cause. But when firms are understood as political actors that insert their interests into sociopolitical debates that influence their operations, the firm itself becomes the site pushing for social change. As seen in the case study of B Corps in Chapter 7, frequently – and, apparently, with increasing regularity (Rhodes, 2022) – firms are becoming flag-bearers for movements to bring about social change. Advocacy of this sort was, in previous spirits of capitalism, focused on defending the firm on issues directly associated with a firm's business interests, but contemporary versions of corporate advocacy occur proactively, even in cases where no direct relationship with the firm's business interests exists (Gaither & Austin, 2023). The forces of communicative capitalism summoning this response in assemblages was discussed at several points in the preceding chapters, where I supplied some answers as to why, in addition to claims about corporate citizenship (Moon et al, 2005), firms might engage in social issue advocacy. But the question I'd like to take up in this subsection is this: *what happens to a firm when it decides to become an advocate for a social cause?*

Given the theory I've outlined throughout this book, there are a few obvious points to interrogate in that question in the context of exploring firms' deterritorializing. First is the notion of the 'it': precisely what is meant by the firm and where its boundaries are to be located are issues made problematic – and thus framed as persistent questions rather than theoretical axioms – in any consideration of corporate advocacy. That's been a central claim of this book. Second is the issue of decidability: how are decisions to become an advocate for a given cause made – where, by what/whom and when, and employing which resources of authority? (The Coinbase case at the beginning of this chapter illustrates this issue.) Third is the 'what happens' part: where should analysts look for evidence of modification resulting from advocacy?

Using the CTF as a guide for responding to the italicized question in this subsection would start with a recognition that what are to be considered 'social causes' are forces of desire coursing through an assemblage's relations. Think issues like climate change, LGBTQIA+ rights, transnational migration, anti-racism, women's rights, and wealth inequality: each has a long history of desiring alternative social arrangements. The desires become manifest in social movements that move through assemblages by activating a myriad of nodes and relations (the vision is thus not merely one of 'civil society' imploring corporations to change). And, importantly, no social movement is unitary: each desire is countered by alternatives and converses; every stream has multiple, and sometimes conflicting, currents. The CTF provides a useful analytical device, however, since it encourages researchers to recognize that whether a vital desire activates any given firm is a matter of the narrative that firm's authoritative text projects. Because that narrative of the 'we' (what we are, what we're not, where we're going [and why], and how we're going to get there) underwrites decision-making, the first step is to examine how those outside a firm articulate the movement's desire to align with the interests encoded into the firm's authoritative text. This suggests that activists seeking to influence firms would be wise to examine a target firm's authoritative text (recalling that such texts are not reducible to public pronouncements and, as expressions of purpose, are ontologically multiple) to enhance the potential to align the desire animating the activism with the narrative underlying the firm's interest advocacy (Jensen et al, 2017).

This point highlights the key theme pointed up by the CTF with respect to advocacy: the authoring of a firm's authoritative text. The CTF holds that participants throughout an assemblage vie for influence over what gets inscribed on that text, and when a firm takes as a facet of its purpose(s) that it is an advocate for a cause, the firm simultaneously signals its interdependence with the elements of the broader assemblage. It is a recognition of co-production as a mode of attachment (Callon, 2007).

Becoming an advocate for a cause that is not merely an outgrowth of a firm's business interests thus carries the possibility for deterritorialization. I acknowledge that this is a radically different vision than is typical in studies of corporate activism and advocacy, which are dominated by the idea that corporations are akin to persons who/that push for their interests (which are generally rendered in the singular) in a broader social arena or that firms are shaped by internal activists moving a firm's purpose in one direction or another (Davis & White, 2015). Along these lines, McDonnell (2016) found that firms generally participate in activism only when they're facing reputational threats in the public domain, and that doing so appears to reduce activist challenges to the firm in the future. The image is one of firms establishing a wall of defence against the incursion of activists, with the proviso that a battle tactic appropriating some challenger's practice might succeed in 'co-opting allies within the population of contentious activists who, in addition to becoming themselves less likely to target the firm, will also work to dissuade other activists in their network from targeting the firm' (McDonnell, 2016, p 54).

The point in this section, in contrast, is to pursue a different metaphor, one suggesting the *possibility* of becoming less arborescent in firm governance. When a firm engages in advocacy, it may well also be opening itself to an interdependence with the forces of desire moving through an assemblage, along with the (non)human participants activated by that flow. Existing models of firm governance, however, are likely to guard against such openness, since that may be understood by the human actors who claim the firm as their property as abdicating their authoring capacity (and also their responsibility). Nevertheless, advocacy signals participation in an unconventional stream of desire, and new assemblage relations are likely to result.

To the extent that advocacy is a mode of branding, it thus also implies the reconfiguration of the firm's binding and boundarying; analysts should thus expect unintended consequences of advocacy on a firm's conception of value and what is to be considered 'proper' firm practice (and whose property the firm's practices are to be considered). The authoritative text is the analytical device to trace the competition for inscription of the firm's trajectory over time; it is the index of the firm's wanting, and advocacy opens up the possibility that the firm might be made to want in a new register. And that opening up carries with it the possibility of becoming other via practices that re-inscribe a firm's authoritative text.

Summary

Across these three themes – the digital undertow, dwelling in the natural realm, and becoming advocate – this section speculated on potentialities for firm deterritorialization. If, in keeping with the desire articulated by the likes of Deleuze, firms need to capitalize on purpose multiplicity to ongoingly become other, these three routes offer opportunities to build on the forces existing in (an) assemblage to satisfy such an interest. The effort, then, is to posit answers to the 'so what' question regarding the CTF in the future tense, to think not normatively but in terms of virtual potentialities for firms' becoming through the lens of the problem of purpose.

A final word

For the OS field, what's the value of another foray into theory? Recently, some in the field, and particularly its management-focused arm, have expressed scepticism about the fascination with *theory*. Despite disagreements about what the floating signifier 'theory' means (Sandberg & Alvesson, 2021), the requirement that every journal article make a unique and significant contribution to theory, the development of theory-focused journals, and the status afforded to a small cadre of theorists exemplifies, to critics, that

OS has drifted toward theorizing for its own sake, thus drifting away from value-generating scholarship (see, for example, Tourish, 2020). Some fixate upon data as an answer to this drift, suggesting that stronger empirical work – work freed from a need to make theoretical claims – would push the field toward greater relevance (Pfeffer, 2014). To a subset of critics, the larger problem is that we have too little testing of too many existing theories (Davis & Marquis, 2005), too little 'knowledge' available to accumulate, or too few generative mechanisms identified in those theories (Newton et al, 2011). When applied to the problem of purpose, there are some, like Mayer (2021), who argue that we can understand 'why [a] business exists and is created, what a business is and desires to be come, namely its purpose' (p 888) by unearthing *general* answers that apply across all firms.

Other critics of theory and theorizing in OS advance *anti*-theory arguments, often based on the bodies the field (though 'the field' is rarely explicitly defined) *allows* to engage in activity coded as theory development. The field's practices of theory development and valorizing theorists has, according to these critics, produced a highly gendered and raced system of theory production along with a narrow band of what counts as 'theoretical' (Cunliffe, 2022; Maingi Ngwu, 2022). Taken together with the preceding paragraph, whether the source of OS's theory fetish is a desire to compensate for the field's feeling of comparative inadequacy, the dream of certainty some versions of theory promise, or the desire to create a sorting procedure for people and research, commentators increasingly register concern for the field's preoccupation with theory.

There are undoubtedly several intersecting issues motivating this set of concerns, but it would appear that these critiques intersect with a contemporary version of critical theorizing mentioned in the Introduction. Part of what pushed critical studies from negative critique to affirmative engagement with futures – the coupling of incisive analyses of managerial power to explorations of novel organizational possibilities – was a desire to inform practice. The shared inspiration is not conversation among and across theorists, nor is it the illusory quest for the stock of knowledge that would definitively answer all our questions, nor is it a desire to police what counts as 'theory.' The inspiration here is instead performative in orientation, where theory does not mirror the world but is a contributor to the production of the new (Callon, 2007).

Provoking the production of the new is precisely the impulse guiding this book. Such a production would include critiques of shifting notions of property and value, as seen in firms' tireless search for invasive means of capitalizing on persons' privacy as well as the feebly anti-racist 'woke-washing' of corporate branding.

The argument toward the new started with two recognitions: that firms and their purposes are ontologically multiple, and that the spirit of capitalism has shifted to be thoroughgoingly communicative. From there, the book developed a rationale for this venture into theory, which is that the two recognitions make it imperative to understand (a) what and how corporations want, and (b) how we might bring tools of imagination to bear in understanding how firms, as assemblages within assemblages, operate. The CTF's aim is thus not toppling governance and competence theories of the firm; it is to highlight the potential for firms' becoming-other via novel constitutive communicative practice. The novel combination of CCO theory and Deleuzian new materialism(s), and the concomitant framing of communication as the very *being* of any organization, led to a sharp break with existing thinking on the firm.

Given that novelty, it's important to note that, in governance and competence theories of the firm, the notion that resources and strategies need to be managerially arranged to meet the purpose of profitability is not at all *wrong*; indeed, there is a mountain of evidence suggesting that such configurations, even though they differ across firm types and industries, are necessary to accomplish preferred ends. The problem is that such configurations work only for a particular conception of performance, as measured by agreed-upon metrics that align only with that narrow vision. As OS scholars have noted, however, the metrics assessing profitability/ performance are arbitrary and unstable, such that a given resource configuration may only temporarily serve the aims it was designed to accomplish (see Chapter 4).

On top of that, the ontological multiplicity of purpose suggests that what a firm wants, what it desires to become, are also likely to transform, refracting over time and across audiences. Existing theories of the firm tend to be uninterested in multiplicity and arbitrariness, yet these forces have become more palpable under communicative capitalism. And communicative capitalism, via its practices of affect capture, platformization, and branding, makes corporations *want* (makes them deploy models of authority in the pursuit of purpose) in ways that interfere with the very becomings that would be generative responses to the challenges they confront. The CTF addresses how attention to the constitutive force of communication both fosters an awareness of the need for continual becoming that confronts complex firms under communicative capitalism.

This book, in the end, is based on a dual hope. It longs for a vision of firms that honours their ontological multiplicity, refusing to reduce their complexity as sociomaterial practices to the metaphors proffered by governance and competence theories. It also aspires to name communication *the* practice constituting firms, a move aided by a recognition that new developments in capitalism foreground communication phenomena. If firms are to respond to the myriad demands communicative capitalism foists upon them, communication becomes both the site for making sense of the trajectories and the site where firms can become anew. And that ongoing *becoming* is key to the future of the assemblages through which firms have their being. Authority, and the authoritative texts upon which it operates, produces that being and becoming.

As it turns out, the question guiding this book, *what do corporations want?*, is neither a simple matter (they don't want profits alone) nor is it an act of unfounded anthropomorphism. It is, instead, a provocation that forces analysts to grapple with the complexity of firms' existence and of their desiring. For if we cannot explain what (and how) firms want, we cannot ask that more pressing question brought up in the Introduction: *what's worth wanting?* Although governance and competence approaches are relatively agnostic on that count, taking it up will shape the tool for imagination that can underwrite the becoming of the Communicative Theory of the Firm.

References

Abbott, A. (2014). The problem of excess. *Sociological Theory*, *32*, 1–26.

Abboud, L. (2021, 18 January). Activist fund Bluebell Capital takes aim at Danone. *Financial Times*. Retrieved from https://www.ft.com/content/2df158fb-357a-499a-b51c-025b4f1d5c97

Aghion, P., & Tirole, J. (1997). Formal and real authority in organizations. *Journal of Political Economy*, *105*, 1–29.

Ahrne, G., & Brunsson, N. (2011). Organization outside organizations: The significance of partial organization. *Organization*, *18*, 83–104.

Alchian, A. A., & Demsetz, H. (1972). Production, information costs, and economic organization. *American Economic Review*, *62*, 777–95.

Alvesson, M., & Deetz, S. A. (2006). Critical theory and postmodern approaches to organizational studies. In S. Clegg, C. Hardy, T. Lawrence, & W. Nord (Eds), *The Sage Handbook of Organization Studies*. Thousand Oaks, CA: Sage, pp 255–83.

Alvesson, M., & Roberston, M. (2006). The best and the brightest: The construction, significance and effects of elite identities in consulting firms. *Organization*, *13*, 195–224.

Ambrosini, V., & Altintas, G. (2019). Dynamic managerial capabilities. In D. D. Bergh (Ed.), *Oxford Research Encyclopedias of Business and Management*. Oxford, UK: Oxford University Press, pp 1–17.

Andrejevic, M. (2013). Estranged free labor. In T. Scholz (Ed.), *Digital Labor: The Internet as Playground and Factory*. New York: Routledge, pp 149–64.

Aplin, L. M. (2019). Culture and cultural evolution in birds: A review of the evidence. *Animal Behaviour*, *147*, 179–87.

Appels, M. (2023). CEO sociopolitical activism as a signal of authentic leadership to prospective employees. *Journal of Management*, *49*(8), 2727–65.

Argenti, P. A. (2022). Integrating multiple voices when crafting a corporate brand narrative. In O. Iglesias, N. Ind, & M. Schultz (Eds), *The Routledge Companion to Corporate Branding*. London: Routledge, pp 1–22.

Armstrong, B. (2020, 27 September). Coinbase is a mission focused company. *The Coinbase Blog* (Vol. 2021). San Francisco: Coinbase, Inc.

Arrow, K. (1999). Foreword. In G. Carroll & D. J. Teece (Eds), *Firms, Markets, and Hierarchies*. New York: Oxford University Press, pp vi–vii.

Arvidsson, A. (2005). Brands: A critical perspective. *Journal of Consumer Culture, 5*, 235–58.

Arvidsson, A., & Colleoni, E. (2012). Value in informational capitalism and on the internet. *The Information Society, 28*(3), 135–50.

Arvidsson, A., & Peitersen, N. (2013). *The Ethical Economy: Rebuilding Value After the Crisis.* New York: Columbia University Press.

Ashcraft, K. L. (2021). Communication as constitutive transmission? An encounter with affect. *Communication Theory, 21*(4), 571–92.

Ashcraft, K. L. (2022). *Wronged and Dangerous: Viral Masculinity and the Populist Pandemic.* Bristol, UK: Bristol University Press.

Ashcraft, K. L., Kuhn, T., & Cooren, F. (2009). Constitutional amendments: 'Materializing' organizational communication. In A. Brief & J. Walsh (Eds), *The Academy of Management Annals* (Vol. 3). New York: Routledge, pp 1–64.

Axley, S. R. (1996). *Communication at Work: Management and the Communication-Intensive Organization.* Westport, CT: Quorum Books.

B Corporation (2022a, 3 May). A blueprint for racial equity in business: building a just future together. Retrieved from https://www.youtube.com/watch?v=caKyj12rAvU

B Corporation (2022b, 18 March). Behind the B: What it means to be a B Corp. Retrieved from https://www.youtube.com/watch?v=NRLnW3WbtCE

B Lab (2021, 2 June). State of the B: Uniting around our Theory of Change. [Zoom Presentation]. Retrieved from https://zoom.us/rec/play/66yvdb KeRCqWwRruEcJ0d1keFb1ng4Suo7NsctmwSD62KHmaUCgyzFni7 4f66yfaMcP413aQrHqRkRIH.CLmupQvofO9R17ru?continueMode= true&_x_zm_rtaid=IMiTsgEgRWGB7JFcVKtvVA.1622658975486.9f752 32a4024185108d27ac2dc05a40c&_x_zm_rhtaid=503

B Lab (2023a). About B Corp certification: Measuring a company's entire social and environmental impact. Retrieved from https://www.bcorporat ion.net/en-us/certification/

B Lab (2023b). About B Lab: B Lab is the nonprofit network transforming the global economy to benefit all people, communities, and the planet. Retrieved from https://www.bcorporation.net/en-us/movement/ about-b-lab

B Lab (2023c). Theory of change: Imagine a world where all stakeholders – not just shareholders – are valued and prioritized. Retrieved from https:// www.bcorporation.net/en-us/movement/theory-of-change

Baars, G., & Spicer, A. (Eds) (2017). *The Corporation: A Critical, Multi-disciplinary Handbook.* Cambridge, UK: Cambridge University Press.

Bakker, K. (2022). How to speak honeybee. NOEMA. Retrieved from https://www.noemamag.com/how-to-speak-honeybee/

Barad, K. (2003). Posthuman performativity: Toward an understanding of how matter comes to matter. *Signs, 28*, 801–31.

Barad, K. (2007). *Meeting the Universe Halfway: Quantum Physics and the Entanglement of Matter and Meaning.* Durham, NC: Duke University Press.

Barad, K. (2012). Nature's queer performativity. *Women, Gender and Research, 1–2,* 25–53.

Barber, G. (Producer). (2020, 5 October). The turmoil over 'Black Lives Matter' and political speech at Coinbase. *Wired.* Retrieved from https://www.wired.com/story/turmoil-black-lives-matter-political-speech-coinbase/

Barendt, E. (1997). Is there a United Kingdom constitution? *Oxford Journal of Legal Studies, 17*(1), 137–46.

Barnard, C. I. (1938). *The Functions of the Executive.* Cambridge, MA: Harvard University Press.

Barney, J. (1991). Firm resources and sustained competitive advantage. *Journal of Management, 17,* 99–120.

Barney, J. (1996). The resource-based theory of the firm. *Organization Science, 7,* 469.

Barney, J., & Clark, D. N. (2007). *Resource-Based Theory: Creating and Sustaining Competitive Advantage.* Oxford, UK: Oxford University Press.

Barrett, L. F. (2017). *How Emotions are Made: The Secret Life of the Brain.* Boston: Houghton Mifflin Harcourt.

Basque, J., Bencherki, N., & Kuhn, T. (Eds) (2022). *The Routledge Handbook of the Communicative Constitution of Organization.* New York: Routledge.

Bayart, J.-F. (2000). Africa in the world: A history of extraversion. *African Affairs, 9,* 217–67.

Bean, H., & Buikema, R. J. (2015). Deconstituting al-Qa'ida: CCO theory and the decline and dissolution of hidden organizations. *Management Communication Quarterly, 29*(4), 512–38.

Beckert, J. (2021). The firm as an engine of imagination: Organizational prospection and the making of economic futures. *Organization Theory, 2,* 1–21.

Beery, S., Mennel, J., & Mitchell, K. (2022). C-suite insights: How purpose delivers value in every function and for the enterprise. Deloitte. Retrieved from https://www2.deloitte.com/us/en/pages/about-deloitte/articles/how-purpose-delivers-value.html

Bencherki, N., & Snack, J. P. (2016). Contributorship and partial inclusion: A communicative perspective. *Management Communication Quarterly, 30*(3), 279–304.

Bencherki, N., & Bourgoin, A. (2019). Property and organization studies. *Organization Studies, 40*(4), 497–513.

Bencherki, N., & Elmholdt, K. T. (2022). The organization's synaptic mode of existence: How a hospital merger is many things at once. *Organization, 29*(4), 521–43.

Bennett, J. (2010). *Vibrant Matter: A Political Ecology of Things.* Durham, NC: Duke University Press.

Bennis, W. G., Berkowitz, N., Affinito, M., & Malone, M. (1958). Authority, power, and the ability to influence. *Human Relations, 11*, 143–55.

Berle, A., & Means, G. (1932). *The Modern Corporation and Private Property*. New York: MacMillan.

Bernthal, B. (2016). Investment accelerators. *Stanford Journal of Law, Business, & Finance, 21*(2), 139–91.

Best, S., & Kellner, D. (1991). *Postmodern Theory: Critical Interrogations*. New York: Guilford Press.

Beunza, D., & Stark, D. (2004). How to recognize opportunities: Heterarchical search in a trading room. In K. K. Cetina & A. Preda (Eds), *The Sociology of Financial Markets*. Oxford, UK: Oxford University Press, pp 84–101.

Bhagat, S., & Hubbard, G. (2022). Rule of law and purpose of the corporation. *Corporate Governance: An International Review, 30*(1), 10–26.

Blagoev, B., Costas, J., & Kärreman, D. (2019). 'We are all herd animals': Community and organizationality in coworking spaces. *Organization, 26*(6), 894–916.

Blake, R. (1999). *Jardine Matheson: Traders of the Far East*. London: Weidenfeld & Nicholson.

Blaschke, S., Frost, J., & Hattke, F. (2014). Towards a micro foundation of leadership, governance, and management in universities. *Higher Education, 68*, 711–32.

Blok, A. (2015). Attachments to the common-place: pragmatic sociology and the aesthetic cosmopolitics of eco-house design in Kyoto, Japan. *European Journal of Cultural and Political Sociology, 2*(2), 122–45.

Boatright, J. R. (1996). Business ethics and the theory of the firm. *American Business Law Journal, 34*, 217–38.

Boivin, G., Brummans, B. H. J. M., & Barker, J. (2017). The institutionalization of CCO scholarship: Trends from 2000 to 2015. *Management Communication Quarterly, 31*(3), 331–55.

Boltanski, L., & Chiapello, E. (2005). *The New Spirit of Capitalism* (G. Elliott, Trans.). London: Verso.

Boltanski, L., & Thévenot, L. (1991/2006). *On Justification: Economies of Worth* (C. Porter, Trans.). Princeton, NJ: Princeton University Press.

Bourdieu, P. (1986). The forms of capital. In J. Richardson (Ed.), *Handbook of Theory and Research for the Sociology of Education*, New York: Greenwood, pp 241–58.

Bourgoin, A., Bencherki, N., & Faraj, S. (2020). 'And who are you?' A performative perspective on authority in organizations. *Academy of Management Journal, 63*(4), 1134–65.

Brandsen, T., Steen, T., & Verschuere, B. (Eds) (2018). *Co-Production and Co-Creation: Engaging Citizens in Public Services*. New York: Routledge.

Brennan, N. (2006). Boards of directors and firm performance: Is there an expectations gap? *Corporate Governance, 14*(6), 577–93.

Brooks, D. (2012, 13 April). Sam Spade at Starbucks. *New York Times*, p A31. Retrieved from https://www.nytimes.com/2012/04/13/opinion/brooks-sam-spade-at-starbucks.html

Brown, T. M. (2023, 22 October). Look who's on the scent: Corporations you might not expect are commissioning their own signature fragrances. *New York Times*, p BU8.

Brummans, B. H. J. M. (2007). Death by document: Tracing the agency of a text. *Qualitative Inquiry*, *13*, 711–27.

Brummans, B. H. J. M. (Ed.) (2018). *The Agency of Organizing: Perspectives and Case Studies*. New York: Routledge.

Brummans, B. H. J. M., Cooren, F., Robichaud, D., & Taylor, J. R. (2014). Approaches to the communicative constitution of organizations. In L. L. Putnam & D. K. Mumby (Eds), *The SAGE Handbook of Organizational Communication* (3rd ed.). Los Angeles: Sage, pp 173–94.

Bruni, F., & Douthat, R. (Producers) (2020, 13 August). The argument. Is individualism America's religion? *New York Times*. Retrieved from https://www.nytimes.com/2020/08/13/opinion/the-argument-coronavirus-catholic-covid.html?

Bruton, G. D., Pryor, C., & Cerecedo Lopez, J. A. (in press). Lean start-up in settings of impoverishment: The implications of the context for theory. *Journal of Management*. doi:10.1177/01492063231204869

Çalişkan, K., & Callon, M. (2010). Economization, part 2: A research programme for the study of markets. *Economy and Society*, *39*, 1–32.

Callon, M. (2007). What does it mean to say that economics is performative? In D. MacKenzie, F. Muniesa, & L. Siu (Eds), *Do Economists Make Markets? On the Performativity of Economics*. Princeton, NJ: Princeton University Press, pp 311–57.

Callon, M. (2017). Afterword: The devices of attachment. In F. Cochoy, J. Deville, & L. McFall (Eds), *Markets and the Arts of Attachment*. London: Routledge, pp 180–95.

Cameron, K. (1980). Critical questions in assessing organizational effectiveness. *Organizational Dynamics*, *9*(2), 66–80.

Cameron, K. S. (1984). The effectiveness of ineffectiveness. In B. M. Staw & L. L. Cummings (Eds), *Research in Organizational Behavior*. Greenwich, CT: JAI, pp 270–95.

Cameron, K. S. (1986). Effectiveness as paradox: Consensus and conflict in conceptions of organizational effectiveness. *Management Science*, *32*, 539–53.

Chandler, A. D. (1962). *Strategy and Structure: Chapters in the History of the Industrial Enterprise*. Cambridge, MA: MIT Press.

Chaparro, F. (2020, 29 September). Coinbase offers exit package for employees not comfortable with its mission. *The Block*. Retrieved from https://www.theblock.co/post/79247/coinbase-offers-exit-package-for-employees-not-comfortable-with-its-mission

Chertkovskaya, E., & Paulsson, A. (2021). Countering corporate violence: Degrowth, ecosocialism and organising beyond the destructive forces of capitalism. *Organization*, *28*(3), 405–25.

Christensen, L. T., Morsing, M., & Thyssen, O. (2013). CSR as aspirational talk. *Organization*, *20*, 372–93.

Ciepley, D. (2013). Beyond public and private: Toward a political theory of the corporation. *American Political Science Review*, *107*(1), 139–58.

Coase, R. H. (1937). The nature of the firm. *Economica*, *4*, 386–405.

Coase, R. H. (1960). The problem of social cost. *The Journal of Law & Economics*, *3*, 1–44.

Coase, R. H. (1988). The nature of the firm: Origin. *Journal of Law, Economics, and Organization*, *4*, 3–47.

Cochoy, F., Trompette, P., & Araujo, L. (2016). From market agencements to market agencing: An introduction. *Consumption Markets & Culture*, *19*, 3–16.

Collins, J. (2001). *Good to Great: Why Some Companies Make the Leap … And Others Don't*. New York: HarperCollins.

Coole, D., & Frost, S. (Eds) (2010). *New Materialisms: Ontology, Agency, and Politics*. Durham, NC: Duke University Press.

Cooper, R. (1986). Organization/disorganization. *Social Science Information*, *25*, 299–335.

Cooren, F. (2012). Communication theory at the center: Ventriloquism and the communicative constitution of reality. *Journal of Communication*, *62*, 1–20.

Cooren, F. (2016). Ethics for dummies: Ventriloquism and responsibility. *Atlantic Journal of Communication*, *24*, 17–30.

Cooren, F. (2018). Acting for, with, and through: A relational perspective on agency in MSF's organizing. In B. H. J. M. Brummans (Ed.), *The Agency of Organizing: Perspectives and Case Studies*. New York: Routledge, pp 142–69.

Cooren, F. (2020). A communicative constitutive perspective on corporate social responsibility: Ventriloquism, undecidability, and surprisability. *Business and Society*, *59*(1), 175–97.

Cooren, F., & Sandler, S. (2014). Polyphony, ventriloquism, and constitution: In dialogue with Bakhtin. *Communication Theory*, *24*, 225–44.

Cooren, F., Kuhn, T., Cornelissen, J. P., & Clark, T. (2011). Communication, organization, and organizing: An overview and introduction to the special issue. *Organization Studies*, *32*, 1149–70.

Cornelissen, J. P., & Kafouros, M. (2008). Metaphors and theory building in organization theory: What determines the impact of a metaphor on theory? *British Journal of Management*, *19*, 365–79.

Cornelissen, J. P., Akemu, O., Jonkman, J. G. F., & Werner, M. D. (2021). Building character: The formation of a hybrid organizational identity in a social enterprise. *Journal of Management Studies*, *58*(5), 1294–330.

Cornell, B., & Shapiro, A. C. (2021). Corporate stakeholders, corporate valuation and ESG. *European Financial Management*, *27*, 196–207.

Costas, J., & Kärreman, D. (2013). Conscience as control: Managing employees through CSR. *Organization*, *20*(3), 394–415.

Cowling, K., & Sugden, R. (1998). The essence of the modern corporation: Markets, strategic decision-making and the theory of the firm. *The Manchester School*, *66*(1), 59–86.

Cronkhite, G. (1984). Ferment in the field: Communications scholars address critical issues and research tasks of the discipline. *Quarterly Journal of Speech*, *70*(4), 468–73.

Crumley, C. (2015). Heterarchy. In R. Scott & S. Kosslyn (Eds), *Emerging Trends in the Social and Behavioral Sciences*. New York: John Wiley & Sons, pp 1–14.

Cruz, J. M., & Sodeke, C. U. (2021). Debunking Eurocentrism in organizational communication theory: Liquidities in postcolonial contexts. *Communication Theory*, *31*(3), 528–48.

Cunliffe, A. L. (2022). Must I grow a pair of balls to theorize about theory in organization and management studies? *Organization Theory*, *3*, 1–28.

Cyert, R. M., & March, J. G. (1963). *A Behavioral Theory of the Firm*. Englewood Cliffs, NJ: Prentice-Hall.

Czarniawska, B. (2008). *A Theory of Organizing*. Northampton, MA: Edward Elgar.

Davis, G. F. (2016a). Can an economy survive without corporations? Technology and robust organizational alternatives. *Academy of Management Perspectives*, *30*(2), 129–40.

Davis, G. F. (2016b). Organization theory and the dilemmas of a post-corporate economy. In J. Gehman, M. Lounsbury, & R. Greenwood (Eds), *How Institutions Matter!* (Vol. 48B). New York: Emerald Group Publishing, pp 311–22.

Davis, G. F. (2016c). *The Vanishing American Corporation: Navigating the Hazards of a New Economy*. New York: Berrett-Koehler.

Davis, G. F. (2021a). Are corporations inevitably evil? A research agenda for B academics. Paper presented at the B Academics Research Conference, online. Retrieved from https://www.youtube.com/watch?v=DDzv03v3OoQ

Davis, G. F. (2021b). Corporate purpose needs democracy. *Journal of Management Studies*, *58*(3), 902–13.

Davis, G. F., & Marquis, C. (2005). Prospects for organization theory in the early twenty-first century: Institutional fields and mechanisms. *Organization Science*, *16*, 332–43.

Davis, G. F., & White, C. J. (2015). The new face of corporate activism. *Stanford Social Innovation Review*, *13*(4), 2–7.

Davis, G. F., & Kim, S. (2017). The corporation in sociology. In G. Baars & A. Spicer (Eds), *The Corporation: A Critical, Multi-Disciplinary Handbook*. Cambridge, UK: Cambridge University Press, pp 97–110.

Davis, G. F., & DeWitt, T. (2021). Organization theory and the resource-based view of the firm: The great divide. *Journal of Management*, 47(7), 1684–97.

Dawson, V. R. (2017). Communicative theory of the firm. In C. R. Scott & L. Lewis (Eds), *The International Encyclopedia of Organizational Communication*. New York: Wiley, pp 1–7.

Dawson, V. R., & Bencherki, N. (2022). Federal employees or rogue rangers: Sharing and resisting organizational authority through Twitter communication practices. *Human Relations*, 75(11), 2091–121.

de Botton, A. (2009). *The Pleasures and Sorrows of Work*. New York: Pantheon.

De Kosnik, A. (2013). Fandom as free labor. In T. Scholz (Ed.), *Digital Labor: The Internet as Playground and Factory*. New York: Routledge, pp 98–111.

de Laet, M., & Mol, A. (2000). The Zimbabwe bush pump: Mechanics of a fluid technology. *Social Studies of Science*, 30, 225–63.

Deakin, S. (2017). The corporation in legal studies. In G. Baars & A. Spicer (Eds), *The Corporation: A Critical, Multi-Disciplinary Handbook*. Cambridge, UK: Cambridge University Press, pp 47–63.

Dean, J. (2005). Communicative capitalism: Circulation and the foreclosure of politics. *Cultural Politics*, 1, 51–74.

Deetz, S., & Simpson, J. L. (2004). Critical organizational dialogue: Open formation and the demand of 'otherness'. In R. Anderson, L. Baxter, & L. Cissna (Eds), *Dialogue: Theorizing Difference in Communication Studies*. Thousand Oaks, CA: Sage, pp 141–58.

Dekker, E., & Kuchar, P. (2021). Heterarchy. In A. Marciano & G. B. Ramello (Eds), *Encyclopedia of Law and Economics*. New York: Springer, pp 1–5.

Delaware Code Annual, Title 8, § 1: General Corporation Law (amended 2019–2020). Retrieved from https://delcode.delaware.gov/title8/index.html

Del Fa, S., & Vásquez, C. (2020). Existing through differentiation: A Derridean approach to alternative organizations. M@n@gement, 22(4), 559–83.

DeLanda, M. (2016). *Assemblage Theory*. Edinburgh: Edinburgh University Press.

Deleuze, G. (1992). Postscript on the societies of control. *October*, 59, 3–7.

Deleuze, G. (1995). *Negotiations, 1972–1990* (M. Joughin, Trans.). New York: Columbia University Press.

Deleuze, G., & Guattari, F. (1983). *Anti-Oedipus: Capitalism and Schizophrenia* (R. Hurley, Trans.). Minneapolis: University of Minnesota Press.

Deleuze, G., & Guattari, F. (1987). *A Thousand Plateaus: Capitalism and Schizophrenia* (B. Massumi, Trans.). Minneapolis: University of Minnesota Press.

Denrell, J. (2005). Should we be impressed with high performance? *Journal of Management Inquiry*, *14*, 292–8.

Dey, P., & Steyaert, C. (2015). Tracing and theorizing ethics in entrepreneurship: Toward a critical hermeneutics of imagination In A. Pullen & C. Rhodes (Eds), *The Routledge Companion to ethics, politics and organizations* (pp 231–48). London: Routledge.

Dobusch, L., & Schoeneborn, D. (2015). Fluidity, identity, and organizationality: The communicative constitution of Anonymous. *Journal of Management Studies*, *52*, 1005–35.

Dobusch, L., & Kapeller, J. (2018). Open strategy-making with crowds and communities: Comparing Wikimedia and Creative Commons. *Long Range Planning*, *51*(4), 561–79.

Dosi, G., & Teece, D. (1998). Organizational competencies and the boundaries of the firm. In R. Arena & C. Longhi (Eds), *Markets and Organizations*. New York: Springer-Verlag, pp 281–301.

Dosi, G., Faillo, M., & Marengo, L. (2008). Organizational capabilities, patterns of knowledge accumulation and governance structures in business firms: An introduction. *Organization Studies*, *29*, 1165–85.

Douglas, M. (1966). *Purity and Danger: An Analysis of Pollution and Taboo*. London: Routledge and Keegan Paul.

Drucker, P. F. (1946). *The Concept of the Corporation*. New York: The New American Library.

Dutta, M. J., & Elers, S. (2020). Public relations, indigeneity and colonization: Indigenous resistance as dialogic anchor. *Public Relations Review*, *46*, 1–9.

Ehrnström-Fuentes, M., & Böhm, S. (2023). The political ontology of corporate social responsibility: Obscuring the pluriverse in place. *Journal of Business Ethics*, *185*, 245–61.

Emirbayer, M. (1997). Manifesto for a relational sociology. *American Journal of Sociology*, *103*, 281–317.

Etzioni, A. (1988). *The Moral Dimension: Toward a New Economics*. New York: The Free Press.

Fairhurst, G. T., & Putnam, L. L. (2004). Organizations as discursive constructions. *Communication Theory*, *14*, 5–26.

Fairhurst, G. T., & Putnam, L. L. (2024). *Performing Organizational Paradoxes*. New York: Routledge.

Farrington, A. (2002). *Trading Places: The East India Company and Asia 1600–1834*. London: The British Library.

Feld, B. (2012). *Startup Communities: Building an Entrepreneurial Ecosystem in Your City*. New York: Wiley.

Fergnani, A. (2022). Corporate foresight: A new frontier for strategy and management. *Academy of Management Perspectives*, *36*(2), 820–44.

Finn, E. (2017). *What Algorithms Want: Imagination in the Age of Computing.* Cambridge, MA: MIT Press.

Fiol, C. M. (2001). Revisiting an identity-based view of sustainable competitive advantage. *Journal of Management, 27,* 691–9.

Fisch, J. E., & Solomon, S. (2021). Should corporations have purpose? *Texas Law Review, 99*(7), 1309–46.

Fleming, P. (2012). The birth of biocracy. In T. Diefenbach & R. Todnem (Eds), *Reinventing Hierarchy and Bureaucracy: From the Bureau to Network Organizations (Research in the Sociology of Organizations, vol. 35).* Bingley, UK: Emerald, pp 205–7.

Fligstein, N., & Freeland, R. (1995). Theoretical and comparative perspectives on corporate organization. *Annual Review of Sociology, 21,* 21–43.

Flyverbom, M., & Garsten, C. (2021). Anticipation and organization: seeing, knowing and governing futures. *Organization Theory, 2,* 1–25.

Follett, M. P. (1940). *Dynamic Administration: The Collected Papers of Mary Parker Follett* (E. M. Fox & L. Urwick Eds). London: Pitman Publishing.

Ford, J., & Harding, N. (2004). We went looking for an organization but could find only the metaphysics of its presence. *Sociology, 38,* 815–30.

Fortado, B. (1994). Informal supervisory social control strategies. *Journal of Management Studies, 31*(2), 251–74.

Foss, N. (1999). Research in the strategic theory of the firm: 'isolationism' and 'integrationism'. *Journal of Management Studies, 36,* 725–55.

Foss, N., & Linder, S. (2017). The changing nature of the corporation and the economic theory of the firm. In T. Clarke, J. O'Brien, & C. R. T. O'Kelley (Eds), *The Oxford Handbook of the Corporation.* Oxford, UK: Oxford University Press, pp 539–62.

Foucault, M. (1977). *Language, Counter-memory, Practice: Selected Essays and Interviews.* Ithaca, NY: Cornell University Press.

Fournier, V., & Grey, C. (2000). At the critical moment: Conditions and prospects for critical management studies. *Human Relations, 53,* 7–32.

Fox, N. J., & Alldred, P. (2017). *Sociology and the New Materialism: Theory, Research, Action.* London: SAGE.

Frankfurt, H. G. (2005). *On Bullshit.* Princeton, NJ: Princeton University Press.

Freeman, R. E., Dmytriyev, S. D., & Phillips, R. A. (2021). Stakeholder theory and the resource-based view of the firm. *Journal of Management, 47*(7), 1757–70.

Freiling, J. (2004). A competence-based theory of the firm. *Management Revue, 15,* 27–52.

French, P. A. (1979). The corporation as a moral person. *American Philosophical Quarterly, 16,* 207–15.

French, P. A. (2017). The diachronic moral responsibility of firms In E. W. Orts & N. C. Smith (Eds), *The Moral Responsibility of Firms*. Oxford, UK: Oxford University Press, pp 53–65.

Friedman, M. (1970, 13 September). A Friedman doctrine: The social responsibility of business is to increase its profits. *New York Times Magazine*, pp SM17–SM21.

Fuchs, C. (2020). *Communication and Capitalism: A Critical Theory*. London: Westminster Press.

Furedi, F. (2013). *Authority: A Sociological History*. Cambridge, UK: Cambridge University Press.

Gabriel, Y. (1998). Psychoanalytic contributions to the study of the emotional life of organizations. *Administration & Society*, *30*, 291–314.

Gaither, B. M., & Austin, L. (2023). Corporate social advocacy. In A. O'Connor (Ed.), *The Routledge Handbook of Corporate Social Responsibility Communication*. New York: Routledge, pp 177–90.

Gallup (2022). *Force for Good Report*. Retrieved from https://www.bentley.edu/files/gallup/Bentley-Gallup_Force_for_Good_Report_final.pdf

Ganesh, S., & Wang, Y. (2015). An eventful view of organizations. *Communication Research and Practice*, *1*, 375–87.

Gartenberg, C., & Zenger, T. (2023). the firm as a subsociety: purpose, justice, and the theory of the firm. *Organization Science*, *34*(5), 1965–80.

Garud, R., & Gehman, J. (2019). Performativity: Not a destination but an ongoing journey. *Academy of Management Review*, *44*(3), 679–84.

Gehman, J., Grimes, M. G., & Cao, K. (2019). Why we care about certified B Corporations: From valuing growth to certifying values practices. *Academy of Management Perspectives*, *5*(1), 97–101.

Gehman, J., Sharma, G., & Beveridge, A. (2022). Theorizing institutional entrepreneuring: Arborescent and rhizomatic assembling. *Organization Studies*, *43*(2), 289–310.

George, G., Haas, M. R., McGahan, A. M., Schillebeeckx, S. J. D., & Tracey, P. (2023). Purpose in the for-profit firm: A review and framework for management research. *Journal of Management*, *49*(6), 1841–69.

Gergen, K. J., Gergen, M. M., & Barrett, F. J. (2005). Dialogue: Life and death of the organization. In D. Grant, C. Hardy, C. Oswick, & L. L. Putnam (Eds), *The Sage Handbook of Organizational Discourse*. London: Sage, pp 39–59.

Gerlitz, C. (2017). Interfacing attachments: The multivalence of brands. In F. Cochoy, J. Deville, & L. McFall (Eds), *Markets and the Arts of Attachment*. London: Routledge, pp 72–88.

Gherardi, S. (2016). To start practice theorizing anew: The contribution of the concepts of agencement and formativeness. *Organization*, *23*, 680–98.

Ghosal, S., & Moran, P. (1996). Bad for practice: A critique of the transaction cost theory. *Academy of Management Review*, *21*, 13–47.

Gilbert, J. C. (2018, 30 August). Are B Corps an elite charade for changing the world? *Forbes*. Retrieved from https://www.forbes.com/sites/jaycoen gilbert/2018/2008/2030/are-b-corps-an-elite-charade-for-changing-the-world-part-2011/?sh=192315747151

Gilman, G. (1962). An inquiry into the nature and use of authority. In M. Haire (Ed.), *Organizational Theory in Industrial Practice*. New York: Wiley, pp 105–42.

Girard, M., & Stark, D. (2003). Heterarchies of value in Manhattan-based new media firms. *Theory Culture & Society*, *20*(3), 77–105.

Glasgow Caledonian New York College (2022). B Lab and the purpose of the corporation. Retrieved from https://www.youtube.com/watch?v=HhDpz88tisI

Golant, B. D., & Sillince, J. A. A. (2007). The constitution of organizational legitimacy: A narrative perspective. *Organization Studies*, *28*, 1149–67.

Golsorkhi, D., Rouleau, L., Seidl, D., & Vaara, E. (2015). Introduction: What is strategy as practice? In D. Golosorkhi, L. Rouleau, D. Seidl, & E. Vaara (Eds), *The Cambridge Handbook of Strategy as Practice* (2nd ed.). Cambridge, UK: Cambridge University Press, pp 1–29.

Gond, J.-P., Cabantous, L., Harding, N., & Learmonth, M. (2015). What do we mean by performativity in organizational and management theory? The uses and abuses of performativity. *International Journal of Management Reviews*, *18*, 440–63.

Góral, A. (2023). Women in public cultural organizations and their professional paths strategies: A rhizomatic approach. *Gender, Work, and Organization*, *30*(3), 937–56.

Gourevitch, P. A., & Shinn, J. J. (2005). *Political Power and Corporate Control: The New Global Politics of Corporate Governance*. Princeton, NJ: Princeton University Press.

Grandori, A. (2022). A rightholding perspective on the firm and principled governance: 10 memos. In M. Pirson, D. M. Wasieleski, & E. Steckler (Eds), *Alternative Theories of the Firm*. New York: Routledge, pp 56–71.

Grant, R. A. (2019). *Contemporary Strategy Analysis* (10th ed.). New York: Wiley.

Grant, R. M. (1996). Toward a knowledge-based theory of the firm. *Strategic Management Journal*, *17*, 109–22.

Grattarola, A., Gond, J.-P., & Haefliger, S. (2024). Traduttore, traditore?: Gains and losses from the translation of the economies of worth. *International Journal of Management Reviews*, *26*, 137–59. doi:10.1111/ijmr.12344

Greenfield, K. (2007). *The Failure of Corporate Law: Fundamental Flaws and Progressive Possibilities*. Chicago: University of Chicago Press.

Grimes, A. J. (1978). Authority, power, influence and social control: A theoretical synthesis. *Academy of Management Review*, *3*, 724–35.

Grossberg, L. (1982). Does communication theory need intersubjectivity? Toward an immanent philosophy of interpersonal relations. In M. Burgoon (Ed.), *Communication Yearbook 6*. Beverly Hills, CA: Sage, pp 171–205.

Grossman, S. J., & Hart, O. D. (1986). The costs and benefits of ownership: A theory of vertical and lateral integration. *Journal of Political Economy*, *94*, 691–719.

Gulati, R., & Gargiulo, M. (1999). Where do interorganizational networks come from? *American Journal of Sociology*, *104*(5), 1439–93.

Hacking, I. (1995). *Rewriting the Soul: Multiple Personality and the Sciences of Memory*. Princeton, NJ: Princeton University Press.

Hallen, B. L., Cohen, S. L., & Bingham, C. B. (2020). Do accelerators work? If so, how? *Organization Science*, *31*(2), 378–414.

Hanlon, G., & Fleming, P. (2009). Updating the critical perspective on corporate social responsibility. *Sociology Compass*, *3*(6), 937–48.

Haraway, D. (2003). *The Companion Species Manifesto*. Chicago: Prickly Paradigm Press.

Hart, O., & Moore, J. (1990). Property rights and the nature of the firm. *Journal of Political Economy*, *98*, 1119–58.

Heiland, H., & Schaupp, S. (2021). Breaking digital atomization: Resistant cultures of solidarity in platform-based courier work In P. V. Moore & J. Woodcock (Eds), *Augmented Exploitation. Artificial Intelligence, Automation and Work*. London: Pluto Press, pp 138–48.

Heller, M. A., & Salzman, J. (2021). *Mine!: How the Hidden Rules of Ownership Control our Lives*. New York: Doubleday.

Henisz, W. J. (2023). The value of organizational purpose. *Strategy Science*, *8*(2), 159–69.

Heracleous, L. (2004). Boundaries in the study of organization. *Human Relations*, *57*, 95–103.

Heracleous, L., & Barrett, M. (2001). Organizational change as discourse: Communicative actions and deep structures in the context of information technology implementation. *Academy of Management Journal*, *44*, 755–78.

Hernes, T. (2003). Enabling and constraining properties of organizational boundaries. In T. Hernes & N. Paulsen (Eds), *Managing Boundaries in Organizations*. New York: Palgrave Macmillan, pp 35–54.

Heugens, P. (2005). A neo-Weberian theory of the firm. *Organization Studies*, *26*, 547–67.

Hill, D. W. (2015). *The Pathology of Communicative Capitalism*. Basingstoke, UK: Palgrave Macmillan.

Hill, D. W. (2021). Trajectories in platform capitalism. *Mobilities*, *16*(4), 569–83.

Hitt, M. A., Arregle, J. L., & Holmes, R. M. (2021). Strategic management theory in a post-pandemic and non-ergodic world. *Journal of Management Studies*, *58*(1), 259–64.

Hochschild, A. R. (1983). *The Managed Heart: Commercialization of Human Feeling*. Berkeley: University of California Press.

Hodder, I. (2012). *Entangled: An Archaeology of the Relationships Between Humans and Things*. Malden, MA: Wiley-Blackwell.

Holm, F., & Fairhurst, G. T. (2018). Configuring shared and hierarchical leadership through authoring. *Human Relations*, 71(5), 692–721.

Holmström, B., & Milgrom, P. (1991). Multitask principal-agent analyses: Incentive contracts, asset ownership, and job design. *Journal of Law, Economics, and Organization*, 7, 24–52.

Hsu, S.-w. (2022). At the critical moment: The rhizomatic organization and 'Democracy to Come'. *Scandinavian Journal of Management*, 38(4), 1–12.

Huising, R. (2015). To hive or to hold? Producing professional authority through scut work. *Administrative Science Quarterly*, 60, 263–99.

Husted, B. W., & Allen, D. B. (2000). Is it ethical to use ethics as strategy? *Journal of Business Ethics*, 27, 21–31.

Husted, E., Just, S. N., duPlessis, E. M., & Dahlman, S. (2023). The communicative constitution of atomization: Online prepper communities and the crisis of collective action. *Journal of Communication*, 73(4), 368–81.

Hyvärinen, M., Hydén, L.-C., Saarenheimo, M., & Tamboukou, M. (2010). Beyond narrative coherence: An introduction. In M. Hyvärinen, L.-C. Hydén, M. Saarenheimo, & M. Tamboukou (Eds), *Beyond Narrative Coherence*. Amsterdam: John Benjamins, pp 1–15.

Iglesias, O., & Bonet, E. (2012). Persuasive brand management: How managers can influence brand meaning when they are losing control over it. *Journal of Organizational Change Management*, 25(2), 251–64.

Illouz, E. (2007). *Cold Intimacies: The Making of Emotional Capitalism*. Cambridge, UK: Polity.

Illouz, E. (2018). Introduction: Emodities or the making of emotional commodities. In E. Illouz (Ed.), *Emotions as Commodities: Capitalism, Consumption and Authenticity*. New York: Routledge, pp 1–30.

Illouz, E., & Benger Alaluf, Y. (2019). Emotions in consumer studies. In F. F. Wherry & I. Woodward (Eds), *The Oxford Handbook of Consumption*. Oxford, UK: Oxford University Press, pp 238–52.

Jackson, J. P. (2017). Cognitive/evolutionary psychology and the history of racism. *Philsophy of Science*, 84, 296–314.

Jacobs, C. D., Steyaert, C., & Ueberbacher, F. (2013). Anticipating intended users: Prospective sensemaking in technology development. *Technology Analysis & Strategic Management*, 25, 1027–43.

Jensen, A. F. (2023). The philosophical history of projectification: The project society. In M. Fred & S. Godenhjelm (Eds), *Projectification of Organizations, Governance and Societies: Theoretical Perspectives and Empirical Implications*. Cham, Switzerland: Springer, pp 17–37.

Jensen, A., Maagard, C. A., & Rasmussen, R. K. (2017). 'Speaking through the other': Countering counter-narratives through stakeholders' stories. In S. Frandsen, T. Kuhn, & M. W. Lundholt (Eds), *Counter-Narratives and Organization*. New York: Routledge, pp 83–101.

Jensen, M. C., & Meckling, W. (1976). Theory of the firm: Managerial behavior, agency costs, and ownership structure. *The Journal of Financial Economics*, *3*, 305–60.

Jessop, B. (1992). Fordism and post-Fordism: A critical reformulation. In M. Storper & A. J. Scott (Eds), *Pathways to Industrialization and Regional Development*. London: Routledge, pp 42–62.

Jones, L. (2021, 12 November). Shein suppliers' workers doing 75-hour week, finds probe. *BBC News*. Retrieved from https://www.bbc.com/news/business-59245708

Kahn, W. A., & Kram, K. E. (1994). Authority at work: Internal models and their organizational consequences. *Academy of Management Review*, *19*, 17–50.

Karikari, E. (2023). Conceptualizing organization: hybridity and the naturalizing of dis/order. *Journal of Multicultural Discourses*, *18*(2), 95–109.

Kärreman, D., & Rylander, A. (2008). Managing meaning through branding: The case of a consulting firm. *Organization Studies*, *29*, 103–25.

Kazis, S. (2022, 20 January). How fast-fashion giant Shein used big tech to change the way we shop. Vice.com. Retrieved from https://www.vice.com/en/article/93bq7z/how-fast-fashion-giant-shein-used-big-tech-to-change-the-way-we-shop

Kelley, L. (2023, 25 October). The murky logic of companies' Israel-Hamas statements. *The Atlantic Daily*. Retrieved from https://www.theatlantic.com/newsletters/archive/2023/10/companies-statements-israel-hamas-war/675776/?utm_campaign=atlantic-daily-newsletter&utm_source=newsletter&utm_medium=email&utm_content=20231025&utm_term=The+Atlantic+Daily

Kjellberg, H. (2017). Acquiring associations: On the unexpected social consequences of possessive relations. In F. Cochoy, J. Deville, & L. McFall (Eds), *Markets and the Arts of Attachment*. London: Routledge, pp 162–79.

Klein, E. (Producer). (2021, 5 February). The Ezra Klein Show. An appalled Republican considers the future of the G.O.P. *New York Times*. Retrieved from https://www.nytimes.com/2021/02/05/opinion/ezra-klein-podcast-yuval-levin.html?

Kliff, S. (2011, 20 September). The Internet is, in fact, a series of tubes. *Washington Post*. Retrieved from https://www.washingtonpost.com/blogs/wonkblog/post/the-internet-is-in-fact-a-series-of-tubes/2011/09/20/gIQALZwfiK_blog.html

Kohtamäki, M., Whittington, R., Vaara, E., & Rabetino, R. (2022). Making connections: Harnessing the diversity of strategy-as-practice research. *International Journal of Management Reviews*, *24*(2), 210–32.

Korczynski, M., Shire, K., Frenkel, S., & Tam, M. (2000). Service work in consumer capitalism: Customers, control, and contradictions. *Work, Employment & Society*, *14*, 669–87.

Kornberger, M. (2010). *Brand Society: How Brands Transform Management and Lifestyle*. Cambridge, UK: Cambridge University Press.

Koschmann, M. (2012). The communicative constitution of collective identity in interorganizational collaboration. *Management Communication Quarterly*, *27*, 61–89.

Koschmann, M., & Burk, N. (2016). Accomplishing authority in collaborative work. *Western Journal of Communication*, *80*, 393–413.

Koschmann, M., Kuhn, T., & Pfarrer, M. (2012). A communicative framework of value in cross-sector partnerships. *Academy of Management Review*, *37*, 332–54.

Kraaijenbrink, J., Spender, J.-C., & Groen, A. J. (2010). The resource-based view: A review and assessment of its critiques. *Journal of Management*, *36*, 349–72.

Kuhn, T. (2008). A communicative theory of the firm: Developing an alternative perspective on intra-organizational power and stakeholder relationships. *Organization Studies*, *29*, 1227–54.

Kuhn, T. (2017a). Developing a communicative imagination under contemporary capitalism: The domain of organizational communication as a mode of explanation. *Management Communication Quarterly*, *31*, 116–22.

Kuhn, T. (2017b). Communicatively constituting organizational unfolding through counter-narrative. In S. Frandsen, T. Kuhn, & M. Lundholt (Eds), *Counter-Narratives and Organization*. New York: Routledge, pp 17–42.

Kuhn, T. (2021). (Re)moving blinders: Communication-as-constitutive theorizing as provocation to practice-based organization scholarship. *Management Learning*, *52*(1), 109–21.

Kuhn, T. (2022). What are corporations for?: Contemporary capitalism, authority, and a communicative theory of the firm. In M. Pirson, D. M. Wasieleski, & E. Steckler (Eds), *Alternative Theories of the Firm*. New York: Routledge, pp 120–50.

Kuhn, T., & Deetz, S. A. (2008). Critical theory and corporate social responsibility: Can/should we get beyond cynical reasoning? In A. Crane, A. McWilliams, D. Matten, J. Moon, & D. Siegel (Eds), *The Oxford Handbook of Corporate Social Responsibility*. Oxford, UK: Oxford University Press, pp 173–96.

Kuhn, T., & Jackson, M. (2008). Accomplishing knowledge: A framework for investigating knowing in organizations. *Management Communication Quarterly*, *21*, 454–85.

Kuhn, T., & Burk, N. (2014). Spatial design as sociomaterial practice: A (dis)organizing perspective on communicative constitution. In F. Cooren, E. Vaara, A. Langley, & H. Tsoukas (Eds), *Language and Communication at Work: Discourse, Narrativity, and Organizing*. Oxford, UK: Oxford University Press, pp 149–74.

Kuhn, T., & Putnam, L. L. (2014). Discourse and communication. In P. Adler, P. DuGay, G. Morgan, & M. Reed (Eds), *The Oxford Handbook of Sociology, Social Theory, and Organization Studies*. Oxford, UK: Oxford University Press, pp 414–46.

Kuhn, T., & Rennstam, J. (2016). Expertise as a practical accomplishment among objects and values. In J. Treem & P. Leonardi (Eds), *Where Is Expertise?: Communication and Organizing in the Information Age*. Oxford, UK: Oxford University Press, pp 25–43.

Kuhn, T., Ashcraft, K. L., & Cooren, F. (2017). *The Work of Communication: Relational Perspectives on Working and Organizing in Contemporary Capitalism*. New York: Routledge.

Kurie, P. (2018). *In Chocolate We Trust: The Hershey Company Town Unwrapped*. Philadelphia: University of Pennsylvania Press.

Laapotti, T., & Raappana, M. (2022). Algorithms and organizing. *Human Communication Research*, *48*(3), 491–515.

Land, C., & Taylor, S. (2010). Surf's up: Work, life, balance and brand in a new age capitalist organization. *Sociology*, *44*, 395–413.

Latour, B. (2005). *Reassembling the Social: An Introduction to Actor-Network Theory*. Oxford, UK: Oxford University Press.

Law, J. (2002). *Aircraft Stories: Decentering the Object in Technoscience*. Durham, NC: Duke University Press.

Lazonick, W., & O'Sullivan, M. (2000). Maximizing shareholder value: A new ideology for corporate governance. *Economy and Society*, *29*, 13–35.

Ledingham, J. A., & Bruning, S. D. (2000). *Public Relations as Relationship Management: A Relational Approach to the Study and Practice of Public Relations*. Mahwah, NJ: Erlbaum.

Lee, J. Y., Bansal, P., & Barbosa, A. M. (2023). Seeing beyond the here and now: How corporate purpose combats corporate myopia. *Strategy Science*, *8*(2), 302–10.

Leonardi, P. M. (2013). Theoretical foundations for the study of sociomateriality. *Information and Organization*, *23*, 59–76.

Leonardi, P. M., & Treem, J. W. (2020). Behavioral visibility: A new paradigm for organization studies in the age of digitization, digitalization, and datafication. *Organization Studies*, *41*, 1601–25.

Lincoln, B. (1994). *Authority: Construction and corrosion*. Chicago: University of Chicago Press.

Linstead, S., & Thanem, T. (2007). Multiplicity, virtuality, and organization: The contribution of Gilles Deleuze. *Organization Studies*, *28*, 1483–501.

Llewellyn, N., & Hindmarsh, J. (2013). The order problem: Inference and interactive service work. *Human Relations*, *66*, 1401–26.

Lo, D. (2022, 15 July). Influencers are out – authenticity is in. Fast Company. Retrieved from https://www.fastcompany.com/90768656/ugc-influenc ers-content-marketing

Loacker, B. (2021). Challenging thought at ephemera: Attempting to think and organize differently. *Ephemera: Theory and Politics in Organization*, *21*(4), np.

Loxley, J. (2007). *Performativity*. London: Routledge.

Lucas, D. S., Grimes, M. G., & Gehman, J. (2022). Remaking capitalism: The strength of weak legislation in mobilizing B Corporation certification. *Academy of Management Journal*, *65*(3), 958–87.

Luce, R. A., Barber, A. E., & Hillman, A. J. (2001). Good deeds and misdeeds: A mediated model of the effect of corporate social performance on organizational attractiveness. *Business & Society*, *40*(4), 397–415.

Lury, C. (2004). *Brands: The Logos of the Global Economy*. London: Routledge.

Lury, C. (2009). Brand as assemblage. *Journal of Cultural Economy*, *2*(1–2), 67–82.

Luyckx, J., Schneider, A., & Kourula, A. (2022). Learning from alternatives: Analyzing alternative ways of organizing as starting points for improving the corporation. *Research in the Sociology of Organization*, *78*, 209–31.

Macey, J. (2013). Sublime myths: An essay in honor of the shareholder value myth and the Tooth Fairy. *Texas Law Review*, *91*, 911–24.

Magnuson, W. (2022). *For Profit: A History of Corporations*. New York: Basic Books.

Maia, F. (2022). *Trading Futures: A Theological Critique of Financialized Capitalism*. Durham, NC: Duke University Press.

Maingi Ngwu, N. (2022). Toward a fluid, shape-shifting methodology in organizational communication inquiry: African feminist organizational communication historiography. *Review of Communication*, *22*(1), 42–59.

Maitland, I. (2017). How insiders abuse the idea of corporate personality. In E. W. Orts & N. C. Smith (Eds), *The Moral Responsibility of Firms*. Oxford, UK: Oxford University Press, pp 106–22.

March, J. G., & Sutton, R. I. (1997). Organizational performance as a dependent variable. *Organization Science*, *8*, 698–706.

Marquis, C. (2020). *Better Business: How the B Corp Movement is Remaking Capitalism*. New Haven, CT: Yale University Press.

Marshak, R. J. (1998). A discourse on discourse: Redeeming the meaning of talk. In D. Grant, T. Keenoy, & C. Oswick (Eds), *Discourse and Organization*. Thousand Oaks, CA: Sage, pp 15–30.

Martin, J. (1992). *Cultures in Organizations: Three Perspectives*. New York: Oxford University Press.

Matheson, B. (2014). Compatibilism and personal identity. *Philosophical Studies*, *170*, 317–34.

Matsakis, L., Tobin, M., & Chen, W. (2021, 14 December). How Shein beat Amazon at its own game – and reinvented fast fashion. RestofWorld.org. Retrieved from https://restofworld.org/2021/how-shein-beat-amazon-and-reinvented-fast-fashion/

May, T. (2005). *Gilles Deleuze: An Introduction*. Cambridge: Cambridge University Press.

Mayer, C. (2021). The future of the corporation and the economics of purpose. *Journal of Management Studies*, *58*(3), 887–901.

Mazzarol, T., & Reboud, S. (2020). Planning, business models and strategy. In T. Mazzarol & S. Reboud (Eds), *Entrepreneurship and Innovation: Theory, Practice and Context*. Berlin: Springer Nature, pp 191–225.

Mazzei, L. A. (2013). A voice without organs: interviewing in posthumanist research. *International Journal of Qualitative Studies in Education*, *26*(6), 732–40.

McDonnell, M.-H. (2016). Radical repertoires: The incidence and impact of corporate-sponsored social activism. *Organization Science*, *27*, 53–71.

McFall, L., Cochoy, F., & Deville, J. (2017). Introduction: Markets and the arts of attachment. In F. Cochoy, J. Deville, & L. McFall (Eds), *Markets and the Arts of Attachment*. London: Routledge, pp 1–21.

McPhee, R. D., & Zaug, P. (2000). The communicative constitution of organizations: A framework for explanation. *The Electronic Journal of Communication/La Revue Electronique de Communication*, *10*(1, 2).

Mease, J. J. (2021). Techniques and forces and the communicative constitution of organization: A Deleuzian approach to organizational (in)stability and power. *Management Communication Quarterly*, *35*, 226–55.

Meier, F., & Carroll, B. (2023). Ventriloquial reflexivity: Exploring the communicative relationality of the 'I' and the 'it'. *Human Relations*, *76*(7), 1081–107.

Mellett, K. (2017). Marketing and the domestication of social media. In F. Cochoy, J. Deville, & L. McFall (Eds), *Markets and the Art of Attachment*. London: Routledge, pp 55–71.

Mercado III, E. (2021). Song morphing by humpback whales: Cultural or epiphenomenal? *Frontiers in Psychology*, *11*, np.

Milan, S. (2017). Data activism as the new frontier of media activism. In V. W. Pickard & G. Yang (Eds), *Media Activism in the Digital Age*. New York: Routledge, pp 151–63.

Miller, D., & Shamsie, J. (1996). The resource-based view of the firm in two environments: The Hollywood film studios from 1936 to 1965. *Academy of Management Journal*, *39*, 519–43.

Mocsary, G. A. (2016). Freedom of corporate purpose. *Brigham Young University Law Review*, *2016*(5), 1319–95.

Mol, A. (2002). *The Body Multiple: Ontology in Medical Practice*. Durham, NC: Duke University Press.

Moldaschl, M., & Fischer, D. (2004). Beyond the management view: A resource-centered socio-economic perspective. *Management Revue*, *15*, 122–51.

Mooallem, J. (2017). Neanderthals were people, too. *New York Times Magazine*. Retrieved from https://www.nytimes.com/2017/01/11/magaz ine/neanderthals-were-people-too.html#

Moon, J., Crane, A., & Matten, D. (2005). Can corporations be citizens?: Corporate citizenship as a metaphor for business participation in society. *Business Ethics Quarterly*, *15*, 429–53.

Moor, L. (2022). *Communication and Economic Life*. Cambridge, UK: Polity.

Morin, C. (2011). Neuromarketing: The new science of consumer behavior. *Society*, *48*, 131–5.

Moroz, P. W., Branzei, O., Parker, S. C., & Gamble, E. N. (2018). Imprinting with purpose: Prosocial opportunities and B Corp certification. *Journal of Business Venturing*, *33*(2), 117–29.

Morrison, A. D., & Mota, R. (2023). A theory of organizational purpose. *Academy of Management Review*, *48*(2), 203–19.

Mumby, D. K. (1987). The political function of narrative in organizations. *Communication Monographs*, *54*, 113–27.

Mumby, D. K. (1997). Modernism, postmodernism, and communication studies: A rereading of an ongoing debate. *Communication Theory*, 7, 1–28.

Mumby, D. K. (2016). Organizing beyond organization: Branding, discourse, and communicative capitalism. *Organization*, *23*, 884–907.

Mumby, D. K. (2019). Communication constitutes capital: Branding and the politics of neoliberal dis/organization. In C. Vásquez & T. Kuhn (Eds), *Dis/organization as Communication: Exploring the Disordering, Disruptive, and Chaotic Properties of Communication*. New York: Routledge, pp 125–47.

Mumby, D. K. (2020). Theorizing struggle in the social factory. *Organization Theory*, *1*, 1–14.

Mutch, A., Delbridge, R., & Ventresca, M. (2006). Situating organizational action: The relational sociology of organizations. *Organization*, *13*, 607–25.

Nathues, E., van Vuuren, M., & Cooren, F. (2021). Speaking about vision, talking in the name of so much more: A methodological framework for ventriloquial analyses in organization studies. *Organization Studies*, *42*(9), 1457–76.

Neff, G., & Stark, D. (2004). Permanently beta: responsive organization in the internet era. In P. N. Howard & S. Jones (Eds), *Society Online: The Internet in Context*. Thousand Oaks, CA: SAGE, pp 173–88.

Nelson, R. R., & Winter, S. G. (1982). *An Evolutionary Theory of Economic Change*. Cambridge, MA: Harvard University Press.

Newton, T., Deetz, S., & Reed, M. (2011). Responses to social constructionism and critical realism in organization studies. *Organization Studies*, *32*, 7–26.

Nguyen, T. (2021). Shein is the future of fast fashion. Is that a good thing? *Vox*. Retrieved from https://www.vox.com/the-goods/22573682/shein-future-of-fast-fashion-explained

Nicolini, D. (2012). *Practice Theory, Work, and Organization: An Introduction*. Oxford, UK: Oxford University Press.

Nicolini, D. (2016). Is small the only beautiful?: Making sense of 'large phenomena' from a practice–based perspective. In A. Hui, T. Schatzki, & E. Shove (Eds), *The Nexus of Practices: Connections, Constellations, Practitioners*. New York: Routledge, pp 98–113.

Nilsson, E. (2023). The instrumentalization of CSR by rent-seeking governments: Lessons from Tanzania. *Business & Society*, *62*(6), 1173–200.

Ocasio, W. (1997). Towards an attention-based view of the firm. *Strategic Management Journal*, *18*(S1), 187–206.

Ocasio, W., Laamanen, T., & Vaara, E. (2018). Communication and attention dynamics: An attention-based view of strategic change. *Strategic Management Journal*, *39*, 155–67.

Ocasio, W., Kraatz, M., & Chandler, D. (2023a). Making sense of corporate purpose. *Strategy Science*, *8*(2), 123–38.

Ocasio, W., Yakis-Douglas, B., Boynton, D., Laamanen, T., Rerup, C., Vaara, E., & Whittington, R. (2023b). It's a different world: A dialog on the Attention-Based View in a post-Chandlerian world. *Journal of Management Inquiry*, *32*(2), 107–19.

Oinas, P. (2006). The many boundaries of the firm. In M. Taylor & P. Oinas (Eds), *Understanding the Firm: Spatial and Organizational Dimensions*. Oxford, UK: Oxford University Press, pp 35–60.

Ongweso, E. (2020, 16 October). Coinbase's new 'direction' is censorship, leaked audio reveals. *Vice*. Retrieved from https://www.vice.com/en/article/5dpmp8/coinbases-new-direction-is-censorship-leaked-audio-reveals

Orishede, F. (2021). Relationship between competitive advantage and value creation and profitability in the firm. *African Journal of Social and Behavioural Sciences*, *11*(2). Retrieved from https://journals.aphriapub.com/index.php/AJSBS/article/view/1343

Orlikowski, W. J. (2007). Sociomaterial practices: Exploring technology at work. *Organization Studies*, *28*, 1435–48.

Orlikowski, W. J., & Scott, S. V. (2008). Sociomateriality: Challenging the separation of technology, work and organization. In J. P. Walsh & A. P. Brief (Eds), *The Academy of Management Annals* (Vol. 2). New York: Routledge, pp 433–74.

Orlikowski, W. J., & Scott, S. V. (2023). The digital undertow and institutional displacement: A sociomaterial approach. *Organization Theory*, *4*, 1–16.

Orts, E. W., & Smith, N. C. (Eds). (2017). *The Moral Responsibility of Firms*. Oxford, UK: Oxford University Press.

Painter-Morland, M. (2011). Rethinking responsible agency in corporations: Perspectives from Deleuze and Guattari. *Journal of Business Ethics, 101*, 83–95.

Parker, M. (2022). Weeds: Classification, organization, and wilding. *Organization Theory, 3*(4), 1–16.

Parker, S. C., Gamble, E. N., Moroz, P. W., & Branzei, O. (2019). The impact of B Lab certification on firm growth. *Academy of Management Perspectives, 5*(1), 57–77.

Parkinson, J. (2003). Models of the company and the employment relationship. *British Journal of Industrial Relations, 41*, 481–509.

Patriotta, G. (2021). The future of the corporation. *Journal of Management Studies, 58*(3), 879–86.

Patriotta, G., Gond, J.-P., & Schultz, F. (2011). Maintaining legitimacy: Controversies, orders of worth, and public justifications. *Journal of Management Studies, 48*, 1804–36.

Pellizzioni, L. (2015). *Ontological Politics in a Disposable World: The New Mastery of Nature*. Burlington, VT: Ashgate.

Penrose, E. T. (1959). *The Theory of the Growth of the Firm*. Oxford, UK: Basil Blackwell.

Peters, J. D. (1999). *Speaking Into the Air: A History of the Idea of Communication*. Chicago: University of Chicago Press.

Peters, J. D. (2015). *The Marvelous Clouds: Toward a Philosophy of Elemental Media*. Chicago: University of Chicago Press.

Peters, T. (Producer). (1997, 31 August). The brand called you. Fast Company. Retrieved from https://www.fastcompany.com/28905/brand-called-you

Petit, P. (2017). The conversable, responsible corporation. In E. W. Orts & S. N. Craig (Eds), *The Moral Responsibility of Firms*. Oxford, UK: Oxford University Press, pp 15–35.

Petrin, M. (2013). Reconceptualizing the theory of the firm: From nature to function. *Penn State Law Review, 118*, 1–53.

Pfeffer, J. (2014). The management theory morass: Some modest proposals. In J. A. Miles (Ed.), *New Directions in Management and Organization Theory*. Newcastle upon Tyne, UK: Cambridge Scholars Publishing, pp 457–68.

Pfister, M. (2020). Corporate social responsibility and organizational attraction: A systematic literature review. *American Journal of Management, 20*(2), 96–111.

Phillips, J. (2006). Agencement/assemblage. *Theory Culture and Society, 23*, 108–9.

Phillips, M. J. (1992). Corporate moral personhood and three conceptions of the corporation. *Business Ethics Quarterly, 2*, 435–59.

Pickering, A. (1995). *The Mangle of Practice: Time, Agency, and Science*. Chicago: University of Chicago Press.

Pignot, E. (2023). Who is pulling the strings in the platform economy? Accounting for the dark and unexpected sides of algorithmic control. *Organization Studies*, *30*, 140–67.

Pine, J., & Gilmore, J. H. (2011). *The Experience Economy* (Updated ed.). Boston: Harvard Business School Press.

Pirson, M., Wasieleski, D. M., & Steckler, E. L. (Eds). (2022). *Alternative Theories of the Firm*. New York: Routledge.

Pistor, K. (2019). *The Code of Capital: How the Law Creates Wealth and Inequality*. Princeton, NJ: Princeton University Press.

Pitelis, C. N., & Teece, D. J. (2009). The (new) nature and essence of the firm. *European Management Review*, *6*(1), 5–15.

Plotnikof, M., & Bencherki, N. (2023). The communicative constitution of organizational continuity and change in, through and over time. In T. Hernes & M. Feuls (Eds), *A Research Agenda for Organisational Continuity and Change*. Cheltenham, UK: Edward Elgar, pp 103–24.

Plotnikof., M., Vásquez, C., Kuhn, T., & Mumby, D. K. (2022). Towards a politics of dis/organization: Relations of dis/order in organization theory and practice. *Ephemera: Theory and Politics in Organization*, *22*(1), 1–26.

Pollman, E. (2021). The history and revival of the corporate purpose clause. *Texas Law Review*, *99*(7), 1423–52.

Poole, M. S., & Van de Ven, A. H. (1989). Using paradox to build management and organization theories. *Academy of Management Review*, *14*, 562–78.

Pope, S., & Kim, J. (2022). Where, when, and who: Corporate social responsibility and brand value – a global panel study. *Business & Society*, *61*(6), 1631–83.

Popper, N. (2020a, 29 December). Cryptocurrency start-up underpaid women and black employees, data shows. *New York Times*. Retrieved from https://www.nytimes.com/2020/12/29/technology/coinbase-pay-employees.html?action=click&module=Well&pgtype=Homepage&section=Technology

Popper, N. (2020b, 27 November). 'Tokenized': Inside black workers' struggles at the king of crypto start-ups. *New York Times*. Retrieved from https://www.nytimes.com/2020/11/27/technology/coinbase-cryptocurrency-black-employees.html

Potts, A. (2004). Deleuze on Viagra (or, what can a Viagra-body do?). *Body & Society*, *10*, 17–36.

Powell, W. W. (1990). Neither market nor hierarchy: Network forms of organization. *Research in Organizational Behavior*, *12*, 295–336.

Pratt, M. G., & Hedden, L. N. (2023). Accounts and accountability: On organizational purpose, organizational identity, and meaningful work. *Strategy Science*, *8*(2), 182–92.

Priem, R. L., & Butler, J. E. (2001a). Is the resource-based 'view' a useful perspective for strategic management research? *Academy of Management Review*, *26*, 22–40.

Priem, R. L., & Butler, J. E. (2001b). Tautology in the resource-based view and the implications of externally determined resource value: Further comments. *Academy of Management Review, 26*(1), 57–66.

Putnam, L. L., & Boys, S. (2006). Revisiting metaphors of organizational communication. In S. Clegg, C. Hardy, T. Lawrence, & W. Nord (Eds), *The Sage Handbook of Organization Studies*. Thousand Oaks, CA Sage, pp 541–76.

Putnam, L. L., Phillips, N., & Chapman, P. (1996). Metaphors of communication and organization. In S. R. Clegg, C. Hardy, & W. R. Nord (Eds), *Handbook of Organization Studies*. Thousand Oaks, CA: Sage, pp 375–408.

Putnam, L. L., Fairhurst, G. T., & Banghart, S. G. (2016). Contradictions, dialectics, and paradoxes in organizations: A constitutive approach. *Annals of the Academy of Management, 10*, 1–107.

Quinn, R. E., & Rohrbaugh, J. (1983). A spatial model of effectiveness criteria: Towards a competing values approach to organizational analysis. *Management Science, 29*, 363–77.

Radford, G. P. (2005). *On the Philosophy of Communication*. Belmont, CA: Thomson Wadsworth.

Rajak, D. (2011). *In Good Company: An Anatomy of Corporate Social Responsibility*. Stanford, CA: Stanford University Press.

Ramaswamy, V., & Ozcan, K. (2022). Brands as co-creational lived experience ecosystems: An integrative theoretical framework of interactional creation. In S. Markovic, R. Gyrd-Jones, S. v. Wallpach, & A. Lindgreen (Eds), *Research Handbook on Brand Co-creation* (pp. 47–64). Cheltenham, UK: Edwin Elgar.

Reckwitz, A. (2002). Toward a theory of social practices: A development in culturalist theorizing. *European Journal of Social Theory, 5*, 243–63.

Regnér, P. (2015). Relating strategy as practice to the resource-based view, capabilities perspectives and the micro-foundations approach. In D. Golosorkhi, L. Rouleau, D. Seidl, & E. Vaara (Eds), *Cambridge Handbook of Strategy as Practice* (2nd ed.). Cambridge, UK: Cambridge University Press, pp 301–16.

Rehn, A., & O'Doherty, D. (2007). Organization: On the theory and practice of excess. *Culture and Organization, 13*, 99–113.

Rekret, P. (2018). The head, the hand, and matter: New materialism and the politics of knowledge. *Theory Culture & Society, 35*(7–8), 49–72.

Rhee, R. J. (2008). Corporate ethics, agency, and the theory of the firm. *Journal of Business & Technology Law, 3*, 1101–24.

Rhodes, C. (2022). *Woke Capitalism: How Corporate Morality is Sabotaging Democracy*. Bristol, UK: Bristol University Press.

Ribstein, L. E. (2003). LLCs: Is the future here? Business Law Today, Nov/Dec, 11–13.

Ries, E. (2011). *The Lean Startup: How Today's Entrepreneurs Use Continuous Innovation to Create Radically Successful Businesses.* New York: Crown Business.

Riordan, M. H., & Williamson, O. E. (1985). Asset specificity and economic organization. *International Journal of Industrial Organization, 3*(4), 365–78.

Ritzer, G., & Jurgenson, N. (2010). Production, consumption, prosumption: The nature of capitalism in the age of the digital 'prosumer'. *Journal of Consumer Culture, 10*(1), 13–36.

Roach, S. (2022, 10 June). Coinbase employees are targeting top execs. Brian Armstrong called it 'really dumb'. *Protocol.* Retrieved from https://www.protocol.com/bulletins/coinbase-employees-petition

Roberts, J. (2004). *The Modern Firm: Organizational Design for Performance and Growth.* New York: Oxford University Press.

Robins, N. (2012). *The Corporation That Changed the World: How the East IndiaCompany Shaped the Modern Multinational* (2nd ed.). London: Pluto.

Rodrigues, C., Brandão, A., & Rodrigues, P. (2021). I can't stop hating you: An anti-brand-community perspective on Apple brand hate. *Journal of Product & Brand Management, 30*(8), 1115–33.

Rorty, R. (1979). *Philosophy and the Mirror of Nature.* Princeton, NJ: Princeton University Press.

Rose, N. (1999). *Governing the Soul: The Shaping of the Private Self* (2nd ed.). London: Free Association Books.

Rosenbaum, M. S., Otalora, M. L., & Ramírez, G. C. (2017). How to create a realistic customer journey map. *Business Horizons, 60*(1), 143–50.

Rosenblat, A., Barocas, S., Levy, K., & Hwang, T. (2016). Discriminating tastes: Uber's customer ratings as vehicles for workplace discrimination. *Policy and Internet, 9*(3), 256–79.

Rosiek, J. L. (2013). Pragmatism and post-qualitative futures. *International Journal of Qualitative Studies in Education, 26*(6), 692–705.

Sandberg, J., & Alvesson, M. (2021). Meanings of theory: Clarifying theory through typification. *Journal of Management Studies, 58*(2), 487–516.

Savignac, E. (2016). Role-playing games at work: About management, gamification and effectiveness. In M. Dymek & P. Zackariasson (Eds), *The Business of Gamification: A Critical Analysis.* New York: Routledge, pp 3–20.

Schatzki, T. (2001). Introduction: Practice theory. In T. Schatzki, K. Knorr-Cetina, & E. von Savigny (Eds), *The Practice Turn in Contemporary Theory.* London: Routledge, pp 1–14.

Schatzki, T. (2006). On organizations as they happen. *Organization Studies, 27*, 1863–73.

Schmeltz, L., & Kjeldsen, A. K. (2022). Corporate brand management and multiple voices: Polyphony or cacophony? In O. Iglesias, N. Ind, & M. Schultz (Eds), *The Routledge Companion to Corporate Branding.* London: Routledge, pp 1–19.

Schoeneborn, D. (2011). Organization as communication: A Luhmannian perspective. *Management Communication Quarterly*, *25*, 663–89.

Schoeneborn, D., Kuhn, T., & Kärreman, D. (2019). The communicative constitution of organization, organizing, and organizationality. *Organization Studies*, *40*(4), 475–96.

Scott, S., & Lane, V. R. (2000). A stakeholder approach to organizational identity. *Academy of Management Review*, *25*, 43–62.

Scott, S., & Orlikowski, W. (2022). The digital undertow: How the corollary effects of digital transformation affect industry standards. *Information Systems Research*, *33*(1), 311–36.

Segrestin, B., Hatchuel, A., & Levillain, K. (2021). When the law distinguishes between the enterprise and the corporation: The case of the new French law on corporate purpose. *Journal of Business Ethics*, *171*, 1–13.

Sennett, R. (1980). *Authority*. New York: Knopf.

Shanahan, G. (2023). 'No decision is permanent!': Achieving democratic revisability in alternative organizations through the affordances of new information and communication technologies. *Human Relations*, *76*(10), 1661–86.

Sharkey, A., Kovács, B., & Hsu, G. (2023). Expert critics, rankings, and review aggregators: The changing nature of intermediation and the rise of markets with multiple intermediaries. *Academy of Management Annals*, *17*(1), 1–36.

Sheldrake, M. (2020). *Entangled Life: How Fungi Make Our Worlds, Change Our Minds & Shape Our Futures*. New York: Random House.

Shepherd, G. J., St. John, J., & Striphas, T. (2006). *Communication as…: Perspectives on Theory*. Thousand Oaks, CA: Sage.

Simmel, G. (1907/1978). *The Philosophy of Money* (T. Bottomore & D. Frisby, Trans., 2nd ed.). London: Routledge and Keegan Paul.

Simon, H. A. (1964). On the concept of organizational goal. *Administrative Science Quarterly*, *9*(1), 1–22.

Simon, H. A. (1997). *Administrative Behavior: A Study of Decision-making Processes in Administrative Organizations* (4th ed.). New York: The Free Press.

Singer, A. (2019). *The Form of the Firm: A Normative Political Theory of the Corporation* Oxford, UK: Oxford University Press.

Sirmon, D. G., Hitt, M. A., & Ireland, R. D. (2007). Managing firm resources in dynamic environments to create value: Looking inside the black box. *Academy of Management Review*, *32*, 273–92.

Slager, R., Gond, J.-P., & Sjöström, E. (in press). Mirroring and switching authoritative personae: A ventriloquial analysis of shareholder engagement on carbon emissions. *Human Relations*.

Smith, W. R. (2024). 'No dig, no ride': The communicative constitution and consequences of imperfect authoritative texts in fluid collective organizing. *Management Communication Quarterly*, *38*(1), 147–70. doi:10.1177/08933189231173076

Sobande, F. (2019). Woke-washing: 'intersectional' femvertising and branding 'woke' bravery. *European Journal of Marketing, 54*(11), 2723–45.

Spee, A. P., & Jarzabkowski, P. (2011). Strategic planning as a communicative process. *Organization Studies, 32*, 1217–46.

Spender, J.-C. (2014). *Business Strategy: Managing Uncertainty, Opportunity, and Enterprise*. Oxford, UK: Oxford University Press.

Spoelstra, S. (2005). Robert Cooper: Beyond organization. *The Sociological Review, 53*, 106–19.

Srnicek, N. (2017). *Platform Capitalism*. Cambridge, UK: Polity.

Starbuck, W. H. (2005). Performance measures: Prevalent and important but methodologically challenging. *Journal of Management Inquiry, 14*, 280–6.

Stark, D. (2009). *The Sense of Dissonance: Accounts of Worth in Economic Life*. Princeton, NJ: Princeton University Press.

Stayton, J., & Mangematin, V. (2019). Seed accelerators and the speed of new venture creation. *Journal of Technology Transfer, 44*, 1163–87.

Stohl, C., & Stohl, M. (2011). Secret agencies: The communicative constitution of a clandestine organization. *Organization Studies, 32*, 1197–216.

Swanepoel, D. (2021). Does artificial intelligence have agency? In R. W. Clowes, K. Gärtner, & I. Hipólito (Eds), *The Mind-Technology Problem*. Berlin: Springer, pp 83–104.

Taylor, J. R. (2009). Organizing from the bottom up? Reflections on the constitution of organization in communication. In L. L. Putnam & A. M. Nicotera (Eds), *Building Theories of Organization: The Constitutive Role of Communication*. New York: Routledge, pp 153–86.

Taylor, J. R. (2011). Organization as an (imbricated) configuring of transactions. *Organization Studies, 32*, 1273–94.

Taylor, J. R., & Van Every, E. (2014). *When Organization Fails: Why Authority Matters*. New York: Routledge.

Taylor, J. R., Cooren, F., Giroux, H., & Robichaud, D. (1996). The communicational basis of organization: Between the conversation and the text. *Communication Theory, 6*, 1–39.

Teece, D. J., Pisano, G., & Shuen, A. (1997). Dynamic capabilities and strategic management. *Strategic Management Journal, 18*, 509–33.

Teeling, R. (2021, 17 November). Shein: The most addictive cult of fast fashion. HerCampus.com. Retrieved from https://www.hercampus.com/school/nottingham/shein-the-most-addictive-cult-of-fast-fashion/

Terranova, T. (2000). Free labor: Producing culture for the digital economy. *Social Text, 18*(2), 33–58.

Testa, J. (2022, 1 September). The people's republic of Shein. *New York Times*. Retrieved from https://www.nytimes.com/2022/09/01/style/shein-clothing.html

Thanem, T., & Linstead, S. (2006). The trembling organisation: Order, change, and the philosophy of the virtual. In M. Fuglsang & B. M. Sorensen (Eds), *Deleuze and the Social*. Edinburgh: Edinburgh University Press, pp 39–57.

Thévenot, L. (2001). Pragmatic regimes governing the engagement with the world. In K. Knorr-Cetina, T. Schatzki, & E. von Savigny (Eds), *The Practice Turn in Social Theory*. London: Routledge, pp 56–73.

Thévenot, L., Moody, M., & Lafaye, C. (2000). Forms of valuing nature: arguments and modes of justification in French and American environmental disputes. In M. Lamont & L. Thévenot (Eds), *Rethinking Comparative Cultural Sociology: Repertoires of Evaluation in France and the United States*. Cambridge: Cambridge University Press, pp 229–72.

Thompson, T. A., & Davis, G. F. (1997). The politics of corporate control and the future of shareholder activism in the United States. *Corporate Governance*, 5(3), 152–9.

Thrift, N. (2005). *Knowing Capitalism*. London: Sage.

Tourish, D. (2020). The triumph of nonsense in management studies. *Academy of Management Learning and Education*, 19(1), 99–109.

Treem, J. W. (2012). Communicating expertise: Knowledge performances in professional-service firms. *Communication Monographs*, 79, 23–47.

Tsai, L.-C., Zhang, R., & Zhao, C. (2019). Political connections, network centrality and firm innovation. *Finance Research Letters*, 28, 180–4.

Turco, C. J. (2016). *The Conversational Firm: Rethinking Bureaucracy in the Age of Social Media*. New York: Columbia University Press.

Vallas, S., & Schor, J. B. (2020). What do platforms do? Understanding the gig economy. *Annual Review of Sociology*, 46(1), 273–94.

Vandaele, K. (2021). Collective resistance and organizational creativity amongst Europe's platform workers: A new power in the labour movement? In J. Haidar & M. Keune (Eds), *Work and Labour Relations in Global Platform Capitalism*. London: Edwin Elgar, pp 206–35.

Vargo, S. L., Maglio, P. P., & Akaka, M. A. (2008). On value and value co-creation: A service systems and service logic perspective. *European Management Journal*, 26, 145–52.

Vasconcelos, L., & Rua, O. L. (2021). Personal branding on social media: The role of influencers. *E-Revista De Estudos Interculturais*, 3(9), np. doi:10.34630/erei.v3i9.4232

Vásquez, C., & Kuhn, T. (2019). Introduction. In C. Vásquez & T. Kuhn (Eds), *Dis/organization as Communication: Exploring the Disordering, Disruptive, and Chaotic Properties of Communication*. New York: Routledge, pp 1–13.

Vásquez, C., Brummans, B. H. J. M., & Groleau, C. (2012). Notes from the field on organizational shadowing as framing. *Qualitative Research in Organizations and Management*, 7(2), 144–65.

Vásquez, C., Schoeneborn, D., & Sergi, V. (2016). Summoning the spirits: Organizational texts and the (dis)ordering properties of communication. *Human Relations, 69,* 629–59.

Vásquez, C., Kuhn, T., & Plotnikof, M. (2022). Disrupting CCO thinking: A communicative ontology of dis/organization. In J. Basque, N. Bencherki, & T. Kuhn (Eds), *The Routledge Handbook of the Communicative Constitution of Organization.* New York: Routledge, pp 119–33.

Vogel, D. (2005). *The Market for Virtue: The Potential and Limits of Corporate Social Responsibility.* Washington, DC: Brookings Institution Press.

Walt, V. (2021, 22 November). A top CEO was ousted after making his company more environmentally conscious. Now he's speaking out. Time. com. Retrieved from https://time.com/6121684/emmanuel-faber-danone-interview/

Weber, M. (1947). *The Theory of Social and Economic Organization* (A. M. Henderson & T. Parsons, Trans.). New York: The Free Press.

Weber, M. (1978). *Economy and Society: An Outline of Interpretive Sociology* (Vols 1 & 2). Berkeley: University of California Press.

Weick, K. E. (1979). *The Social Psychology of Organizing* (2nd ed.). New York: McGraw-Hill.

Weick, K. E. (1995). *Sensemaking in Organizations.* Thousand Oaks, CA: Sage.

Weil, D. (2014). *The Fissured Workplace: Why Work Became So Bad For So Many and What Can Be Done to Improve It.* Cambridge, MA: Harvard University Press.

Werner, A. (2015). Corporations are (white) people: How corporate privilege reifies whiteness as property. *Harvard Journal on Racial and Ethnic Justice, 31,* 129–47.

Wernerfelt, B. (1984). A resource-based view of the firm. *Strategic Management Journal, 5,* 171–80.

Wheeler, W. (2014). Natural play, natural metaphor, and natural stories: Biosemiotic realism. In S. Iovino & S. Oppermann (Eds), *Material Ecocriticism.* Bloomington: Indiana University Press, pp 67–79.

Whitehead, H., Smith, T. D., & Rendell, L. (2021). Adaptation of sperm whales to open-boat whalers: Rapid social learning on a large scale? *Biology Letters, 17,* 1–5.

Wilhoit, E. D., & Kisselburgh, L. G. (2015). Collective action without organization: The material constitution of bike commuters as collective. *Organization Studies, 36,* 573–92.

Wilken, N. (2015, 28 June). The B (S?) Corporation. Retrieved from https://wilkencpas.wordpress.com/

Williamson, O. E. (1988). The logic of economic organization. *Journal of Law, Economics, and Organization, 4,* 65–94.

Williamson, O. (1999). Strategy research: Governance and competence perspectives. *Strategic Management Journal, 20,* 1087–108.

Williamson, O. (2002). The theory of the firm as governance structure: From choice to contract. *Journal of Economic Perspectives, 16,* 171–95.

Winkler, A. (2007). Corporate personhood and the rights of corporate speech. *Seattle University Law Review, 30,* 863–73.

Winkler, A. (2018). *We the Corporations: How American Businesses Won Their Civil Rights.* New York: Liveright.

Winter, S. G. (2003). Understanding dynamic capabilities. *Strategic Management Journal, 24,* 991–5.

Wise, J. M. (2011). Assemblage. In C. J. Stivale (Ed.), *Gilles Deleuze: Key Concepts* (2nd ed.). New York: Routledge, pp 91–102.

Woods, C. S. (2016). The implications of the B Corp movement in the business and human rights context. *Notre Dame Journal of International & Comparative Law, 6*(1), 77–99.

Wright, A., Kuhn, T., Michailova, S., & Hibbert, P. (2023). Ventriloquial authority in management learning and education: A communication as constitutive of learning and education perspective. *Academy of Management Learning and Education, 22*(2), 312–30.

Wright, C., & Nyberg, D. (2015). *Climate Change, Capitalism, and Corporations: Processes of Creative Self-Destruction.* Cambridge: Cambridge University Press.

Wright, P. M. (2023). Woke corporations and worldview: The perils of CEOs making moral proclamations from shaky moral foundations. *Academy of Management Perspectives, 37*(3), 252–69.

Zhang, R., Voronov, M., Toubiana, M., Vince, R., & Hudson, B. A. (in press). Beyond the feeling individual: Insights from sociology on emotions and embeddedness. *Journal of Management Studies.* doi:10.1111/joms.12976

Zheng, Y. (2003). The social life of opium in China, 1483–1999. *Modern Asian Studies, 37,* 1–39.

Zuboff, S. (2019). *The Age of Surveillance Capitalism: The Fight for a Human Future at the New Frontier of Power.* New York: PublicAffairs.

Zwick, D., Bonsu, S. K., & Darmody, A. (2008). Putting consumers to work: 'Co-creation' and new marketing govern-mentality. *Journal of Consumer Culture, 8,* 163–96.

Index

Note: References to figures appear in *italic* type; those in **bold** type refer to tables. References to endnotes show both the page number and the note number (83n13).